I0892164

The Modernist as Philosopher

The Modernist as Philosopher

Selected Writings of Marcel Hébert

Translated by C. J. T. Talar and Elizabeth Emery

Edited by C. J. T. Talar

The Catholic University of America Press

Washington, DC

Copyright © 2011
The Catholic University of America Press
All rights reserved

The paper used in this publication meets the minimum requirements of American National Standards for Information Science—Permanence of Paper for Printed Library Materials, ANSI Z39.48-1984.
∞

Designed and composed by Kachergis Book Design

Library of Congress Cataloging-in-Publication Data
Hébert, Marcel, 1851–1916.
[Selections. English]
The modernist as philosopher : selected writings of Marcel Hébert / translated by C.J.T. Talar and Elizabeth Emery ; edited by C.J.T. Talar.
p. cm.
Includes bibliographical references and index.
Includes a translation of the complete second edition of the author's Pragmatisme.
ISBN 978-0-8132-1879-3 (cloth : alk. paper) 1. Hébert, Marcel, 1851–1916. Pragmatisme. 2. Pragmatism. 3. Philosophy, French—19th century 4. Philosophy, French—20th century I. Talar, C. J. T., 1947– II. Emery, Elizabeth (Elizabeth Nicole) III. Hébert, Marcel, 1851–1916. Pragmatisme. 2nd ed. IV. Title.
B832.H43 2011
194—dc23 2011022278

Contents

Preface vii

Introduction by C. J. T. Talar 1

Part I. Articles

1. Thomism and Kantianism 27
2. Memories of Assisi 49
3. The Last Idol: Study of the "Divine Personality" 70
4. Anonymous or Polyonymous: Second Study on the "Divine Personality" 85
5. The Bankruptcy of Despotic Catholicism 106

Part II. *Pragmatism: A Study of Its Various Forms, Anglo-American, French, and Italian, and of Its Religious Value*

Foreword 135

1. Mr. Peirce's "Pragmatism" 137
2. Mr. James's "Pragmatism" 149
3. Mr. F. C. S. Schiller's "Humanism" 161
4. Pragmatism: "A New Name for Some Old Ways of Thinking" 179
5. Religious Pragmatism 193

Notes 217

Appendix I. Pragmatism and Aesthetics 217

Appendix II. Pragmatism and Morality 217

Appendix III. Notes on J.-J. Rousseau and Chateaubriand 218

Appendix IV. What Pragmatism Means to M. Le Roy 221

Contents

Appendix V. Origins of Pragmatism according to M. R. Berthelot 223
Appendix VI. The Social Pragmatism of M. Durkheim 225
Mr. James's Response (William James) 226
Author's Reply 233

Part III. Review of Hébert's *Le Pragmatisme*

1. Pragmatism 241
Eugène Ménégoz

Bibliography 247

Index 251

Preface

Where Hébert has quoted Vatican documents with no other reference than their title, notes give page references to an English translation. Where needed, Scripture references have been supplied. In general, where Hébert quotes foreign works in French translation, we have adhered closely to the French, providing references to standard English translations for readers wishing to locate the context of the citation. When the English translation has been used, that is noted. His bibliographical references tend to be brief, most often limited to author and title. Where possible, publication data are amplified. Lastly, when a page or section reference is inaccurately cited in the original, correction has been made without further notation.

"Thomism and Kantianism" originally appeared as "Thomisme et Kantisme," *Annales de philosophie chrétienne* 13 (January 1896): 364–84.

"Memories of Assisi" was originally printed as a booklet for private circulation, *Souvenirs d'Assise* (Paris: Impr. Bour, 1899) and subsequently published as "Souvenirs d'Assise," *Revue blanche* 29 (1903): 81–95.

"The Last Idol: Study of the 'Divine Personality'" appeared as "La Dernière Idole. Étude sur la 'personalité divine,'" *Revue de Métaphysique et de* Morale 10 (July 1902): 397–408.

"Anonymous or Polyonymous: Second Study on the 'Divine

Personality'" was published as "Anonyme ou polyonyme. Seconde étude sur la 'personalité divine,'" *Revue de Métaphysique et de Morale* 11 (March 1903): 231–47.

"The Bankruptcy of Despotic Catholicism" was published as "La Faillite du catholicisme despotique," *Revue blanche* 30 (March 1903): 439–57.

Pragmatism: A Study of Its Various Forms, Anglo-American, French. and Italian, and of Its Religious Value was published as *Le pragmatisme. Étude de ses diverses formes, anglo-américaines, françaises, italiennes et de sa valeur religieuse* (Paris: Émile Nourry, 1908). A second, expanded edition appeared from the same publisher in 1910, which included a French translation of a review of *Le Pragmatisme* by William James that originally appeared in the *Journal of Philosophy, Psychology and Scientific Methods* 5 (December 3, 1908): 689–94. James included this review in his *The Meaning of Truth* (New York: Longmans, Green, and Co., 1914), chap. 12, 230–45, with some small modifications, under the title "Professor Hébert on Pragmatism." The 1910 edition also published Hébert's reply to James's review.

We wish to acknowledge Christine E. Thirlway's careful reading of the translation and her many suggestions that greatly improved it.

The Modernist as Philosopher

Introduction

C. J. T. TALAR

Roman Catholic Modernism, in France, was prominently represented by scholars whose interests were, in significant measure, historical.[1] Louis Duchesne, Alfred Loisy, and Albert Houtin come readily to mind.[2] Where philosophy was concerned, Mau-

1. The historiography of Roman Catholic Modernism begins with those who were involved with the movement. Among early contributions may be found Paul Sabatier, *Modernism* (New York: Charles Scribner, 1908); Albert Houtin, *Histoire du modernisme catholique* (Paris: chez l'auteur, 1913); Maude D. Petre, *Modernism: Its Failure and Its Fruits* (London: T. C. & E. C. Jack, 1918); and Jean Rivière, *Le Modernisme dans l'église* (Paris: Letouzey, 1929). More recent studies include Thomas Loome, *Liberal Catholicism, Reform Catholicism, Modernism* (Mainz: Matthias-Grünewald-Verlag, 1979); Gabriel Daly, *Transcendence and Immanence: A Study in Roman Catholic Modernism and Integralism* (Oxford: Clarendon Press, 1980); Marvin O'Connell, *Critics on Trial: An Introduction to the Catholic Modernist Crisis* (Washington, D.C.: The Catholic University of America Press, 1998); *Catholicism Contending with Modernity: Roman Catholic Modernism and Anti-Modernism in Historical Context*, ed. Darrell Jodock (Cambridge: Cambridge University Press, 2000); Maurilio Guasco, *Il modernismo. I fatti, le idee, i personaggi* (Rome: San Paulo Edizioni, 1995), French trans. *Le Modernisme. Les faits, les idées, les hommes* (Paris: Desclée de Brouwer, 2007); and Claus Arnold, *Kleine Geschichte des Modernismus* (Freiburg: Herder, 2007). There are several good regional studies of the movement, which include Lawrence Barmann, *Baron Friedrich von Hügel and the Modernist Crisis in England* (Cambridge: Cambridge University Press, 1972); R. Scott Appleby, *"Church and Age Unite": The Modernist Impulse in American Catholicism* (South Bend, Ind.: University of Notre Dame Press, 1992); Pierre Colin, *L'Audace et le soupcon. La crise du modernisme dans le catholicisme français 1893–1914* (Paris: Desclée de Brouwer, 1997); Pietro Scoppola, *Crisi modernista e rinnovamento cattolico in Italia* (Bologna: Il Mulino, 1969); Lorenzo Bedeschi, *Il modernismo italiano. Voci e volti* (Cinisello Balsamo, 1995); and Otto Weiss, *Der Modernismus in Deutschland, Ein Beitragzur Theologie-geschichte* (Regensburg: Pustet, 1995).

2. Louis Duchesne (1843–1922) was a historian of the early church. He taught at the Institut catholique de Paris (1877–1895) and at the École pratique des hautes études (1885–1895) before becoming director of the École française de Rome from 1895 until his death. His three-

rice Blondel was largely successful in distancing himself from the movement as it grew more radical and was condemned by Rome in 1907.[3] Though suspected by Scholastic critics of conceding too much to the subjectivity of human knowing, too little to the gratuity of the supernatural, Blondel managed to escape ecclesiastical sanction—unlike his collaborator, Lucien Laberthonnière, whose work found its way onto the Index and who was eventually silenced.[4] Marcel Hébert (1851–1916) stands at the confluence of

volume *Histoire ancienne de l'Église* (1906–1910) was placed on the Index in 1912. See Brigitte Waché, *Monseigneur Louis Duchesne (1843–1922), historien de l'Église, Directeur de l'École française de Rome* (Rome: École Française de Rome, 1992). Alfred Loisy (1857–1940): called to the Institut catholique de Paris in 1881 by Louis Duchesne, he taught there until his dismissal in 1893 for his advanced views in biblical scholarship. His *L'Évangile et l'Église* can be said to have precipitated the modernist crisis. Excommunicated in 1908, the following year he was elected to the chair of the history of religions at the Collège de France where he taught until his retirement in 1931. See Alfred Loisy, *Mémoires pour server à l'histoire religieuse de notre temps,* 3 vols. (Paris: Émile Nourry, 1930–1931). A survey of Loisy's modernist writings and of critical responses to them may be found in Émile Poulat, *Histoire, dogme et critique dans la crise moderniste* (Tourani: Casterman, 1962). The bibliography of studies on Loisy in English is extensive and may be accessed at http://alfred.loisy.free.fr. Albert Houtin (1867–1926) is best known for his two volumes on the history of the biblical question. His involvement in modernism is told in the first volume of his autobiography, *Une Vie de prêtre. Mon experience, 1867–1912* (Paris: F. Rieder, 1926), Eng. trans. by Winifred Whale, *The Life of a Priest: My Own Experience, 1867–1912.* (London: Watts & Co., 1927). A bibliography of his writings may be found in the autobiography's second volume, *Mon expérience. II. Ma vie laïque, 1912–1926. Documents et souvenirs* (Paris: F. Rieder, 1928). In addition to Houtin's autobiography, see C. J. T. Talar, "Identity Formation, Reconstruction, and Transformation: The Autobiographical Trajectory of Albert Houtin," in *Personal Faith and Institutional Commitments: Roman Catholic Modernist and Anti-Modernist Autobiography*, ed. Lawrence Barmann and Harvey Hill (Scranton, Pa.: University of Scranton Press, 2002), 39–65.

3. Maurice Blondel (1861–1949). Blondel's doctoral thesis *L'Action* (1893) identified his work with the "new apologetics" then emerging, an identification reinforced by his *Lettre sur les exigences de la pensée contemporaine en matière d'apoloétique et sur la méthode de la philosophie dans l'étude du problème religieux* (1896). In his attempt to develop a truly philosophical apologetic he drew criticism from theologians who identified his method of immanence with an immanentism. On Blondel's involvement in the modernist movement, see René Virgoulay, *Maurice Blondel et le modernisme* (Paris: Cerf, 1980) and Oliva Blanchette, *Maurice Blondel: A Philosophical Life* (Grand Rapids, Mich.: William B. Eerdmans, 2010). For a bibliography on Blondel, consult René Virgoulay and Claude Troisfontaines, *Maurice Blondel, Bibliographie analytique et critique, Vol. 1: Oeuvres de Maurice Blondel* (1880–1973); *Vol. 2: Études sur Maurice Blondel* (1893–1975) (Louvain: Institut Supérieure de Philosophie/Peeters, 1975–1976).

4. Lucien Laberthonnière (1860–1932). Oratorian, professor of philosophy at the Collège

these two tendencies. His appreciation of the exegesis of Scripture and its subsequent development in Church tradition was importantly shaped by both Loisy and Duchesne. And like Blondel and Laberthonnière, he felt the insufficiency of Scholasticism to speak to minds formed by modernity, to formulate an adequate response to the philosophical legacy of Kant. He acknowledged his debt to Duchesne and Loisy in history, but regarded himself, though an autodidact, their superior in philosophy. As Loisy may represent a case study of how modern historical consciousness impacted a mind formed by traditional Catholic theology and piety, so Hébert may serve as a case study in the impact of modern philosophical consciousness on one also formed by traditional Catholicism.

The essays selected for translation that form part I of this volume begin with "Thomism and Kantianism," which reflects Hébert's wrestling with a problem that engaged a broad spectrum of philosophical minds at the fin de siècle—the search for a critical realism that sought to go beyond a naive realism in acknowledging the deforming character of concepts while admitting their necessity.[5] "Memories of Assisi"[6] places those epistemological concerns within the framework of a modernity reflecting the post-1859 world of Darwin, evolution, and the centrality of scientific ideology in the French "positivist Republic."[7] For Hébert,

de Juilly (1887–1896), then head of the Collège Massillon (1897–1899), he became superior at Juilly in 1903. From 1905 he assumed direction of the *Annales de philosophie chrétienne* until 1913 when the *Annales* was condemned by Rome and Laberthonnière was silenced. Laberthonnière awaits a definitive biography. For his early formation, see Giacomo Losito, *Cristianesimo e modernità. Studio sulla formazione del personalismo di Laberthonnière—1880–1893* (Naples: Edizioni "La Città del Sole," 1999).

5. Marcel Hébert, "Thomisme et Kantisme," *Annales de philosophie chrétienne* 13 (January 1886): 364–84.

6. Marcel Hébert, "Souvenirs d'Assise," *Revue blanche* 29 (1903): 81–95.

7. See Henry W. Paul, *The Edge of Contingency: French Catholic Reaction to Scientific Change from Darwin to Duhem* (Gainesville: University of Florida, 1979), and *From Knowledge*

an evolutionary interpretation of Catholicism pointed a way forward, beyond the traditional—and professedly inadequate—theodicies, while preserving the legacy of the past through a symbolist understanding of dogma. "The Last Idol" and "Anonymous or Polyonymous" apply that mode of interpretation to a critique of classical theism and pose necessary modifications to its approach to God for minds formed by modernity.[8] If philosophical concerns are uppermost in these essays, "The Bankruptcy of Despotic Catholicism" exhibits the importance of critical historical scholarship, both for Hébert's own evolving position and for Catholicism's future.[9] While "Memories of Assisi" retains hope for a renewed—hence renewable—Catholicism, by the time he wrote "The Bankruptcy of Despotic Catholicism" Hébert judged that the Church had missed its chance with its condemnation of Loisy's efforts. The decision to publish "Memories of Assisi" and "The Last Idol" in secular journals sealed Hébert's break with the Church. "The Bankruptcy of Despotic Catholicism" constituted a kind of post-mortem on missed opportunity.

Hébert's preoccupation with the subjective dimension of human knowing, one he shared with others linked to Modernism such as Blondel and Édouard Le Roy,[10] evidently motivated his

to Power: The Rise of the Science Empire in France, 1860–1939 (Cambridge: Cambridge University Press, 1985).

8. Marcel Hébert, "La Dernière Idole. Étude sur la 'personalité divine,'" *Revue de Métaphysique et de Morale* 10 (July 1902): 397–408; Marcel Hébert, "Anonyme ou polyonyme. Seconde étude sur la 'personalité divine,'" *Revue de Métaphysique et de Morale* 11 (March 1903): 231–47.

9. Marcel Hébert, "La Faillite du catholicisme despotique," *Revue blanche* 30 (March 1903): 439–57.

10. Edouard Le Roy (1870–1954): Mathematician, philosopher. He succeeded Henri Bergson at the Collège de France in 1921. Le Roy achieved notoriety with his article "Qu-est-ce qu'un dogme?" which appeared in *La Quinzaine* in 1905. He reprinted the article, together with critical responses and his answer, in *Dogme et critique* (Bloud, 1907), which was placed on the Index. The controversy surrounding these works is set out in Guy Mansini, *What Is a Dogma? The Meaning and Truth of Dogma in Edouard Le Roy and His Scholastic Opponents* (Rome: Pontifica Universita Gregoriana, 1985).

interest in the work of the Anglo-American pragmatists, especially that of William James.[11] There are a number of concerns that are common to modernists and pragmatists—to the point that critics at the time could argue for a basic solidarity in views between the two movements, seeing a common source in Kant's philosophy. In *Pragmatisme, Modernisme, Protestantisme* Albert Leclère concluded that Modernism's essentials were "well defined by the expression 'Catholic religious pragmatism.'"[12] Given Hébert's own emphasis on the subjectivity of knowledge, there were critics who were surprised—and edified—to find him breaking ranks, as it were, and accusing pragmatism of failing to adequately preserve the objective element in knowing. In *Le Pragmatisme* Hébert positions other Catholic thinkers identified with Modernism. In doing so he contributes to our understanding of the diversity and complexity of that movement, as well as broader issues that connected it to currents of thought beyond Catholicism.

From Scholasticism to Modernism

Although urged by several friends to write an account of his life, Hébert declined to do so. The primary access to his life remains *Un Prêtre symboliste. Marcel Hébert (1851–1916)* written by his friend and literary executor Albert Houtin.[13] Raised in an at-

11. William James (1842–1910). In addition to his contribution to pragmatism James is remembered for his work in psychology and for his *Varieties of Religious Experience* (1902). Recent biographies of James include Richard D. Richardson, *William James: In the Maelstrom of American Modernism* (Boston: Houghton Mifflin, 2007), and Linda Simon, *Genuine Reality: A Life of William James* (New York: Harcourt, Brace and Company, 1998). Also see Gerald E. Meyers, *William James: His Life and Thought* (New Haven, Conn.: Yale University Press, 1986).

12. Albert Leclère, *Pragmatisme, Modernisme, Protestantisme* (Paris: Librairie Bloud, 1909), 90n.

13. Albert Houtin, *Un Prêtre symboliste. Marcel Hébert (1851–1916)* (Paris: F. Rieder, 1925). On Houtin's biography, see C. J. T. Talar, "An Ideal Modernist: Marcel Hébert," in Harvey Hill et al., *By Those Who Knew Them: French Modernists Left, Right, and Center* (Washington, D.C.:

mosphere of exemplary piety, Hébert was attracted to the priesthood. The prospect of having to support his widowed mother and sister, combined with his fragile health, made the realization of that desire rather doubtful for a time. Indeed, when eventually he did enter the seminary its austere regime proved too rigorous for him. However, given his intellectual gifts and responsiveness to seminary formation, accommodations were made that enabled him to be ordained to the priesthood in June 1876. Given his strong interests in science and philosophy and his initiative in independent study, ordinarily Hébert would have been a candidate for a seminary faculty. Health considerations were once again a factor and instead he was assigned to a country parish. His pastoral responsibilities left him ample time for continued study and he was able to pursue his strong interest in Scholastic philosophy.[14]

In 1879 Hébert secured a position that returned him to Paris and provided a venue in which he could further develop his knowledge of philosophy while not overtaxing his physical resources. He joined the staff of the École Fénelon, a school that provided a Catholic education for sons of the well-to-do bourgeoisie. Students in its upper divisions attended the Lycée Condorcet, returning to the school for their religious formation and to have their studies monitored by a priest-director. The philosophy taught in French universities over the period was strongly impregnated with Kantianism, and this was especially true of the Lycée Condorcet. Placed in charge of students following a course of study in philosophy, Hébert expanded his philosophical horizons in the course of his tutoring.[15] A growing respect for

The Catholic University of America Press, 2008). Those wishing further particulars regarding Hébert's life may consult these two sources.

14. See Houtin, *Un Prêtre symboliste*, chaps. 1–3.

15. Ibid., chap. 4–5.

Kant's work set him at odds with clerical contemporaries who regarded Kant as the destroyer of metaphysics. This negative reading of Kant became dominant in Catholic circles and the dangers of Kantianism surfaced in critiques of individual thinkers such as Blondel as well as Vatican admonitions to remain faithful to the Thomist prescriptions of *Aeterni Patris* (1878).[16] In his analysis of Modernism in France, Pierre Colin reminds us that more than the positions of a given philosopher are at stake here.

> The true line of division does not pass between Thomists and non-Thomists, or even between Kantians and non-Kantians, but separates the acceptance or refusal of the Kantian problematic insofar as this problematic exhibits the values of modernity.... There exists between Kant and modernity a bond so strong that it may be difficult to gain a deep understanding of modernity without at least passing through Kant.... Reciprocally, moreover, the refusal of Kant can signify the conscious or unconscious refusal of modernity. The anti-Kantian resistance of Catholic adversaries of Kant is an anti-modern resistance at the same time as it is an anti-Protestant resistance.[17]

Hébert acquired a reputation as a Kantian of questionable orthodoxy. Already by the mid-1880s, when Mgr. Maurice d'Hulst invited Hébert's participation in the recently revived Société de Saint-Thomas d'Aquin, he alluded to the "problematic" orthodoxy of the invitee.[18] D'Hulst's intention in reforming the société was one of enlarging the horizons of Thomism through comparison with other philosophical systems. Thus he desired Hébert's participation as a way of furthering those aims. A mark

16. See Colin, *L'audace et le soupcon*, chap. 6.

17. Ibid., 201.

18. Maurice Le Sage d'Hauteroche d'Hulst (1841–1896). Named rector of the Institut catholique de Paris in 1881, his article on "La Question biblique" (1892) catalyzed controversy over biblical inspiration and precipitated Roman intervention with the encyclical *Providentissimus Deus* (1893). On d'Hulst, see Alfred Baudrillart, *Vie de Mgr d'Hulst*, 2 vols. (Paris: De Gigord, 1914). Also see Francesco Baretta, *Monseigneur d'Hulst et la science chrétienne. Portrait d'un intellectual* (Paris: Beauchesne, 1996).

of Hébert's growing commitment to Kantianism is evident in the first of his writings translated for this volume, "Thomisme et Kantisme," read before the society in 1885 and published in the *Annales de philosophie chrétienne* the following year.

Here he attempts to establish common ground between Thomism and Kant's thought, emphasizing the objective basis of the latter in sensation and the active role played by the agent intellect in the former. He also remarks that a distinction may be drawn between Kant and Kantianism; the excesses of the latter do not necessarily vitiate the real contributions of the former. Nor, for that matter, do the very real exaggerations of Kant himself in making his case. And an intellectual humility before the profound nature of things must not be confused with a thoroughgoing skepticism. Hébert even seeks to defend Kant at what many perceived was a major point of vulnerability: certitude. Increasingly this had become a moral question, as well as an intellectual one, in which the heart and the will would play a prominent role. Here he sees a possible complementarity with the intellectual emphasis put forward by Thomism, each philosophy serving to balance and correct the other.

From the published accounts of the société's discussions, which also appeared in the *Annales de philosophie chrétienne,* it is apparent that Hébert found few sympathizers, let alone converts to his views.[19] Those views underwent further development through his contact with evolutionary thought, particularly in its Darwinian form.

Along with many of his contemporaries, Hébert experienced the challenge of reconciling the fact of a superfluity of pain, waste, and loss in nature and the affirmation of a particular Prov-

19. Houtin profiles the société's membership, summarizes reactions to Hébert's communication, and exhibits his growing disaffection and eventual disaffiliation in chap. 6.

idence.[20] The problem of theodicy in its Darwinian form made it difficult to harmonize the providential care of a benevolent Creator with a nature "red in tooth and claw." The acute perception of evil and suffering in the world induced a kind of philosophical crisis in Hébert. His way of resolving the difficulty was to distinguish between what may be termed "speculative" and "regulative" modes of relating to God, between the reality of the infinite, the perfect, and the images of human personality used to represent that reality and to relate to it. The images traditionally used to represent God, while speculatively false, are regulatively true, insofar as they serve as a guide orienting us to action. The distinction between the idea of the infinite and the attributes of personality that are its image places the problem on another footing. Like other contemporaries Hébert found a resolution of his dilemma in transforming Darwin by injecting into evolution a benevolence and an inevitable progress.[21] As encapsulated by Houtin, "With the Kant of practical reason, he identified God and the 'Moral Law'; with evolutionism, he made this law 'the Great Law,' 'the Orientation of universal activity,' thus keeping together the two terms he sought to reconcile: a profound reality which is the ground of evolution, of the world's tendency toward an ideal of perfection."[22] Hébert gave expression to these ideas in a dialogue he entitled "Platon et Darwin" that appeared in the *Annales*

20. As John Haught has observed, it was not only the sheer fact of suffering that made an impact, but the great length of time over which it occurred that challenged a benign cosmic vision governed by a divine providence. Moreover, the theory of natural selection, with its random variations, appeared more compatible with a relentlessly impersonal universe than one governed by a compassionate deity. See John F. Haught, *God after Darwin: A Theology of Evolution* (Boulder, Col.: Westview Press, 2000), 20, 23–24.

21. James C. Livingston provides an extensive account of the problems posed by Darwin's thought for divine providence, design, miracles, and theodicy in his *Religious Thought in the Victorian Age* (New York: T & T Clark, 2007), and the range of solutions that were attempted in the face of those problems.

22. Houtin, *Un Prêtre symboliste*, 88–89.

de philosophie chrétienne in 1893.[23] He would continue to refine this "symbolist" compromise over the course of the 1890s. It appeared to him a way of preserving the form of Catholicism while investing it with new content.[24] If its doctrines were no longer adequate intellectually, they nevertheless retained their power to touch the heart.

As is the case with Kant, the impact of Darwin represents more than the powerful consequences of a theory, and the replacement of one theory by another. Hébert's intellectual development is also reflective of a change in what Charles Taylor has called the "cosmic imaginary": a change in the "whole background understanding and feel of the world."[25] For Taylor it is a matter of how the universe figures not just in theory, but in moral and aesthetic imaginations. From this perspective, the appeal of the scientific viewpoint is not a matter solely or even primarily of convincing proofs; "it is rather that one whole package: science, plus a picture of our epistemic-moral predicament in which science represents a mature facing of hard reality, beats out another package: religion, plus a rival picture of our epistemic-moral predicament in which religion, say, represents true humility, and many of the claims of science unwanted arrogance."[26] He argues that the decisive consideration in an abandonment of (traditional) religious belief was the picture of the moral predica-

23. "Platon et Darwin" appeared in English translation as *Plato and Darwin: A Philosophical Dialogue,* trans. William Gibson (Longmans, Green & Co., 1899). It was originally my intention to include it in this collection of Hébert's writings, as it had become very rare. However, it has recently come back into print by Kessinger Publishing, 2007, and is once again available.

24. In February 1893 Hébert was able to write to Abbé John Hogan, his former mentor at the seminary, "I am thankful that I have come through the crisis, in which so many others have foundered, with a creed whose formulas have been slightly modified, but in which all that is fundamental remains"; quoted in Houtin, *Un Prêtre symboliste,* 92n.

25. Charles Taylor, *A Secular Age* (Cambridge, Mass.: Belknap Press of Harvard University Press, 2007), 325.

26. Ibid., 366.

ment proposed by "science," which resonated with a person's experience, rather than the actual findings of science. This picture "offered a more convincing story about his moral/spiritual life."[27] In line with this, it is clear from Hébert's writings and from Houtin's biography that such moral considerations loomed large in his intellectual development. In that sense Hébert's own life reflects his convictions expressed in "Thomisme et Kantisme" regarding the moral grounds of certitude.

In 1899, after a trip to Umbria, Hébert composed another symbolist dialogue, "Souvenirs d'Assise," translated here as "Memories of Assisi." If "Platon et Darwin" expressed hopes for reconciliation between modernity and the Catholicism of the present, this writing appears more critical of the latter and invests hopes in a Catholicism of the future.

Like *Platon et Darwin, Souvenirs d'Assise* originally was printed as a booklet intended for private circulation. Both were written for a type of Catholic whose mind had been impacted by the findings of modern science and critical history, but "who willingly accepted that intelligent priests provide them with the means to live in peace with official Catholicism, the old national Church."[28] Hébert did not encounter this mind-set only in the abstract; *Souvenirs* was written for a specific family whom he thought could profit from its proffered solution in a symbolist reading of doctrine. When he met with similar cases he cautiously made the booklet available as a possible resolution of their difficulties. However, *Souvenirs d'Assise* goes beyond a relatively circumscribed circle of those whose secular education had outstripped their catechism. Its ambitions encompass a transformed Catholicism of the future, a day "when—the discoveries of criticism and

27. Idem.
28. Houtin, *Un Prêtre symboliste,* 94.

the natural sciences having been popularized—the Church will take them into account in its formulas and its teaching." The effects of historical criticism of the Scriptures emerge in the dialogue's treatment of the Resurrection of Christ. If, under the impact of that criticism "the Resurrection ceases to be considered a fact of the physical order, it remains a fact of the ideal order and conserves, under its imaginative covering, all its value." This is hailed as a process of purification, not one of destruction. Indeed, "the true sense, the high moral significance of the dogmas, the ceremonies that come to us from Christ" will then become manifest.[29] The question naturally arises, how could its author seriously entertain such hopes? Again, it is Houtin who provides a clue, in this instance from his account of his own life in which he cites a climate of "dogmatic anarchy" among the French clergy as the nineteenth century drew to its close, a climate that sustained aspirations for far-reaching reform of the Church and its teaching.[30] How widely shared this climate actually was in fact remains conjectural. Houtin later provided some documentation in his *La Crise du clergé*.[31] *Souvenirs* gives testimony that it influenced Hébert to the degree that he considered his symbolist proposal a serious option. At the end of the dialogue his protagonist

29. "Memories of Assisi," 68, 65, and 68. The brief reference to the Resurrection is symptomatic of the significant impact Loisy's exegetical work made upon Hébert. While critical philosophy provided the primary impetus for his symbolist reading of doctrine, Loisy's parallel work with critical exegesis was a strong stimulus to a sense that the traditional formulas could no longer be understood with the literalness of previous generations.

30. Albert Houtin, *Une Vie de prêtre*, 266; *The Life of a Priest*, 157. Houtin makes this observation in the course of discussing Hébert's difficulties over *Souvenirs d'Assise*. In his autobiography Loisy makes a similar comment relative to the state of the clergy: "I myself perceived the intellectual anarchy that was beginning to invade the Catholic clergy"—referring to the same period as Houtin. See Alfred Loisy, *Choses passées* (Paris: Émile Nourry, 1913), 231; English trans. *My Duel with the Vatican* [1924], trans. Richard Wilson Boynton (New York: Greenwood Press, 1968), 217.

31. Albert Houtin, *La Crise du clergé* (Paris: Émile Nourry, 1907; 2nd ed. 1908), English trans. *The Crisis among the French Clergy*, trans. F. Thorold Dickson (London: David Nutt, 1910).

is exhorted (and through the protagonist, the reader) "not [to] break with the old Catholic tradition; be of those who can say with Christ: 'I have come not to destroy, I have come to bring things to their perfection.'"[32] At the time Hébert did not foresee that his symbolist compromise would prove to be an unstable solution. In just a few years he would move from seeing Catholicism as the highest point in humanity's religious evolution to a stage that was itself in the process of being superseded by those who no longer had need of its symbolic mediation of the truth of things.

Unlike *Platon et Darwin,* Hébert did not rush to publish *Souvenirs.* It was brought to the attention of the hierarchy by a colleague of his who appropriated a copy without Hébert's knowledge and communicated it to the cardinal archbishop of Paris along with its author's identity. The choice between submission or demission was offered him. Hébert resigned as director of the École Fénelon, a position he had held since 1895 and, after a period of protracted negotiations, quietly left the Church. His decision to leave Catholicism and invest his hopes for the progress of humanity in the socialist movement was sealed by the publication of "La Dernière Idole" in 1902—here translated as "The Last Idol."

While his early contact with Kant's thought had challenged his Scholastic confidence in the traditional proofs for the existence of God, in this article he mounts a direct attack on them. With their "unconscious mixing of religious belief and simple reason"[33] they are logically flawed, but indicative of a psychological need to represent the Divine personally. However, in doing so, this mode of understanding risks mistaking the phenomenal, the contingent for "reality such as it is *in itself* and not as it *ap-*

32. "Memories of Assisi," 69.
33. "The Last Idol," 74.

pears in our imperfect, fragmentary experiences."[34] The influence of Kant is readily detectable here. Moreover, insofar as the notion of a personal God bears traces of its authoritarian origins in primitive humanity, insofar as it has legitimated and continues to legitimate abuses of power—be they secular or ecclesiastical—a firm grasp of the idea is necessary to purify the image. An evolved human consciousness is capable of grasping a distinction that earlier generations were incapable of making. For Hébert the development of dogma is radical in its scope, affecting even the anthropomorphic representation of God in Christianity. In the "Second Study on the 'Divine Personality,'" "Anonyme ou polyonyme" (1903), which is also translated here, he continues lines of thought generated in the previous article and affirms: "It would be surprising if so many modern theologians, who have no other means of defending their positions against criticism than the theory of the evolution of dogma, gratuitously limit this evolution and refuse to allow it when it treats the very idea of the Divine and religion."[35]

The last of Hébert's articles to be translated for this collection is "The Bankruptcy of Despotic Catholicism" (1903). While his Catholic faith had steadily given ground under the impact of critical philosophy and that of natural science, critical study of the Scriptures had also played a significant role. The last of these factors comes to the fore in this writing, which showcases the work of Alfred Loisy. In Loisy he finds a kindred spirit, an ally on historical terrain in distinguishing the letter from the spirit. However, he parts company with the exegete in seeing several possible legitimate forms of expression of the gospel. Protestantism, Orthodoxy, and Catholicism can each in its way image the

34. Ibid., 81.
35. "Anonymous or Polyonomous," 100.

Divine Reality, "because it seems impossible that any adaptation of religious life can be considered intrinsically better [perhaps better for a few], for a certain category of minds, at all times and in all places, but it is impossible to prove it."[36] In this respect Hébert sides with Adolf von Harnack [37] rather than Loisy. Moreover, in the continuing evolution of human consciousness, as the Divine transcendence gives way before Divine immanence, dogmatic differences will fade in significance as people achieve greater solidarity in action, working for the betterment of humanity. Little wonder, then, that after his break with the Church Hébert directed his energies toward the advancement of socialism.

With the publication of "La Faillite du Catholicisme despotique" Hébert has clearly moved beyond the reformist intentions of Roman Catholic Modernism. After his break with Catholicism, Hébert took a position in Brussels. While there he became closely associated with the socialist movement, channeling his earlier religious aspirations for the amelioration of humanity into more secular form. He became a regular contributor to socialist newspapers and journals, although his idealistic form of socialism attracted opposition from those who saw it as remaining suffused with a religious tenor. *L'Évolution de la foi catholique* dates from this period. His *Le Divin. Expériences et hypotheses* (1907), originally given as a series of lectures at the Université Nouvelle de Bruxelles, provides a developed synthesis of his positions. [38]

After his return to Paris in 1907 Hébert continued to collaborate with the *Revue de l'Université de Bruxelles* and *Le Peuple*. He

36. "The Bankruptcy of Despotic Catholicism," 124.

37. Adolf von Harnack (1851–1930). Professor of theology at several German universities before becoming rector of the University of Berlin in 1900, and author of a monumental history of dogma, Harnack's *Das Wesen des Christentums* (1900) evoked Loisy's critique in the form of *L'Évangile et l'Église* (1902).

38. Marcel Hébert, *Le Divin. Expériences et hypothèses* (Paris: Félix Alcan, 1907).

also wrote on a variety of subjects, spanning science and the arts. On February 12, 1916, he died of complications following an operation.

Having situated Hébert's principal modernist writings in relation to his own development, it remains to situate him in relation to the modernist movement.

Hébert and Modernism

The two figures who are most prominently associated with the modernist crisis in Roman Catholicism are Alfred Loisy and George Tyrrell.[39] Loisy always protested strongly (if more than a bit disingenuously) against any imputation of conscious philosophizing on his part. He disavowed any interest in the discipline, representing himself as an historian whose conclusions were dictated by critical study of the facts. Although well schooled in Scholastic philosophy and acquainted with the work of both Blondel and Laberthonnière, Tyrrell's main interests resided elsewhere. Yet, although *Pascendi dominici gregis* (1907), the encyclical that condemned Modernism, acknowledges the role played by historical criticism and modern social and political thought, it exposes the roots of this "synthesis of all heresies" as resolutely philosophical. In that regard Hébert, although a secondary figure in the movement, gave substance to Vatican fears of the lengths to which philosophical speculation indebted to Kant could go.

Pascendi conducts an inventory of the modernist personal-

39. George Tyrrell (1861–1909). Tyrrell experienced increasing difficulties with his Jesuit superiors over the tenor of his writings, leading to his dismissal from the society in 1906. He was excommunicated for his public criticism of the antimodernist encyclical *Pascendi* in 1907. On George Tyrrell, see Maude Petre, *Autobiography and Life of George Tyrrell,* 2 vols. (London: Edward Arnold, 1912); Nicholas Sagovsky, *"On God's Side": A Life of George Tyrrell* (Oxford: Clarendon Press, 1990); and David Schultenover, *George Tyrrell: In Search of Catholicism* (Shepherdstown, W. Va.: Patmos, 1981).

ity, giving pride of place to the modernist as philosopher. While critical biblical exegesis and dogmatic revisionism would receive attention in their turn, the encyclical begins with Modernism's philosophical foundations, identified as agnosticism. In consequence, human reason is confined "entirely within the field of *phenomena*, that is to say, to things that appear: it has neither the right nor the power to overstep these limits" (§6).[40] While Kant is not named in the document, his philosophy is not far from view, especially given the consequences that are said to flow from this agnosticism: the demise of natural theology and the exclusion of God from science and from divine intervention in human history.[41] Agnosticism as a limiting principle finds its counterpart in a principle of "vital immanence" (§7). Confined within the phenomenal realm, speculative reason loses contact with the transcendent. That contact is reestablished by the modernist as believer and given expression by the modernist as theologian. Indeed, the latter may be regarded as a kind of synthesis of the philosopher and the believer:

> [T]he Modernist as theologian takes exactly the same principles which we have seen employed by the Modernist philosopher—the principles of *immanence* and *symbolism*—and applies them to the believer. The process is an extremely simple one. The philosopher has declared: *The principle of faith is immanent;* the believer has added: *This principle is God;* and the theologian draws the conclusion: *God is immanent in man.* Thus we have *theological immanence.* So, too, the philosopher regards it as certain that *the representations of the object of faith are merely symbolical;* the believer has likewise affirmed that *the object of faith is God in himself;* and the theologian proceeds to affirm that: *The representations of the divine reality are symbolical.* And thus we have *theological symbolism* (§19).

40. All references to *Pascendi* are taken from Vincent A. Yzermans, ed., *All Things in Christ* (Westminster, Md.: Newman Press, 1954).

41. Herbert Spencer and the positivism of Auguste Comte are also not far from view.

The modernist as historian is also directly dependent upon the philosopher, notwithstanding protests that exegetical and historical conclusions were determined by rigorous application of method, not by an underlying philosophy. The modernist as critic proceeds directly from the historian and thus indirectly from the philosopher: "[T]he philosopher must come in again to enjoin upon the historian the obligation of following in all his studies the precepts and laws of evolution" (§33). And thus in the Scriptures the critic "must admit a *vital evolution*, springing from and corresponding with the evolution of faith" (§34). In sum, "[t]he philosopher leads the way, the historian follows, and then in due order come the internal and textual critics" who practice an "*agnostic, immanentist, and evolutionist* criticism" (§34).

The articles translated for this collection exhibit how the agnosticism, immanentism, and evolutionism that Rome found to be integral to Modernism come to expression in Hébert's work. At this point some additional commentary on the "theological symbolism" censured by the encyclical provides further perspective on his ideas and their significance.

For sheer quantity of published output Loisy and Tyrrell—as but two instances among many—far outstrip Hébert's modernist writings. And while much of Loisy's exegetical work was more technical in nature, books such as *L'Évangile et l'Église* and *Autour d'un petit livre* found a wider readership. For all of that, it is arguable that Hébert's symbolist position became even more widely known in France through Nobel laureate Roger Martin du Gard's novel *Jean Barois* (1913). While a student at the École Fénelon during the period of Hébert's directorship, Martin du Gard underwent a crisis of faith and was one of those with whom the priest shared *Souvenirs d'Assise* in an attempt to preserve his student's relationship to Catholicism on symbolist terms. The initiative was not successful. Nonetheless, Martin du Gard remained on friendly terms with Hébert and modeled one of the characters in his novel, Abbé Schertz, on his former mentor. In the course of the chapter entitled "The Symbolist Compromise" Schertz becomes the mouthpiece for Hébert's position at the time he wrote *Souvenirs,* as Martin du Gard understood it and rendered it in popular form.[42] In the course of an extended conversation with Barois, the priest affirms:

> Human beliefs, like everything else, are subject to the laws of evolution; they steadily progress from the less good to the better. So obviously it's essential that religion should adjust itself to the modern mind.... Don't forget that in every man's belief there is bound to be a subjective element. People are only just beginning to allow for this. It's only quite recently that orthodox believers have admitted that some stories in the Old and New Testaments are to be taken in a figurative sense.... Well, that sort of mental honesty—which calls what is obviously symbolic by its proper name: a symbol—that's what is needed by people like you and me. But we must not apply the principle reluctantly and half-heartedly ... we must apply it to every statement of fact, when the modern mind cannot admit its credibility.... We should concentrate on the truth, not of the literal facts, but of their moral significance.[43]

Since a major portion of *Jean Barois* depicts its protagonist's involvement in the Dreyfus Affair, the novel long remained a staple of student reading lists. Thus, through the medium of a fictionalized character, an important part of Hébert's ideas continued to be diffused to a readership that likely had little contact with their point of origin or appreciation for what they were intended to accomplish in their day. We may ask, what may be

42. Critical analysis of the novel has shown that portions of *Jean Barois* closely reflect Hébert's letters to Martin du Gard, especially those written over the period of its composition. See Réjean Robidoux, *Roger Martin du Gard et la religion* (Paris: Aubier, 1964).

43. Roger Martin du Gard, *Jean Barois,* trans. Stuart Gilbert (Indianapolis, Ind.: Bobbs-Merrill, 1969), 37–38.

learned of Hébert's impact on the movement for theological renewal that was developing in the 1890s and early 1900s? How was he perceived by his theological contemporaries?

Loisy, Duchesne, and Friedrich von Hügel[44] were among those Hébert thought would be sympathetic to his aims in *Souvenirs d'Assise* and with whom he shared the unpublished booklet. Loisy reports that von Hügel was not at all shocked by Hébert's ideas on the Church, but that he expressed reservations on the representation of the Resurrection, and judged the proposals on the personality of God unacceptable. Loisy also states that, prior to acquaintance with this work, Hébert's ideas had not engaged either his or Duchesne's attention. As a result of his exegetical work, Loisy from his side had come to the conclusion that developments in human knowledge had far-reaching implications for the problem of God. However, he found the solution proposed in *Souvenirs* both inopportune and insufficiently thought through.[45] As for Duchesne, who saw little hope for reform, the booklet's very existence was regrettable because of the threat its discovery posed for its author.[46]

When both "Souvenirs d'Assise" and "La Dernière Idole" appeared in journals in 1902 their publication posed a threat well beyond Hébert to those identified as innovators in biblical or historical questions. A threat that apparently had substance, as shortly after the latter article's publication Loisy was informing von Hügel that "the Hébert case has already been exploited

44. In addition to Barmann's *Baron Friedrich von Hügel and the Modernist Crisis in England*, cited in n. 1, see his "Friedrich von Hügel as Modernist and as More Than Modernist," *Catholic Historical Review* 75 (1980): 211–32. Von Hügel (1852–1925) developed a wide range of contacts and was instrumental in diffusing modernist ideas.

45. Alfred Loisy, *Mémoires pour servir à l'histoire religieuse de notre temps*, 3 vols. (Paris: Émile Nourry, 1930), 2.48–52.

46. Cf. Letter of Duchesne to Hébert, 18 January 1900, quoted in Houtin, *Un Prêtre symboliste*, 113–15.

against us."[47] Shortly after Loisy made that observation the editorial note that prefaced "Souvenirs d'Assise" in the *Revue blanche* associated him with its contents. Although normally not one to initiate contact with the hierarchy, Loisy took the rare step of writing to Cardinal Richard, dissociating himself from Hébert's ideas.[48] In light of his previous difficulties with the cardinal over articles that earlier had appeared in the *Revue du clergé français*, he deemed it a prudent measure.

Despite the radical nature of their contents, neither of Hébert's two articles, nor "Anonyme ou polyonyme" or "La Faillite du Catholicisme despotique" received formal censure. This was perhaps in part because of their radicalness, in part because they appeared in laic journals, also in view of their author's liminal status. A work such as Loisy's *L'Évangile et l'Église*, perceived to insinuate its ideas rather than to state them openly, apparently was considered a greater threat.

Our earlier retrieval of *Pascendi*'s characterization of Modernism was intended to note the convergence of themes prominent in Hébert's work with those highlighted in the encyclical, not to suggest the adequacy of that characterization as a definitive definition of Modernism. In current historiography of the modernist movement *Pascendi* is viewed as part of the dynamics of definition, not its term. Indeed, despite the encyclical's insistence on the philosophical aspects of Modernism, the movement has often been portrayed as reflecting the impact of a critical historical consciousness on biblical exegesis and the history of dogma within Catholicism. Rather than attempt to do justice here to the phenomenon of Modernism in its varied aspects, let me simply note that Hébert's writings can broaden our appreciation of

47. Loisy to von Hügel, 26 August 1902, in Loisy, *Mémoires*, 2.128.
48. Loisy to Richard, 17 October 1902, ibid., 2.136–39.

what was at stake. Rather than being an internal affair within Catholicism, Modernism engages catholic (that is, general) concerns bearing on the importance of human experience—how that plays a role in our accounts of the world, the problem of reality—stemming from the role granted human experience in the process of knowing and interpreting reality, and the problem of determinism—following on a century of naturalism and especially given Darwin's impact.

Engagement with Pragmatism

The brief citation above from "The Bankruptcy of Despotic Catholicism" is indicative of what may be termed a "pragmatic" strain within Hébert's thought. Religious imagery is useful for purposes at hand, be they of individuals or collectivities, and possess a psychological (if not metaphysical) validity to that degree. No doubt Kant's second Critique fed this tendency. And Hébert's rejection of a portrayal of Kant as a radical subjectivist is symptomatic of a care to affirm an objective reality that grounds the always inadequate attempts of human reason to grasp it. Thus, on the one hand, it is not surprising that Hébert would experience a certain affinity with the work of philosophical pragmatists insofar as they placed emphasis on the practical dimension of truth. Nonetheless, just as he found it necessary to reject a perception of Kant as having volatilized objective reality into subjective apprehension, so he judged it necessary to counter what he perceived as a subjectivization of knowledge on the part of various pragmatist thinkers. In *Le Pragmatisme. Étude de ses diverses formes anglo-américaines, françaises et italiennes et de sa valeur religieuse* (1908) he surveyed C. S. Peirce and William James as American representatives of pragmatism, F. C. S. Schiller's "humanism" in England (James sometimes felt that he should have called pragmatism humanism), a group of Italian pragmatists associated with the review *Leonardo,* and considered the extent to which various French thinkers, notably a number of those who were identified with the modernist movement, could be judged to manifest this approach.[49]

The agnostic strains critics detected in both pragmatist and modernist thought, coupled with the influences of evolutionism and privileging of experience, facilitated identification of these two movements. This identification was reinforced by a certain anti-intellectualist tendency common to both, and a willingness to rework classical solutions to problems such as evil and suffering, and the very nature of God. In J. Bourdieu's summary judgment "Modernism is an application of pragmatism to religious beliefs."[50] Hébert's study shows this judgment to be too summary: both pragmatism and Modernism are more complex than Bourdeau represents.

On the pragmatist side, Hébert's slim volume gained the attention of William James, who wrote a reply with a view toward countering an imputation of subjectivism to his thought. In a second edition of his book, Hébert modulated some of the statements he had made regarding James in the earlier version, included James's reply reproduced in French, and added his own response. The second edition (1910) serves as the basis for the translation given here.[51]

49. On Charles Sanders Peirce's (1839–1914) life and contributions to philosophy, see Joseph Brent, *Charles Sanders Peirce: A Life* (Bloomington: Indiana University Press, 1998). Ferdinand Canning Scott Schiller (1864–1937) was the primary English representative of pragmatism, spending most of his teaching career at Oxford (1897–1926) before moving to the University of Southern California (1926–1935).

50. J. Bourdeau, *Pragmatisme et modernisme* (Paris: Félix Alcan, 1909), vii.

51. Since I have discussed Hébert's relation to pragmatism in "*Le Critique malgré lui*: Marcel Hébert's *Le Pragmatisme,*" in *The Reception of Pragmatism in France and the Rise of Catholic Modernism, 1890–1914,* ed. David Schultenover (Washington, D.C.: The Catholic University of

In sum, although himself a marginal modernist, Hébert contributes to our understanding of the movement from the ground up—through his own writings and his positioning of others. The writings selected for inclusion in this volume reflect a "left-wing" Modernism—also represented by Albert Houtin and Joseph Turmel.[52] The articles in part I exhibit the inner turmoil that erupted in Catholicism at the time of the modernist crisis and serve as a reminder that orthodox fears of Modernism were not groundless. In part II, the text on pragmatism sheds light on that philosophy's reception in France, especially with respect to the contribution of William James.

Hébert, along with others involved in the modernist movement, engaged human concerns shared with major intellectual movements of the period, indeed perennial concerns that transcend that period, though expressed in the language of the time.

America Press, 2009), 167–84, his study is not treated extensively in this introduction. The second edition of *Le Pragmatisme* has also been republished by Kessinger.

52. Joseph Turmel (1859–1943). A specialist in the history of dogmas, Turmel was a prolific writer, both under his own name and under a veritable team of pseudonyms in which he countered received views in Catholic teaching. Unmasked as the true author of his various pseudonymous writings, he incurred excommunication in 1930. Turmel defended his conduct in his two-volume autobiography, *Comment j'ai donné congé aux dogmes* (Herblay: Éditions de l'idée libre, 1935) and *Comment l'Église romaine m'a donné congé* (Herblay: Éditions de l'idée libre, [1939]); reprinted as *Joseph Turmel. Autobiographie* (Rennes: La Libre Pensée rennaise, 2003). Turmel's extensive bibliography can be found in Kurt-Peter Gertz, *Joseph Turmel (1859–1943). Ein Theologiegeschichtlicher Beitrag zum Problem der Geschichtlichkeit der Dogmen* (Frankfurt: Peter Lang, 1975). See also C. J. T. Talar, "Multiple Identities: Joseph Turmel, *Moderniste Démasqué*," in *Personal Faith and Institutional Commitments*, ed. Barmann and Hill, 67–89.

Part I Articles

1

Thomism and Kantianism

Paper Read to the Société de Saint-Thomas d'Aquin

The encyclical *Aeterni Patris* could be called the generative act of our society. Hence I do not need to defend it before you. But we should not forget that a considerable number of intelligent and influential men see in the "restoration of Thomism" merely an abuse of ecclesiastical power and the triumph of retrograde ideas. This is a deplorable misunderstanding that can perhaps be remedied by highlighting a few passages of the celebrated document.

I

The mere idea of a *traditional* philosophy outrages certain modern thinkers. Philosophy and tradition; are not the two words contradictory? Philosophy is free, autonomous, ever-open exploration; tradition is blind, servile, and sterile submission. And does not Leo XIII unmistakably condemn "*this new pursuit*," that is to say, progress?[1]

["Thomism and Kantianism" originally appeared as "Thomisme et Kantisme," *Annales de philosophie chrétienne* 13 (January 1896): 364–84]

1. Leo XIII, *Aeterni Patris* [Eng. trans. in *The Catholic World* 39 (October 1879–March 1880): 127].

No, we reply; what the Holy Father condemns is the violent break with the past that occurred in the sixteenth and seventeenth centuries, a wrongful, irrational break; for there is a choice: either human intellect had not yet succeeded in resolving any difficulty, an untenable hypothesis; or it was already in possession of certain truths, that it was not allowed to take into account. Leo XIII is thus correct in blaming those who treated their predecessors with such disdain and regarded pagan and Christian wisdom as null and void, "who, throwing aside the patrimony of ancient wisdom, choose rather to build up a new edifice rather than to strengthen and perfect the old."[2] "*To build up a new edifice*," to have the ambition to construct the philosophical edifice anew, from the ground up, with materials absolutely unknown previously, is the "*new pursuit*" the Sovereign Pontiff rejects; but what he is calling for prayerfully is to enrich the old patrimony with new ideas, new perspectives, to formulate the eternal problems better and to direct a brighter and more penetrating light into their deep mysteries. "[*T*]*o strengthen and perfect the old*": there has never been a more correct or more striking expression of the idea of progress. And to make sure of being understood: "In saying this," he adds, "we have no intention of discountenancing the learned and able men who bring their industry and erudition, and, what is more, the wealth of new discoveries, to the service of philosophy; *for, of course, we understand that this tends to the development of learning*."[3] Finally, at the very point at which Leo XIII most warmly recommends "the golden wisdom of Saint Thomas," he says, "we hold that *every word of wisdom, every useful thing by whomsoever discovered or planned, ought to be received by a willing and grateful mind*."[4]

2. [Idem.]
3. [Idem. (emphasis Hébert's).]
4. [Ibid., 130 (emphasis Hébert's).]

There indeed is the broad and comprehensive philosophy understood by Saint Thomas: "It is necessary," he says, "to accept the opinions of the ancients *as they are*. This is helpful for two reasons. First, what is said well we will accept from them insofar as it is helpful for us. Second, what is poorly enunciated we will be cautious of."[5] Elsewhere he expresses the same thought: each one, he says "*looks at that which has been acquired from his predecessors and adds something*. And by this means additions are made to knowledge. In the beginning these additions were moderate, but as time went by, in many diverse ways, little by little these additions progressed greatly. *One felt free to expand the thinking of one's predecessors by adding what was lacking*."[6]

Much later, this was the constant preoccupation of Leibnitz: to find a system that could "unite Plato with Democritus, Aristotle with Descartes, the Scholastics with the moderns, theology and morality with reason; to take the best from all sides and go still farther on. . . . This would be *perennis quaedam philosophia*."[7] A magnificent statement, but one no more illuminating than that of Leo XIII: "*to strengthen and perfect the old*."

Is it possible to carry this out? Is there not an incompatibility of temperament and necessary divorce between the moderns and the Scholastics? Is one not obliged to be entirely one or the other? Here one sees the shrewd smile of an Italian, of Leo XIII himself, if he heard this question asked: Ah the French spirit, which tolerates neither middle terms, nor compromises, and will accept only *all or nothing* in philosophy, in theology, and in many other things!

Is it not more sensible, more honorable for the human mind

5. St. Thomas Aquinas, *De anima*, lect. II.

6. St. Thomas Aquinas, *Ethic*. Lib. I, lect. II. Cf. M. Guthlin, "L'Esprit de la philosophie d'autrefois," *Annales de philosophie chrétienne* (May 1881).

7. G. W. F. Leibnitz, *Nouveaux Essais*, edit. Janet, p. 34.

to affirm that, in every spiritualist system, ancient or modern, a thinker *can* and *must* seek and discover a portion of truth?

This would be all too easy to demonstrate by taking Descartes or Leibnitz as an example; we prefer to choose a philosopher, Immanuel Kant, who is in bad odor with many people but who exerts at present a purportedly exaggerated, but in any case incontestable, influence.

II

Why, then, should not the German philosopher too add his share of ideas to the "perennial philosophy"? Admittedly, he has broken with tradition; he seeks nevertheless to benefit from the work of his predecessors. This is apparent in the way he speaks of Wolff and Hume, and moreover, did he not write these significant lines: "There is no possible use of our powers, however free, and no exercise of reason either that would not lead to unhappy consequences if each of us had always to start from first principles, and if others had not preceded us on the same path, not in order to reduce their successors to (servile) imitators, but in order to help us through their experience to seek out the principles in ourselves and thus to follow in the same path but with greater success."[8]

This is not, we hasten to say, the famous distinction between theoretical reason and practical reason that we consider an assured acquisition of philosophical thought. Scholasticism has been accused of *creating* abstractions; never has a more artificial

8. Immanuel Kant, *Critique du jugement*, 2 vols., trans. Jules Barni (Paris: Librairie philosophique de Ladrange, 1846), vol. 1, pp. 208–09. [Cf. *Critique of the Power of Judgment*, trans. Paul Guyer and Eric Matthews (Cambridge: Cambridge University Press, 2007), 163–64. Translations of Kant's texts are made from the French. References to the *Cambridge Edition of the Works of Immanuel Kant* are given in brackets following the page reference to the French translation for readers wishing to locate quoted material.]

and more dangerous abstraction been created than this division of reason into two other reasons, the first infallible, the second illusory. At the least we must take into account our philosopher's intentions.

Far from being a skeptic, Kant wanted, like Descartes, to strike a blow at these skeptics, these "nomads who abhor all permanent cultivation of the soil,"[9] a blow from which they would never recover;[10] like Descartes, he had recourse to a *desperate* approach, that he wrongly presented as the only true and legitimate method. On the contrary, it is only an *argument ad hominem* that forces the skeptic to rely on his honesty, and from there to admit his belief, believing in duty, that is to say in freedom and good, thus in the soul and in God. As an argument *ad hominem* Kant's approach possesses and will retain an incontestable value; never will a better nor a more decisive argument against materialists and positivists be found.

To what extent, then, has Kant contributed to philosophical progress? To what extent has he influenced the direction of human thought in a real and enduring manner? In our humble opinion, it is above all with regard to the problem of *knowledge* and of *certitude.*

III

The Kantian theory of knowledge differs less from the Thomist theory than is generally believed. For both sides sensible knowledge is the point of departure, the necessary condition for intellectual development. Let us note clearly, in fact, that Kant is not a skeptic relative to the *existence* of the external world, as is

9. Immanuel Kant, *Critique de la raison pure*, trans. Jules Barni (Paris: Germer-Ballière, Librairie-Éditeur, 1869), vol. I, p. 6. [*Critique of Pure Reason,* trans. Paul Guyer and Allen Wood (Cambridge: Cambridge University Press, 1998), 99.]

10. Ibid. I, p. 88 [p. 163], II, p. 46 [468–69].

generally believed. He even devotes a six-page paragraph to refuting Berkeley's idealism.[11] His true thought was not understood even in his own time, and in his preface to the *Critique of Practical Reason* he inserted the following note: "The names given to the groups into which philosophers have been divided have always given rise to a good deal of misapprehension so if someone said, N (Kant is here alluding to himself) was an *idealist* because, although he insists that *real objects*, external things, *correspond to our representations of external things,* he nevertheless holds at the same time that the *form* of intuition of these objects does not depend at all on the objects themselves but on the human mind."[12] Here is the best response to the widespread opinion that Kantianism is the ever-gnawing worm of modern philosophy, the casting off of all scientific character and is, in fact, a dream, an intellectual game that signifies nothing and relates to nothing. No, human thought is not a dream; it does not function in a void; Kant repeats over and over[13] that it *cannot* function thus and that it does not come into play unless "*sensible intuition*" provides "*matter*" for it; this *matter* is "*given*" by experience, it is, as a result, *objective* and does not lose this character just because it is subsequently submitted to the work of the intellect from which it receives its *form.* Do not the Scholastics also admit the action of the *agent intellect* on sensible representation? According to the most plausible interpretation, this means that sensation determines the higher intellectual faculty of the soul to produce in itself, by a virtue proper to it, the abstract general representation

11. Ibid. I, pp. 285ff. [326ff.]. See also p. 81 [159].

12. Emmanuel Kant, *Critique de la raison pratique*, 2 vols., trans. Jules Barni (Paris: Librairie philosophique de Ladrange, 1848), pp. 145–46. [*Practical Philosophy*, trans. Mary J. Gregor and Allen Wood (Cambridge: Cambridge University Press, 1996), 147; emphasis and comment are Hébert's].

13. *Critique de la raison pure* I, pp. 73, 111, 173–276, 114, 215, etc. [172, 193, 254–320, 195, 282, etc.].

of the object of sensation.[14] This new representation is not drawn materially from sensation; it is engendered by the mind itself and yet conserves an *objective* value, since the point of departure, sensation, corresponds to something real. Very well, but the same conclusion must be drawn for Kant's theory, which also places experience, "*intuition,*" at the beginning of all knowledge.

It is true that Kant preferred to speak of an intellectual "spontaneity" acting according to certain laws that he termed *a priori forms, categories, ideas of reason* instead of an *agent intellect* completely engendering abstract ideas, but that is only a secondary point; what is important is that the intellectual spontaneity, the active thought only exerts itself over the *data* of experience; thus knowledge has its objective foundation.[15]

We have said: *active* thought. There are two possibilities: either intellect is a purely passive capacity, incapable of reacting, a "tabula rasa" as the sensualist school would have it: one thus sees knowledge as reproducing the object as it is, without the slightest modification, as a faithful, but inert mirror; or the intellect is active, hence, since all activity is subject to laws, the intellectual act is complex since it is determined simultaneously by external influence and by the laws that govern the activity of the thinking subject. What are these laws? We do not have to state them here; it suffices to have shown that Kant distinguishes with good reason the *matter* and the *form* of knowledge, and that he might willingly subscribe to the formula of Saint Thomas: "the manner of knowing a thing *conforms to the state of the knower, which receives the form in its own way.*"[16]

14. Joseph Kleutgen, *Philosophie scholastique,* vol. I, trans. Constant Sierp (Paris: Gaume Frères et J. Duprey, 1868), No. 74ff. "Determination plus precise de l'abstraction." I q. LXXXV, a. 1.

15. Reread, if necessary, the beginning of the Transcendental Aesthetic and the Transcendental Logic. *Critique de la raison pure,* pp. 73ff., 110ff. [172ff. and 193ff.].

16. St.Thomas Aquinas, *De veritate,* q. X a. 4 [*The Disputed Questions on Truth,* trans. James V. McGlynn (Chicago: Henry Regnary, 1953), 19].

But, if the intellectual act is complex, it can and must be subject to a rigorous analysis in order to distinguish, to separate as much as possible, what comes from things and what comes from the mind. Kant did not waver before so arduous an enterprise, and even if complete success did not crown his efforts, nonetheless it is to his credit that he tried. Henceforth, in fact, philosophers must *critique* thought: to avoid it, under one pretext or another, is to admit one's inadequacy.

Shall it be said that this sort of method leads to skepticism? Pretty nearly, we shall reply, just as the experimental method leads to materialism. The best and most legitimate of things can be abused; induction, analogy, syllogism are abused, but is this a reason to condemn them?

It is too easy, moreover, to avoid a discussion by disqualifying one's adversary with such an accusation of skepticism. The objection is sincere, we know, for certain minds, but it may stem from confusing two things that are very distinct: the affirmation of the *existence* of a thing and the knowledge of its *nature*. For example, to doubt the *existence* of an external world is incontestably skepticism; but to acknowledge one's ignorance about the *intimate nature* of bodies, what Leibnitz termed so well "the inner nature of things,"[17] is proper and sincere humility.

And yet, Kant's objections and negations bear upon the second point and not the first; we have shown this earlier relative to the external world; it would be simple to prove it for the psychological world: "In the synthetic original unity of apperception," he says, "I do not know myself such as I am *in myself*, but am only conscious *that* I am. Now, since the knowledge of ourselves requires, in addition to the act of thinking that brings the various elements of every possible intuition to the unity of appercep-

17. Leibnitz, *Nouveaux Essais*, I, ch. 1, pp. 32–34; III, ch. 6 §36.

tion, a determinate sort of intuition, through which these various elements are given, *my own existence is not indeed appearance (let alone mere illusion)*, but the *determination* of my existence can only occur in correspondence with the forms of inner sense and according to the particular way in which these various elements that I combine is given in inner intuition, and I therefore do not know myself as I am, but only as I appear to myself. *The consciousness of oneself is therefore far from being a knowledge of myself. . . .*"[18]

And yet Saint Thomas also established precisely this distinction between the *fact* of the soul's *existence* and knowledge of its *nature*. "[T]he intellect knows itself not by its essence, but by its act. *This happens in two ways:* In the first place, singularly, as when Socrates or Plato perceives that *he has an intellectual soul* because he perceives that he understands. In the second place, universally, as when we consider the *nature* of the human mind from knowledge of the intellectual act. . . . There is, however, *a difference between these two types of knowledge,* and it consists in this, that the mere presence of the mind suffices for the first, and the mind itself being the principle of action whereby it perceives itself. . . . But as regards the second kind of knowledge, the mere presence of the mind does not suffice, and there is further required a careful and subtle inquiry. Hence many are ignorant of the soul's *nature* and many have erred about it."[19]

It is apparent that Saint Thomas does not in any way admit that the soul knows its own *nature* directly, through an immediate intuition. It establishes only the *fact* of its *existence*. But, one may say that the saintly Doctor admits "a careful and subtle inquiry"

18. *Critique de la raison pure I. Transcendental Analytic*, p. 183. [259–60 (emphasis is Hébert's).]

19. St. Thomas Aquinas, *Summa Theologica* Ia q. 87 §1 [(New York: Benziger Brothers, 1947), 444].

which can lead us to know the nature of the thinking principle. Yes, and here we get to the heart of the problem. "[T]he judgment and force of this knowledge, whereby we know the *nature* of the soul, comes to us according to the derivation of our intellectual light from the Divine Truth which contains the types of all things as above stated."[20] Here is the well-known passage to which Saint Thomas alludes: "[T]he human soul knows all things in the eternal types, since by participation of these types we know all things. For the intellectual light itself which is in us, is nothing else than a participated likeness of the uncreated light, in which are contained the eternal types. Whence it is written (Ps. IV. 6, 7), 'Many say: Who showeth us good things?' Which question the Psalmist answers, 'The light of Thy countenance, O Lord, is signed upon us,' as though he were to say: By the seal of the Divine light in us, all things are made known to us."[21]

The Angelic Doctor could not adopt another theory. How, in fact, would the nature of things be known to us? Would we read, so to speak, essences in the divine intellect which thinks them? Saint Thomas rejects this hypothesis. And would we have the intuition in the things themselves which are their realization? Saint Thomas does not admit this either. We have just seen that, according to him, the soul does not perceive its nature directly. As for material objects, Saint Thomas often repeats that the senses stop at accidents and do not penetrate to substance. Substance, as the very name indicates, remains hidden *under* accidents, which are still, at this point, so distinct from it that divine power, according to the Scholastics, can maintain them as separate. Saint Thomas also teaches that *substantial forms* are not known in themselves: "substantial forms ... in themselves are

20. Ia q. 87 a.1 [Ibid., 444].
21. Ia q. 84 a.5 [Ibid., 427 (emphasis in original)].

unknown to us,"[22] which would not be the case if we had the intuition of substances.[23]

We could highlight the striking resemblance between the *substantial forms in themselves unknown to us* and Kant's *noumena;* let it suffice to conclude that since the essences can neither be known directly in the entities that realize them nor through the intuition of divine ideas, a single resource remained for Saint Thomas: to acknowledge a special power of divine origin responsible for manifesting essences to us: this is the "intellectual light," the "seal of the Divine light in us [through which] all things are made known to us." This mysterious power is activated each time an object makes an impression upon our senses, and it then represents this object to us as it is "in the divine types."

It is always necessary to be suspicious of *special powers;* ordinarily these are but ingenious hypotheses that cover over difficulties instead of resolving them. In similar cases, it is best to abandon abstract discussion as soon as possible, and to reason about a concrete example.

Let us take then the definition of man: rational animal; there is the essence, the "quod quid est" of man; there is man such as he is "in the divine types." Does this not say a great deal? Do not the two terms of this definition, far from manifesting an essence to us, on the contrary convey a series of mysteries, one more impenetrable than the other! First, what is *reason*? Undoubtedly a faculty of knowing superior to the senses, but what is it *in itself,* in its essence? It is impossible to answer. Saint Paul had but to speak of the Resurrection to bring about interminable discussions between Pharisees and Sadducees; a similar thing happens

22. Ia q. 77 a.1 ad 7 [Ibid., 384].

23. Edmond Domet de Vorges, *Essai de Métaphysique positive* (Paris: Didier et Cie, 1883), Ch. III, part 2: "De la substance" and Ch. IV, p. 251.

when one speaks to philosophers of reason, of the origin of ideas, of the notion of the infinite. Would it be thus if we knew them "in the divine types"? But, the second term of the definition is no less pregnant with mystery. What is an *animal*? A *living and sensing being*. What is *sensation*? There are as many systems as philosophers. What is *life*? From this superficial definition—"the immanence of action"—does one imagine one knows its essence? But, the principle of this action, the nature of the matter on which it acts, the nature of the union between it and this matter, must be identified. Lastly, the essence of the created *being* and its distinction from the Creator must be stated. Mysteries, always mysteries! And it is so poor a knowledge that is supposed drawn "in the divine types"!

Let us take another example. Suppose that we declared to a chemist that we know the *essence* of iron, of sulphur, of iodine. The chemist will be quite astonished, for he is aware of the discussions among atomists, monadists, and partisans of continuous matter and knows full well that the greatest philosophers have not been able to settle the question. He will point out that the majority of the notions that we include in the *essence* of a body are quite simply its sensible qualities, that is to say, these complex phenomena of which we spoke earlier and which find their explanation both in the nature of the affected subject, and in the action of the external cause. Thus if we deduct from our knowledge various impressions of sensibility, what is left? The *fact* of the *existence* of an external cause, but we know of this cause only *that it is* and not *what it is;* the famous "quod quid est" escapes us, and what we accept as such is only the notion of being, of cause (which expresses, let us note again, a *fact* and not an *essence*) endowed with certain other notions: color, flavor, weight, movement, etc. . . . that are nothing other than sensible experience generalized.

Some may reply that we are wrong to consider the "intellectual light" as responsible for manifesting essences directly and completely to us; it is a matter of a simple impetus, which leads us to *abstract* essences from sensible qualities. But this interpretation runs up against a double impossibility.

The first has been very well highlighted by a contemporary philosopher, M. Elie Rabier. To subtract from an object or from its qualities their *particular determinations* in order to consider solely the *essence* is an absolutely impossible procedure. Why? "Because the thing to be separated constitutes here an integral part of the thing from which it must be separated. The separation is thus rendered impossible in this case, not by a more or less tenacious association, but by the very law of contradiction; the effort to bring it about would entail the very suppression of the idea. To conceive of a man with a body, arms, legs, but without granting him a size or position is impossible and contradictory, because parts having extension, yet without size and position, are not extended parts. . . . This is no less true for the *relations* conceived by thought than for the *things* themselves among which relations exist. . . . Resemblance cannot be conceived without *similarities,* and similarities cannot be conceived that are not *particulars;* for to conceive terms that are not particular, terms which are absolutely indeterminate, is to conceive nothing at all."[24] In short: to claim to abstract the essence of an object from its particular characteristics is a pure illusion, since in order to be possible every representation must be determined and consequently endowed with particular characteristics. How do we nevertheless form *general* ideas? The question arises naturally, but now is not the time to address it.

24. Elie, Rabier, *Leçons de philosophie,* vol. I: *Psychologie* (Paris: Hachette, 1903), p. 308.

Second impossibility: the passage from accidents to substance. There remains, in fact, a way of avoiding the preceding observations: considering the *accident* as produced by the substance, as the expansion of its activity and consequently the expression of the substance. Hence one could legitimately infer one from the other. But to say that the accident *expresses* the substance is a metaphor which, moreover, accomplishes nothing. Can one, in fact, conceive of the translation of an absolutely unknown language? And yet the *language* of accidents is a foreign idiom for which we do not have and will never have either grammar or lexicon, since substance itself eludes us. Unless, however, admitting, as does Leibnitz, the identity of nature among all beings; one could then give a *psychological* solution to the enigma of the world, but one which would be a pure hypothesis as would the postulate that underlies it.

Not that it is necessary to disdain hypotheses. What would remain of human knowledge if they were suppressed! Kant has written interesting pages on the use that can be made of these insights into the mind.[25] He himself has outlined grandiose and ingenious hypotheses; in his *Universal Natural History and Theory of the Heavens,* he sets forth the famous theory of the formation of the universe since taken up again and developed by Laplace and Herschell, and in the *Critique of Judgment*[26] the transformist hypothesis that would attract such great interest in our time. But, it is no less true that a hypothesis is a hypothesis, and that to take it for reality is to be a victim of an intellectual optical illusion, of a deceiving mirage.

Certainly, in experimental sciences the hypothesis can be transformed into a certain, positive law by means of *induction.*

25. *Critique de la raison pure* ["Transcendental Doctrine of Method," chap. 1, sect. 3.]
26. *Critique du jugement,* §79.

However, one must not delude oneself over the scope of this method. Induction infers from *facts* to *causes*, but experts are the first to warn us that when they use the words: *cause, force, atom,* etc., they do not give them a metaphysical sense; *cause* is simply the phenomenon or the group of phenomena that invariably and unconditionally precede another. The *causes* arrived at through induction are all of the *phenomenal order*: all that induction allows one to say is that given a particular phenomenon, another such phenomenon will follow. Here again it a *fact* which is stated and not an *essence* which is perceived. And this is true even with the special form of induction termed *analogy*. For example, I observe animals, their movements, their cries, and I affirm with certainty that they feel emotions of pleasure and pain just as we do. Am I better informed about their intimate *nature*? They feel the same emotions as we, they have representations, desires, joys, sufferings; very well, but *these are phenomena* and I end up knowing the *essence* of beasts' souls no better than I know those of humans. The same for the external world which is manifested to us through the *phenomena* of tension, pressure, resistance, etc., analogous to those which we ourselves can produce. We may be allowed to suspect, to conjecture that the two kinds of causes resemble one another a great deal, but, truth to tell, we do not know the *nature* of the one any better than that of the other. To affirm that they are endowed with *activity, sensibility,* etc. . . . , is not in any way an advance in knowledge, it is simply to separate, to group the various *phenomena* of activity, sensibility, etc., and to recognize that they have their raison d'être in a reality distinct from these phenomena, at least a partial cause of these phenomena, but about which we do not know how to say anything more. The proof is that a *faculty* can be defined only through its acts, through the phenomena it produces; it is thus not known *in it-*

self, or rather this parceling out of a nature among several faculties shows clearly that we do not know their essence, only the various modes taken by their outward signs.

Thus we can conclude with Suarez: "Nor do I think it inconvenient to concede that *no substance* can be known *in its essence* by us in this life. I do not consider the essence able to be known by sufficient experience. For that which has not been known by such philosophy and such love, by sufficient probability exceeds the natural faculty of human genius. However, I do not see this *essential* knowledge of any substance as something to be known. For that which we see, for the greatest part the soul can know. But such a knowledge is imperfect because its *essence* is not able to be stated. From its accidents what it truly is, is not perceived in itself, this can be easily stated, because from these accidents that knowledge which is perceived in itself is able to be held in higher esteem because it is seen through its own form. But thus far those things do not seem to be known essentially, for anything which shows itself with sufficient clarity, shows what it might be, sound, odor, and similar things."[27]

Kant's merit is to have based this claim, already discussed at the time of the Scholastics, while remaining only a practical observation for them, on a rigorous analysis of thought, thus establishing it *scientifically.*

Henceforth, this capital distinction between knowledge of the *existence* of beings and knowledge of their *nature* has been an acquired part of philosophy.

In this system one does not have to fear the exaggerations of nominalists and conceptualists: our thought, in fact, our general

27. Suarez, *Disp.* XXXV, sect. III, No. 5. We borrow this citation from the work of our honorable vice-president, M. Domet de Vorges, to whom reference has been made earlier: his chapter on "Substance" is an excellent commentary on it.

ideas, our definitions, our classifications have an *objective* value since they represent *objective* realities; it is nonetheless true that they do not enable us to know things as they are *in themselves,* but as our mind subject to their mysterious influence, represents them, in accordance with its own laws.

Kant recognized—as we have proven—the objective aspect of our knowledge, although he left it insufficiently resolved; as with all founders of systems, it was his lot to exaggerate, to force his thought in order to make it more striking; after having admitted *existence* as a fact, he presented it as a simple *category*; it is a case of following Saint Paul's counsel: "But test all things: hold fast *to the good*" (1 Thess. 5.21).

IV

In the numerous works on certitude published over the past thirty years,[28] one tendency emerges with increasing frequency: to make a *moral* question of certitude, in which the heart and the will play an essential role, rather than an indirect, secondary one. Centuries ago Plato said: "We must approach the truth with the *entire* soul"; this was forgotten and certitude was perceived too exclusively under its intellectual and impersonal aspects.

According to the Scholastics, the mind draws from sensible data a certain number of simple notions, such as the idea of being, of unity[29]; it brings them together, compares them, and obtains the first principles, all of which are consequently grounded on the principle of contradiction.[30] And yet, one of Kant's most

28. Charles Chareux, *La Pensée et l'amour* (Paris: Durand et Pédone-Lauriel, 1869); Henri de Cossoles [pseudonym of Mlle Gréard], *Du Doute* (Paris: Didier et Cie, 1867), and *La Certitude philosophique* (Paris: E. Plon, 1883); M. Ollé-Laprune, *La Certitude morale* (Paris: Eugène Belin, 1880); Victor Brochard, *De l'Erreur* (Paris: Félix Alcan, 1897); Gustave Derepas, *Les Théories de l'inconnaissable* (Paris: Ernest Thorin, 1883); the works of MM. Renouvier, Secrétan, etc.

29. St. Thomas Aquinas, *De Magistro,* a1; Opuscule LXIII *Super Boethium.*

30. St. Thomas Aquinas, In lib. I *Metaphycorum,* lect. VI.

original views, a veritable stroke of genius, is the distinction between *analytic* judgments and *synthetic* judgments. In analytic judgments for which the principle of contradiction is the standard, the attribute is contained in the idea of the subject, in such a way that it suffices to analyze the concept of the subject in order to deduce the attribute; for example, when I say: man is reasonable. These judgments do not give rise to any difficulty, for in formulating them, thought is confirmed without recourse to anything other than itself, since the predicate is only the repetition, at least partially, of the subject. On the contrary, in synthetic judgments, one adds to the concept of the subject an attribute which is not contained in it and which no analysis can extricate. For example, when I assert that every being has a sufficient reason, it is obvious that the idea of *sufficient reason* is not included in the idea of *being*. And yet I make the synthesis. On what grounds? Why add something to a concept that is not included in it? Therein lies, says Kant quite correctly, the real problem of pure reason, the life and death question of metaphysics.[31] Let us examine the objections of positivists. They never ask us: Have you the right to assert that the whole is greater than the parts, but: Have you the right to assume that everything has a raison d'être, that an imperfect, contingent being has its sufficient reason beyond itself, that order supposes an intelligent cause, that everything which has a beginning has a cause?[32] The principles under attack are all *synthetic* judgments. Will some say that these syntheses are *evident* of themselves and that the will's intervention in the form of attention suffices for the mind to conceive and acknowledge them? But what exactly is *evidence*? Is it not our objectified certitude? In fact, we call *evident* all propositions

31. *Critique de la raison pure,* Introduction, §6.
32. The formula: *Every effect has a cause,* is but a vain tautology.

of which we are now *certain,* excepting later recognition of their inaccuracy and falsity. To say that synthetic judgments are evident is thus simply to say that we are *certain* of a certitude, it is true, unassailable, imperishable. But from whence derives this certitude? Will some say that thought perfectly knows its conformity with its object because it knows its own nature which is to be *representative* of an object and consequently *conformed* to this object. We are all aware, it has been noted,[33] that our thought exists solely to represent something to us; if it did not have this end, why would it occur? To suppose that it represents nothing would be to suppose that it belies its very nature, that it is contradictory, impossible. But this theory supposes that representation is a servile copy of reality; we have seen earlier that it is, on the contrary, a complex matter: representation, to draw on the language of the School, is the act common to the knower and the known; the knower submits to the influence of the object (this is the *empirical* part of the representation), but he receives it according to his nature, reacting according to laws proper to him. These laws, at whose head we would place the principle of sufficient reason, are the *a priori* element of representation and allow the mind to raise itself above simple sensible data. But, it is the objective value of these laws[34] and not that of the empirical element of representation that is in question, and we cannot explain it through experience: experience is necessary for us to apply unconsciously these laws, for us subsequently to become conscious of them through reflection and analysis, but these laws go beyond it. Leibnitz pointed this out to Locke: first principles are universal and necessary, while experience is always particular and

33. Edmond Domet de Vorges, *Annales de philosophie chrétienne* (July 1885): 416.

34. Laws of *time,* of *space,* of *number,* for example. Here we only *outline* a theory that seems to us more exact than the old one.

contingent. Nor can one account for them clearly through an intuition of divine essence or a supposed perception which would assimilate the first principles to supernatural entities like Plato's *Ideas*. Experience can thus be explained only through an *intellectual necessity*, the mind cannot think otherwise; but then arises the formidable question: Is this necessity grounded in the nature of things or does it belong only to the human mind? It is useless to object: one must renounce philosophical reflection or follow it to this point.

As we have already said, Kant discovered the exact formula of this problem and resolved it with a bold stroke: he abandons theoretical reason and seeks his salvation in practical reason. Would it not be more productive to assimilate these two aspects of reason to one another? It is practical reason itself that obliges us to seek the theoretical explanation of its commandments. "Duty!" exclaims Kant in a celebrated apostrophe, "you that has nothing charming or flattering and that requires submission, without however seeking to move the will by threatening anything that would arouse fear, *what origin* is there worthy of you, and *where is to be found the root of your noble descent*, that root which . . . is the necessary condition of that worth which human beings can give themselves?"[35] Do we not catch him here in the transition from theoretical reason to practical reason? Once again this word "transition" is inexact, for it seems to indicate the anteriority of theoretical reason to practical reason which does not really exist. The notion of *sufficient reason* which grounds theoretical reason is just as primitive and independent as the notion of *duty*, and Kant has only avoided this objection by distorting the notion of sufficient reason and reducing it to that of a phenomenal

35. *Critique de la raison pratique*, p. 269 [209].

causality.[36] Perhaps even, in lightly exploring these fundamental notions, one would see that they all go back to a single idea, that of *perfection,* explanation, sufficient reason of all things in the theoretical order, an obligatory rule in the practical order. Whatever the case may be, these great primary notions which are at the basis of all our reasoning do not impose themselves on the mind *mechanically.* Otherwise agreement would occur in metaphysics as in algebra or in geometry, and minds would be no more divided over the existence of God than over Archimedes' principle or the theorem of the square of the hypotenuse. These eternal debates on the subject of great metaphysical and moral problems are often explained by saying that the mind remains free to give or withhold its attention from even obvious truth. But the most minute, most intense, most sustained attention can only make us notice *that* the principle of causality and that of finality *impose themselves* upon our intellect, it does not explain *how* one moves from this *intellectual necessity* to the *objective value* of said principles. Once again, does the difficulty not stem from the creation of abstractions? In fact, Kant saw in reason only the *voluntary,* obligatory aspect, the duty; older philosophy would consider chiefly evidence, *intellectual* necessity. If we make these two rays converge we shall no doubt have a fuller and truer light: the most important theoretical or practical principles, we may say, show themselves to the mind as necessary syntheses, but on the other hand, the *belief in their objectivity* is presented as a *duty* that must be discharged *freely.* Psychologically speaking, I am free to deny the objectivity of *truth* and of *duty* just as I am free, psychologically and physically speaking, to kill myself, but I am not so *morally.* I *could* avoid the *true* and the *good* by tak-

36. *Critique de la raison pure* I, p. 251 [305]; II, p. 347 [665–66].

ing refuge in a subjectivism irrefutable by the strength of logic alone, but I feel clearly that I *ought* not, and *freely* I *believe* in my reason as I *believe* in my conscience. I believe in them not only because I *submit* to the "brightness of the *mind* seizing *assent*," but because I *freely* yield to the influence on my soul of what appears to me as true and as good, to this attraction that solicits my adherence without extracting it by main force. The *consent* of the *will* stimulated by *love* of the true and the good is thus united to the *assent* of the *intellect;* certitude springs forth from the soul *in its entirety.*[37]

Let us stop here. This subject would require pages and pages. We have only sought to show that it is no less wrong to stop philosophy's development at the thirteenth century than it is to refuse to study these great thinkers known as the Fathers of the Church and the Scholastic Doctors. If human thought is something living, it is not confined to one period or another; it began with humanity, it develops with it, and the motto of the philosopher is indeed that which Leo XIII proposes: "to strengthen and perfect the old."

37. We think it necessary to recall here art. 9 of the rules of the *Société de Saint-Thomas d'Aquin*. "Each member or correspondent bears complete responsibility for his opinions. The publication of the works read in session does not in any way imply the adherence of the society to the ideas that they express."

2

Memories of Assisi

Editor's Note for Revue blanche: For the last few years now, an extremely interesting movement has been growing within the Catholic world and whose long-term consequences can barely be grasped: according to some it will renew the spirit of French Catholicism; others say it may even destroy Catholicism as a religion while reviving it as a philosophical system.

We shall not choose between these two hypotheses. Attentive spectators of the times, we limit ourselves to informing our readers about a development likely to mark the history of French ideas.

This is not just a question of the attempt to establish Christian socialism undertaken by a few priests, concerned, like their great forebears, with bringing religion back to the spirit of the Gospel. It is a parallel effort in which other ecclesiastics, familiar with the methods of criticism and analysis that, in the nineteenth century, so notably advanced philology and history, have begun explaining religious texts with the same rigor, in order to purify them of often crude interpretations.

The upper echelons of the Church were alarmed, thinking,

["Memories of Assisi" was originally printed as a booklet for private circulation as *Souvenirs d'Assise* (Paris: Impr. Bour, 1899), and subsequently published as "Souvenirs d'Assise," *Revue blanche* 29 (1903): 81–95.]

wrongly or rightly, that all of Catholicism, as a religion, would founder because of these breaches and would soon be no more than a philosophical system, seductive, but without a hierarchy and without power, a doctrine of resistance against the powerful of this world at whose service the Church has increasingly placed itself. The Cardinals, perhaps recalling the words of Lacordaire about Lamennais—"I am warning the Church that a war is being prepared and is already being waged against it in the name of Humanity"—have requested condemnations from Rome, have brought all their forces to bear against this proselytism.

They have not curbed it: despite the fact that the learned and courageous Abbé Loisy was judged in this sense too bold in his teaching by the theologians and was brutally excluded from the Institut catholique, each week sees more than twenty of the clergy crowd into the course he has given for two years at the Sorbonne, at the École des Hautes Études, regardless of the disfavor they court in doing so. M. Houtin, a priest attached to Saint-Sulpice, was banished to the provinces (no doubt so that any further work in Paris libraries would be impossible), guilty of having recently published *La Question biblique chez les catholiques de France*, a book of good faith, erudition, and courage, that has nevertheless had considerable success.

Still other men, enjoying great authority and high repute in the Church, are among this movement's initiators:

Canon Hébert, for example, until recently director of the École Fénelon at Paris, where he taught philosophy for twenty years.

The care with which the Church chooses those who teach young people is well known.

Abbé Hébert is not afraid of acknowledging his desire to adapt dogmas to the moral needs of the present and to reconcile his faith with his reason.

In 1899, urged by several former students who asked him: "Can one remain a Catholic without sacrificing one's reason and with complete loyalty to the modern conclusions of philosophy and criticism?," he wrote the following dialogue, *Memories of Assisi,* published below.

How did a copy of this work come to be extracted from one of the rare friends who knew of it and placed in the hands of ecclesiastical authority? The fact remains that the Archbishop of Paris forced Abbé Hébert to resign as director of the École, then, little by little, relieved him of all ecclesiastical faculties because M. Hébert refused to retract these lines, the result of twenty-five years of reflection.

The interest of this dialogue is that it asks aloud a question everyone asks in hushed tones, some seeking its solution in the faith of common folk, others in exegetical tours de force that delude only themselves, others settling it as does M. Hébert, but preferring, out of various motives, to keep quiet about it.

But the question has arisen, and must continue to be asked, and there is no doubt that it is one that preoccupies reflective minds. We thus feel it is our duty to submit it to our readers through this dialogue, so that they may taste the solid and generous thought underlying its poetic charm.

Memories of Assisi

Contemplated from the hill of Assisi, Umbria appears as an immense lake of verdure, an enclosed garden of potent but soothing vegetation, made perfect by the silvered greenery of olive trees. It is in this calm and pleasant valley that the voice of Jesus found its most faithful echo, his examples their most perfect imitator. Nowhere has anyone loved more or better; nowhere has anyone lived a life more truly evangelical, full of purity and goodness, of joy and holy freedom.

I walked the old streets of Assisi, and descended the short, steep, barren way that leads to San Damiano. My first visit would not be to the basilica, a marvelous and overly splendid shrine, containing the bones but not the spirit of Francis; it would be to San Damiano, for San Damiano is Francis himself, his humility and his poverty and his angelic love for the angelic friend. I can still see the poor little chapel that Francis repaired with his hands, the humble refectory where the Canticle of the Sun resounded for the first time, the tiny garden where Saint Claire cultivated a few flowers. San Damiano is still today nearly what it was in the thirteenth century; it has been providentially preserved from the ridiculous embellishments that disfigure and dishonor Saint Mary of the Angels. But what has become of the enthusiasm that filled the hearts of Francis and Claire? What has become of the mystical intoxication, utterly without fanaticism, that exalted them and filled them with an unutterable joy without absorbing them and rendering them less attentive, less compassionate to all misery, all suffering? . . . There, where these souls of fire were consumed with love, would mine remain impervious? There, where the river of the most captivating poetry flowed to the full, would my heart remain as dry as the stony road that I tread once again? . . . I stopped and sat down sadly under an old olive tree. A puff of wind ruffled the foliage; I listened to the slight murmur. It was as if the tree spoke to me: "Poor human brother, why is your heart so sad and discouraged? You seek to revive within yourself the naive simplicity and the transports of a Francis and a Claire? It is no longer possible! Never again will you be able to do so! Six centuries have passed, the world has progressed, the rays of science have penetrated even the most opaque bodies, they have dissipated mirages, made legends and myths disappear. Shed no tears over their passing, my brother; contemplate the divine nature as Francis did. See how when we are young, our trunk is smooth, regular, but soon the implacable sun floods us with its rays. We resist, we protest, we painfully twist ourselves about and our wood splits; there remains of us only tattered shreds of bark and a few roots that scarcely cling to the soil. . . . Are we destroyed? Not a bit; we continue to provide men with our delicate foliage and pleasant fruits. Poor human brother, do the same! Do not be concerned that the irresistible energy of the divine Sun that you call Science or Reason smashes to pieces your feeble ideas and little systems, dear as they may be, as useful and as apparently indispensable as they may be; give your flowers, your fruits to Humanity all the same."

And I thought: Brother Olive Tree is right. And I began to read the Life of the Poverello of Jesus Christ; then, after having cast a final glance at dear San Damiano, I slowly ascended the hill and headed toward the town. Soon I was joined by a good Capucin with whom, in a mixture of Latin, Italian, and French, I engaged in conversation.

I like Capucins, especially the old Capucins, whose experience of souls has replaced Scholastic formulas. Formulas live on in their mind and on their lips, but the living soul stands out as does the body from a custom-made suit; it goes beyond formulas and, unconsciously, disregards them in practice. My old Capucin, even if he was familiar with current systems and knew how to speak their modern language, appreciated and judged things as one of Christ's companions would have judged them, descending the mountain with him. I thus shared the subject that filled my mind.

—I do not like, he replied, to play the role of prophet and predict the future, but I can affirm that this future, if it is not a return to barbarity, to animality, will still acclaim our seraphic Father as an initiator, a precursor. Men understand this more and more clearly: their nature is a double-sided reality: at once individual and collective; they must thus never neglect or sacrifice either of these two aspects. To live in the most intense and most harmonious way and at the same time to live for others; to be oneself, to assert one's personality, but not to isolate oneself from one's brothers, not to claim exemption from this law of association which is the universal law of bodies and of minds, this is what all accept and proclaim, at least in theory, and this is already progress. Yet, no one has been more himself than Saint Francis, more original, more unshakable in his conviction, more ardent in defending his individual inspiration.

"No one," he says in his Testament, "told me what I had to do, but the Most High Himself revealed to me that I should live according to the model of the Holy Gospel."[1] It is this point that generated the popular image of Saint Francis as secular in the modern sense, living outside, but alongside the Church, parallel to it, a kind of proto-Protestant. What a false idea! Remember his relations with Pope Innocent III to whom he hastened to ask confirmation of his rule, and with Cardinal Hugolin, the future Gregory IX; listen to him in his Testament:

"The Lord gave me and gives me still such great faith in priests who live according to the manner of the holy Roman Church, because of their priestly character, so that even if they were to persecute me, I would have recourse to them. And if I possessed

1. [An English translation of Francis's "Testament" may be found in *Francis and Clare: The Complete Works*, trans. Regis J. Armstrong and Ignatius C. Brady (New York: Paulist Press, 1982), 154–55. Translation here is our own, adhering to the French.]

as much wisdom as Solomon, when I came upon poor priests of this world, I would preach in their parish only with their assent. I want to respect, love, and honor them. I do not wish to take account of their sin because I discern the Son of God in them; they are my masters."[2] An individual, yes, certainly, Francis was that in the fullest sense of the term; an individualist, no. He lived in and for the Church; he served it without being reduced to servitude, without ever taking an attitude of pure passivity which, to believe certain poorly informed people, would be normal, obligatory for a Catholic.

—So here, I replied, as in so many other circumstances, antinomies insoluble by theoretical reason alone are resolved by real life. How can one reconcile the individual with the collectivity? And thus we have it that Francis effectively becomes thoroughly individual, wholly developed according to his own law, and perfectly Catholic according to the common law.

—That is it precisely, resumed the Father; his life, indeed, has marvelously resolved the apparent contradiction that torments many consciences; it allows us to speculate about the Catholicism of the future. It will be neither the despotic Catholicism we too often observe, nor individualist Protestantism, nor an appeal solely to subjective consciousness alone, independent of all tradition and of the historical religious development of humanity, but it will be providential social support offered to the individual, respecting him, completing him, never crushing him. "The kings of the Gentiles," said Christ to his apostles, "lord it over them; and they exercise power over them. Be it not so among you: but the greatest among you, let him become as the smallest; and he that is the leader, as a servant."[3]

2. [Ibid., 154. Our translation.]
3. [Cf. Lk. 22.25–26.]

—Oh! What wonderful words, I exclaimed, and how my heart clings to the Catholic Church thus conceived! Confess, Father, that the most meritorious act of faith a Catholic can make in our time is to believe that the current Church contains within it this ideal Church, much as the dark and deformed chrysalis contains the graceful butterfly.

—I do not in any way deny it, my friend; it is to the Ideal, indeed, that our faith must always appeal. This is why those who are tempted to break with the Church make a deplorable mistake; they do not distinguish between the idea of the Church and the outer forms it has taken or takes on; and yet, these external realizations have only, as say our philosophers, an entirely phenomenal, relative, transitory value.

—I understand this, Father, but since you have had the extreme kindness to speak to me with open heart on these delicate matters, allow me a new round of questioning. Do you think that a new Saint Francis could be possible in the future? Just as we, who are civilized, are repulsed by the eccentricities of the fakirs while respecting the spirit that animates them, will not a future humanity be repulsed by this naivety, this admittedly admirable poverty, which is so difficult or even impossible to imitate?

—Exactly so, my dear friend, the new Francis will not appear under the same guise, since he will not grow and blossom under the same conditions. "The grace of God has manifold forms," says Saint Peter; and Saint Paul: "One after this manner, and another after that."[4] I admire the absolute detachment of Saint Francis only because it was his own spontaneous and joyous way of breaking with the barbarous, egotistical society of his day. Since, in fact, everyone understood and admired this approach, since it was effective, let us accept and admire it. But we are not

4. [Cf. 1 Pet. 4.10 and 1 Cor. 7.7.]

in any way obliged to see in it an absolute rule, a universal method, or, most of all, an eternal one. In the life of our holy patriarch, there are a thousand aspects explained by the milieu and the ideas of his time; all that is outmoded, has no meaning for our day, scandalizes instead of edifying, and will not happen again. But go deeper; admire the moral rule that the gentle mystic proclaims with unflagging constancy: Work and Charity! "I have worked with my hands," he says in his Testament, "and I want to continue; and I also want all the other brothers to work at an honest craft. Let those who do not know a craft learn one, not for the purpose of receiving wages for their work but as an example and in order to avoid idleness."[5] Saint Claire, on her deathbed, asked her sisters to raise and support her so that she could continue working. You admit, I believe, that the progress of humanity is oriented toward the meaning of these words: Work, Charity?

—Without a doubt, but what a chasm between the life of a Francis, of a Claire, and that imposed by the industrial progress of our time!

—Assuredly; Francis and his companions were above all mystical artists; their work assumed the form determined by their nature and the milieu in which they lived. They cared for lepers, helped country people harvest wheat, gather grapes, or pick olives; Brother Egidio served when needed as a water carrier or a sweeper; Brother Juniper had an awl and earned his livelihood by repairing shoes. . . . All this scarcely resembles the hard labor of a mine or of a factory, but given, I repeat, the milieu and the circumstances, it is no less the categorical affirmation of the sacred law of work, a duty no one should shirk. When the reformer of the future exclaims: Let us work with our hands! he will only

5. [Cf. "The Testament," 155.]

be repeating the customary recommendation of Francis and his brothers. As for charity. . . .

—Oh! On this point, Father, there is no need for lengthy explanations. I have long understood that the vice of our industrial civilization is not industry, work, or riches, but egoism. If men truly loved one another, seeing their brothers happy would be the condition of their own happiness; from then on, they would no longer seek to increase their fortune without limits, they would not exploit the workers' need when setting wages, they would not take an exorbitant portion from the profits of labor, out of all proportion to their personal effort or individual risk; the point of honor would be to accomplish the noble mission of work in common and not, as today, to display extravagant luxury and try to ruin or destroy their fellow men. All would work, but all would have the time to be educated, to be refreshed, and to profit from the pleasures that life on earth now confers only on privileged souls. And for me, this is what made Francis not only a marvelous organizer, a very prudent and wise administrator, as Saint Vincent de Paul would later be, but a progressive, a true reformer; he did not limit himself to pouring oil and wine on the wound, he wanted to make impossible the existence of those who wound and bruise humanity; he proposed to change, to reform the social condition, not by overturning it through violence, but by destroying the vice that poisoned it: egoism.

—So the saint of the future, although he would not walk barefoot nor wear sackcloth and a cord, could he not, in reality, be a new Francis adapted to different intellectual and social conditions, but animated by the same spirit, following the same impulse?

—I admit this, Father; however, have you yourself not indicated the insurmountable difficulty? You mentioned "intellectual conditions." And yet, is not the progress of reflective thought in flagrant contradiction to all mysticism? Would it not be as impossible for the future Saint Francis to live in our truly intellectual and critical scientific society, as for a bird to exist and fly in the void? Air, light, the indefinite heights of space were necessary for Francis's beloved lark; in the same way the charm and the unboundedness of myths and legends are needful for the mystical soul. Let me speak to you in all honesty, Father, criticism has killed legend, and philosophical reflection has dissipated the old religious myths on which your theology is based.

—Speak, dear son; yes, be honest; it is the primary condition of all Christian virtues; give me some examples which allow me to imagine these difficulties, these impossibilities which you say will henceforth stand in the way of any flourishing of the mystical life.

—Since you are amenable, I shall choose two examples, but I warn you, I am going straight to the heart of the subject. First, an example of criticism applied to the Resurrection of Christ. Please note, Father, that I am not asking myself whether, *a priori,* the thing is possible or impossible. . . . Outside of logical impossibilities, our poor intellects know nothing, absolutely nothing of real impossibilities. "If something exists, it is because it is possible," said the Scholastics, and that is, indeed, all that can be said. But a fact is only a fact when it is properly attested; yet if I open the Gospels without bias, what do I find there about the Resurrection of Christ? Discrepancies and contradictions that can only be overcome by prodigies of subtlety, real exegetical tours de force. The appearance to the Magdalene is told in an entirely different fashion by John than by Matthew and, in order to bring Matthew and Luke into agreement on the subject of the vision of the holy women, we must suppose, simply to meet the needs of the case, that they formed several distinct groups. Luke, moreover, only knows about the appearances at Jerusalem; nothing in Galilee. It is in Galilee, on the contrary, that Jesus meets his apostles according to Matthew and Mark; it is in Galilee that they receive their mission to preach the Gospel throughout the earth, a solemn scene that the author of the ending of Mark seems to have located near Jerusalem. All these contradictory details betray a revision, an alteration of the primitive testimonies, or at the very least the clouding, the overexcitement of the imagination, the absence of the calm and methodical observation without which a fact, especially a supernatural fact, cannot be established. Moreover, the eyes which saw the body of Christ also attributed bodies to angels, bodies brilliant as a flash of lightning and garments white as snow; the Apostles contemplated Christ rising into the air, Saint Paul heard him speak to him from the highest heaven as if the dwelling place of God, according to the ancient Chaldean belief, was situated above the firmament, a solid vault to which the stars were attached. . . . This suffices to determine the true significance, to convey the tone of these Gospel passages; these are clearly visions, not real perceptions. I do not therefore contest the sincerity of the first disciples, nor do I attack their profound and joyous faith in the Resurrection of their Master. I only affirm that we do not have any testimony that requires us to consider this Resurrection as a fact of the material, physical order. It would be easy to extend the use of this critical reflection to analogous questions; but I prefer to turn to the other example, of the metaphysical order, a capital and indeed fundamental subject: the existence of God. You shudder with indignation. . . .

—Not at all, dear son, and I shall tell you in a minute why your boldness leaves me calm and confident.

—You renew my self-confidence. I was afraid that the most venerable of acquired habits would inspire in you an insurmountable repugnance with regard to any criticism applied to this universal and necessary belief of humanity. The expressions I use prove to you that it is not in sacrilege that I touch on the holy ark; endowed with intelligence and reflection, I believe I am paying homage to the Divinity in using this intelligence and this reflection to examine what men have claimed about his existence and his attributes. I could raise once more the eternal objection: the existence of a good God is incompatible with that of all the ills that torture us. In fact, it is only in doing away with the rights of the individual for the profit of the species that this difficulty has been settled. God is supposed to act only through general laws. This is unacceptable, for, in metaphysics, one does not have the right to do away with so much as an atom. Or it is claimed that the individual will be rewarded for his troubles in another existence; yet this is a vicious circle, since the reality of this future life is proven by relying on the idea of a good and just God. But let us leave this difficulty aside and contemplate the set of arguments known as proofs for the existence of God. In truth, they make us aware that there is something beyond phenomena and beyond series of secondary causes; this something is manifested by a feeling *sui generis* that we call a feeling or idea of the absolute, the Infinite, the perfect. We possess this feeling, since we can clearly distinguish the infinite from the indefinite, for example, or from the unknown. Admittedly, but what is this infinite, this absolute, this perfect? Impossible, completely impossible to articulate whatever it is. There are, I know, analogies, images, but in order to make use of them without too many drawbacks it behooves us to append to these notions of psychological origin—power, goodness, causality, etc.—an adverb or an adjective and to say: *infinitely* good, *all* powerful, *first* cause, *sufficient* reason. . . . And yet these adverbs and adjectives reintroduce precisely the notion of the infinite, of the absolute, that we claim to explain. Let us admit, then, that this primitive feeling of the infinite, the absolute, defies all analysis. From the notion of space, the geometer can draw the notions of plane, of line, of point; from the absolute, the metaphysician can draw only the absolute. Let him, if he wants, tell the rich rosary of synonyms: infinite, perfect, ideal,—he simply repeats himself; this is not analysis, it is tautology. The metaphysician ought thus to limit himself to concluding: we have an irreducible notion of the divine, which possesses an objective value in the same way as our sensations. This notion can no more be treated as vain illusion than our categories of time and space, than our sensible impressions. *And that is all.* The rest is image and myth. And yet the image is true insofar as it can be associated with a true feeling; in itself, it is only a fiction and must not be taken for a reality.

—But theologians have always made this distinction between the image and the idea.

—They have made it *in theory;* in practice they have treated the image as objective reality; they have drawn conclusions relative to divine goodness, intelligence, power, as if one could apply logical reasoning to images. God, the king of heaven, conceived as an oriental monarch, dispensing his favors, his *graces,* to those who please him, performing prodigies for the benefit of one or another: there is the antique Chaldean and Judaic image that is at the root of your theology. Instead of viewing this myth as a thing in itself, give it its true value, its *analogical* value of which the theologians themselves speak; then, as long as necessary explanations are given, I no longer oppose its use in chants, poetry, worship, but you must admit that it represents for pure thought only a symbol whose elements are borrowed from a form of civilization long ago surpassed, from a conception of royalty repugnant to us.

—You admit in any case that the infinite is the cause of the finite and that, because the cause is supposed to contain eminently what is in the effect, one has the right to say that God is infinitely good, powerful. . . .

—Applying the concepts of causality, intelligence, goodness, etc., supplied by experience to the Infinite is no more having an idea than saying: squared circle. Infinitely good, infinitely powerful, is equivalent to infinitely finite. Calling God the *first* cause is to subject him to time, as it is to subject him to number to claim with the pantheists that God and the world comprise but *one* substance. From the standpoint of pure intellect, we can and must assert only that the human mind fully expresses its consciousness of being by the double notion of finite *and* infinite, like this other: subjective *and* objective—also quite legitimately. As for the relations between the finite and the infinite, pure thought has nothing to say about it, other than that the finite and the infinite are two aspects of Reality and that they are reconciled in it in a way that remains for us an impenetrable mystery. All the rest is image and myth. And yet these are the images and myths that, taken literally, in naiveté, have incited the enthusiasm, fed the charity of a Francis and a Claire; these myths having disappeared, will mysticism be able to subsist?

—My friend, as long as man is not to be a pure spirit, pure thought will remain an abstraction. Imagination and sensitivity are as essential for man as reason. The "God perceptible to the heart" symbolized by the somewhat dull images of metaphysics or by religion's more colorful ones, is therefore nowhere near disappearing from Humanity's consciousness. I say as much of the feeling of our dependence on the infinite, a dependence symbolized by prayer disguised as petition. Moreover, do you not attribute to symbol, to myth, greater importance than is proper? Mirrors do not confer beauty upon the face and myths do not give value to the soul. Brother Elias accepted the same myths as Saint Francis and their lives were so different! It is the living soul, good and beautiful, which, in interpreting myth, confers goodness and beauty upon it. And when it can no longer find itself, recognize itself in a myth and make use of it, as your scholars say, through autosuggestion, it abandons it and creates others. This marvelous power of the human soul to idealize and create has no bounds, and this is why I am not anxious about the saints of the future.

—But what do you yourself think, Father?

—I belong, my dear son, to a generation that has also taken metaphorical and mythical formulas quite literally. I shall never easily disengage my mind from them; nevertheless, I understand the requirements of a better trained, more thorough mind, and you yourself have recognized that if theologians have continued in the old popular ways, in theory they have already made the distinctions of which modern philosophy is so proud. An equivalent to the formula: "God does not exist; he is" can be found in the writings of Pseudo-Dionysius the Areopagite, and it is Saint Paul who spoke of the "Divine" to Athenians on the hill of the Areopagus. Here we find milestones and as it were building blocks for the constructions of the future. Besides, what are the results of your implacable criticism? Jesus was not materially resuscitated; but who today still claims that he "descended into the lower regions of the earth" as Saint Paul nevertheless taught? You do not deny the actual fact of the visions confirmed by all these testimonies so contradictory in their details; and yet, to employ an expression belonging to one of your thinkers, nothing stands in the way of considering these visions as "veridical hallucinations." They could have been produced by the apostles' and disciples' imaginations under the influence of their conviction—

a conviction justified by the facts and thus having an objective value—that Christ henceforth lived in the true life and acted in them and through them to found his Church. The same mysterious and divine force which created Christianity through them created these visions in them. It is not surprising that the imaginations of the first Christians were clothed in a very pronounced Judaic character, that the disciples could not represent their Master surviving other than with a material body which, however ethereal Saint Paul tells us it is, is no less a body, and that this survival has consequently taken the form of a resurrection. If the Resurrection thus ceases to be considered a fact of the physical order, it remains a fact of the ideal order and conserves, under its imaginative covering, all its value. Your criticism, far from destroying dogmas, purifies them; it re-creates, reinvents them, reclothes them in new, less material and more psychological forms, and still the same divine center of consciousness finds expression in them. I will say the same of your metaphysics: the myth of God personified has vanished, the feeling of the existence of the Divine subsists unshaken, unassailable. If, to satisfy your imagination as a philosopher, instead of saying: I believe in God,—you prefer to say: I believe in the objective value of the idea of God,—I see no difficulty, unless you are speaking to simple folk who will not understand you.

—It is not my imagination as a philosopher that I am satisfying, Father, I am easing my conscience. Well then! We no longer want this infinitely just God who punishes our crimes for four generations and indulges in every kind of arbitrariness and favoritism; this infinitely good God who tortures for all eternity those who have not loved him! We claim to seek and to find a way of objectivizing our sense of the Divine, a way less dangerous, less subject to abuse. This primary formula modified, the others will transform themselves. For example, if we used the Stoic image, instead of the popular image—you see, Father, I do not delude myself; I accept the necessity of our being unable to think without image—if, I say, instead of speaking of a personal God, we spoke of an eternal Law according to which beauty, goodness, justice are accomplished in the world, Prayer would no longer be the supplication of a self-interested beggar, but the energetic effort, accompanied by words and aspirations, for this accomplishment of the Good; the Miracle being this accomplishment in itself from which clearly shines forth a force superior to those we see at work in purely mechanical combinations. . . .

—And the Gospel, Morality?

—The Gospel, Father, would thus be freed from its setting of popular beliefs and magical tricks; it would become the incontestable revelation of the Divine through the life and death of Christ, the incomparable proclamation of the Law of justice and love; from then on it would be accepted by every upright conscience. And morality would become a true morality, for man would willingly submit himself to its Law, not because a master imposes it, but because he senses its value. In your own case, would you entrust yourself to a man who would be just because a God changed water into wine? The God-policeman that the catechism preaches is suitable for savages, not for free beings. But alas! So much worry about making the popular masses intelligent and free! Conservatives, on the contrary, who have domesticated religion to their profit, so to speak, seek to restrict and hinder reflection, out of fear that the old images on which their privileges and moral conventions rest may be affected. As for the simple, the humble, you well know that I have no intention of separating myself from them. I believe too strongly in the intimate communion of all beings to shut myself up in my personality, prideful yet so morally wanting. I want to pray with them; all I ask is the right to view their manner of speaking of God as relative and transient, consequently reformable. I am not agnostic since I affirm the Divine; but what is this Divine? The conception I form of it is imperfect and subordinated to my physical and intellectual constitution; from here I can find the absolute and definitive neither in Christ himself nor in the Church which represents and continues him. I recognize that the truth is in Christ and in the Church, but it resides there only in the general direction given to thought and activity; we must adapt this direction to the scientifically established conditions of reality.

—But, dear son, Saint Paul proclaimed long ago: "We see now through a glass darkly, later we shall see face to face. . . . Then, prophecies shall be made void, . . . tongues shall cease, . . . knowledge will disappear. For we know in part, and we prophesy in part, but when that which is perfect shall come, that which is in part shall disappear. . . . Charity alone is eternal."[6]

—Ah! No doubt, Father, but no sooner read than forgotten; the theologian is no less arrogant, the Church no less intolerant, no less despotic, no less imperious in its intention of transforming the believer into a religious automaton.

—My dear child, this is a chance to tell you with Scripture: "Go and see the flowers of the fields, as they 'increase' in a manner slow and imperceptible." This is also the law of progress in Humanity. Seven hundred years before Jesus Christ, the prophet Hosea was already saying in the name of the Lord: "What I desire are not sacrifices, but kindness."[7] And Christian nations are still cutting each other's throats! . . . Thus let us affirm the Ideal, my friend, but, knowing through our personal experience how

6. [1 Cor. 13.12, 8–10.]
7. [Hosea 6.6.]

much it costs to put it into practice, let us not deprive Humanity of means however humble, however imperfect they may be, which help it to accomplish some of its aspects. To those who accept dogmas automatically, through sheer habit or without understanding them, let us explain the true sense, the high moral significance of these dogmas, ceremonies that come from Christ. Believe me, their ideal content is nowhere near exhausted; therefore I can—and I must—use them without being charged with hypocrisy. Further, if I have faith in the Gospel, I have faith in Reason, and I hail the distant day when—the discoveries of criticism and the natural sciences having been popularized—the Church will take them into account in its formulas and its teaching. Leave this great humano-divine organism the time to eliminate certain elements, from now on devoid of value, that it assimilated in Jerusalem, in ancient Rome, in Byzantium, or in medieval Schools, and then the reconciliation of religion and science will come about because their reciprocal role will be clearly understood: for religion should support the soul's sense of the Ideal, what *ought* to be; it is for science to make us clearly understand the requirements of reality; it is for the individual to consciously master these two forces, unite them, regulate them both, and live according to their result. The more Humanity progresses, the better it will be understood that the Gospel and the Church are not machines distributing ready-made truth and moral authority, but providential aids designed to support and encourage the individual in his continual effort toward the best. For nothing is done, no progress is accomplished if not by the individual; on the other hand, as in all true evolution, progress cannot be imposed from without and by the use of violent force: it must come from within. "The Church," one of my friends is wont to say, "the Church, one day, will fashion *its own*

Protestantism, and that will be the end of the other." Once more, then, I commend you, do not break with the old Catholic tradition; be of those who can say with Christ: "I have not come to destroy, I have come to bring things to their perfection."[8] But here is the basilica; let us enter and each, in his own manner, pray!

We entered the lower church and, after glancing with pleasure at the frescoes of Cimabue, Giotto, and Simon Martini, we descended into the crypt constructed at the beginning of this century above the remains of the Poverello of Assisi: Greek columns, gilding, a vault painted green . . . I shrugged my shoulders at the good Capucin. He responded with a smile that signified: Be more indulgent! What exasperates you comes from men; raise your heart higher! . . . I knelt down. The Divine, I thought, is inexhaustible. What form will its new epiphany take? And who will be the chosen, the herald of a Gospel better-understood, filling hearts with joy and love? A poor person, a simple person from Umbria, as before? . . . Or rather, a worker from our factories? . . . And the words of the Psalmist came to my lips: "Send forth your spirit, your creative breath, and you will renew the face of the earth!"[9]

8. [Cf. Mt. 5.17.]
9. [Ps. 104.30.]

3

The Last Idol

Study of the "Divine Personality"

The harrowing problem that troubles many consciences today is this: Must the old belief in the *transcendent God* give way to the affirmation of the *immanent Divine*? Is not the All-Powerful (the "King of Kings") one of these Chaldean metaphors that Christianity has passed on to us along with its doctrine, of much moral stature, but so intermingled, so encumbered with archaic conceptions and comparisons? Metaphysics has done its best to repair this image, increasingly correcting and idealizing it, but it has preserved the notion of personality in such a way that this imaginative construct, made not to resemble our body, but our soul, nonetheless remains, in spite of certain practical advantages, the last idol against which our intellect, informed by so many reflections and experiences, protests.

And yet, it is important to note that many come to think of a personal God only because they desire, they want, a priori, that God to be personal. Unconsciously they replace their reason with their faith. Most of the *major premises* on which the Scholastic

["The Last Idol: Study of the 'Divine Personality'" appeared as "La Dernière Idole. Étude sur la 'personalité divine,'" *Revue de Métaphysique et de Morale* 10 (July 1902): 397–408.]

philosophers based their syllogisms thus contained their diluted belief, incorporated in some principle, more or less experimental or rational; it is not surprising that the conclusion should concur so remarkably with the data of Revelation. Here is a striking example taken from the proofs of the existence of God as developed by Saint Thomas Aquinas in the first part of the *Summa Theologiae.*

I

The principle on which the first proof (proof by the "first mover") is based is expressed in this way: "[W]hatever is in motion is put in motion by another."[1] And, a little farther on: "It is therefore impossible that in the same respect and in the same way a thing should be both mover and moved, i.e., that it should move itself. Therefore whatever is in motion must be moved by another." The conclusion is predictable: "But this cannot go on to infinity. . . . Therefore it is necessary to arrive at a first mover, put in motion by no other; and this everyone understands to be God."[2]

Let us first point out that the problem is badly articulated; Saint Thomas affirms as impossible what the adversaries allow as possible, namely, that nature "moves itself"; a Spinozist would, indeed, reply that it is not "in the same respect and in the same way" that Being is "mover and moved" and would follow up with the famous distinction between "natura naturans" and "natura naturata."[3] Saint Thomas thus commits a *petitio principii.*

1. [When Hébert quotes Aquinas he does so in Latin.]

2. St. Thomas Aquinas, *Summa Theologiae* Ia 2 §3 [Eng. trans. *Summa Theologica* (New York: Benziger Brothers, 1947), 1.13].

3. [Literally "Nature naturing" and "Nature natured." The first term in effect describes an active and changing God, while the second a passive God in which things have already been created.]

It is, moreover, easy to recognize that the apparent lucidity of this proof depends on the introduction of a spatial image into a problem of a metaphysical nature: beings supposed from the outset (without proof) isolated from one another, are juxtaposed as a row of billiard balls in which each communicates movement to the other. Are you surprised then that a "*first* mover" is necessary! This way of arranging things, of deciding the question by an image, is another form of the same *petitio principii,* unconscious no doubt, but real.

But still, one might reply, the Spinozist is required to distinguish between "natura naturans" and "natura naturata"; a kind of equivalent to the distinction between creator and creature. No, we shall answer, for the first theory *distinguishes* while the second *separates.* Likewise the monistic idealist will, in fact, speak of the Ideal and its realization, but nonetheless he will not place the Ideal on one side and the world on the other. The affirmation of the Ideal satisfies his need for "sufficient reason"; as for the famous principle of causality, verifiable only by our fragmentary experiences, he refrains from unduly carrying it beyond experience, as Saint Thomas once more does in the second proof.

Let us finish what we have to say regarding to the first proof in pointing out within it a third *petitio principii.* If the Angelic Doctor effectively ends with a God existing separately from the world, thus its creator, it is because the separate existence is already affirmed in the major: "[W]hatever is in motion is put in motion *by another.*" *By another;* but that is the question! . . . And consequent upon whether or not these two words are introduced into the premises, the transcendent God or the immanent God will be found. Yet nothing, absolutely nothing, warrants preferring *by another* to *by itself;* nothing warrants extending a formula justified only *through* and *in* sensible experience to the essence of things.

The *petitio principii* is more evident still in the *second proof.*

"In the world of sense we find there is an order of efficient causes. There is no case known (neither is it, indeed, possible) in which a thing is found to be the efficient cause of itself; for so it would be prior to itself, which is impossible. Now in efficient causes it is not possible to go on to infinity, because in all efficient causes following in order, the first is the cause of the intermediate cause. . . . Therefore it is necessary to admit a first efficient cause, to which everyone gives the name of God."[4]

Obviously, if the efficient causes are set sequentially in a row in numerical series, it is necessary to go back to number one; but the problem has already been resolved by formulating it in this way. Saint Thomas did not realize that the constitution of said series could be merely a method representing our imperfect intellect, incapable of encompassing the whole and reduced to dividing it up; further he did not perceive that he applied to activity, to life considered *in itself,* a concept of causality borrowed from the experience of *phenomena,* from the experience of the senses: "in the world of sense" a phenomenon may well *condition,* determine another phenomenon; this does not make it in any way the *cause* in a metaphysical sense. *Condition* is not *cause.*

The *third proof* denotes precisely the claim to regard being in itself, to grasp its essential contingency: "We find in nature things that are possible to be and not to be . . . for that which is possible not to be at some time is not." The argument is dense and Saint Thomas concludes with good reason: "[T]here must exist something the existence of which is necessary . . . some being having of itself its own necessity, and not having received it from another, but rather causing in others their necessity. This all men

4. *Summa Theologica* Ia 2 §3, p. 13.

speak of as God."[5] But why, after having affirmed the "existence *of* which is necessary," conclude "necessity *above* the thing," if not by the same unconscious sleight of hand as in the first proof: the "*something* [else] which exists" plays the same role as the "put in motion by an *other*"; separation, once surreptitiously introduced into the major, infallibly reappears in the conclusion. The same observation for the *fourth proof* and the *fifth*, whose major premises are: "'more' and 'less' are predicated of different things, according as they resemble in their different ways *something* which is the maximum." And: "whatever lacks intelligence cannot move toward an end, unless it be directed by *some being* endowed with knowledge and intelligence; as the arrow is shot to its mark by the archer."[6]

Always, one notes, the same a priori separation or personification; always, as a consequence of the unconscious mixing of religious belief with simple reason, the same *petitio principii* to which we shall oppose the Angelic Doctor's reply to the ontological argument of Saint Anselm: "[T]his precisely is not admitted by those who hold that God does not exist."[7]

II

Do Saint Thomas's proofs lose all value?

As syllogistic arguments, they do not retain any value. They are unconscious sophisms. We will not say the same, however, if we regard them less from the *logical* point of view than from the *vital* point of view, as expressions of the psychic life of the person who elaborated and formulated them in accordance with his time. Through the tendencies and beliefs they contain and arouse, they

5. Idem.
6. Ibid., p. 14.
7. *Summa Theologica* Ia 2 §1 ad. 2. Ibid., p. 12.

can be a support for the soul, a stimulus for reflection, a means of establishing the incomplete character of a thought that would persist in thinking and affirming only the phenomenal, the relative, an excellent method for exploring the mysterious beyond; but we repeat, these arguments allow us to arrive at the beyond, the Ideal, the Divine, but not a personal God. What they really prove is that our consciousness of Reality will be completely expressed only if we assert this Reality's absolute, infinite, perfect aspects with its contingent, finite, imperfect aspects, just as our consciousness of the psychic is completely expressed only if we assert the whole set of its unitary and multiple aspects. As for positing the reality of the Absolute, of the Perfect *separately* from the reality of the contingent, of the imperfect, we are no more authorized to do it than actually to separate unity from multiplicity in the soul. Let us *distinguish;* let us not *separate*!

An objection to this may be that we are up against a mystery, that nothing thus allows us to deny the hypothesis of transcendence in order to assert that of immanence.

Immanence and transcendence, the within and the above, always these spatial metaphors so insufficient and so dangerous in such a matter! It is tempting to refuse to take sides and simply to assert the *divine* as one asserts the *beautiful,* the *good,* ultimate mysteries, impenetrable to thought.

Also, it is not a priori, but only a posteriori and with ad hominem argument that one can reply to those who make the divine a separate being, creator of the universe: in the sincerity of your faith, in the ardor of your assertion, you forget the objection of the existence of evil; a satisfactory solution *has never been given;* it has been attempted in the name of reason, but only by evading the very reality of evil, as did Leibnitz, by supposing that physical evil is always a moral test (but then why does the child suffer?), or by suppressing one part of the problem, for example, objections stemming from the suffering of animals: Are these not automatons? asked Malebranche, and Père Bougeant even claimed they might be incarnate demons! . . . We are not so naive as to take seriously the childish pleadings of these so-called *Theodicies*. Once again we would side with Renan: "The general drift of the world is benevolent . . . the spirit of goodness dominates in the universe";[8] in order to make it clearer to the imagination and to the heart, we would gladly *symbolize* this spirit of goodness (itself a symbol) by the "heavenly Father" of the Gospel, but it has become forever impossible to take these words *literally* in saying: I believe in the Heavenly Father, in the Infinite Love that created consumption, the plague, cancer, hurricanes, volcanoes. . . .

Thus let us admit: Reality, insofar as it manifests itself as active power, represents neither an omnipotence, nor an omniscience, nor all goodness, but rather a colossal, an incommensurable force which, by trial and error and without ever tiring, strives unceasingly, through innumerable attempts, toward the best, toward the Ideal. Reality carries within it, as the law of its own evolution, this Ideal, a living law, true life of all life and not an abstract law like those of a physics or chemistry manual; this is why, when all is said and done, the outcome of the world's forces drifts toward the Good.

For those who do not acknowledge, beyond utilitarian ends, any objective value to the qualitative appreciation of beings and things, the problem of the existence of God *does not even arise*. However, from the moment this ideal value is acknowledged to whatever degree, it follows that if, through abstraction, one isolates this ideal from its imperfect always incomplete realization,

8. Ernest Renan, *Feuilles détachées*, article on Amiel, pp. 386–88.

one thereby establishes in reality an aspect as real and as objective as any other aspect of this same reality directly grasped by experience, and there is no reason to raise it up as a *separate being,* as an anthropomorphic idol, for it to respond to the notion of the perfect, of the absolute, that we find in our consciences. The same life, the same law animates our consciences and the world.

III

Conclusion: perfect-imperfect; infinite-finite; absolute-relative, human thought can only express its complete consciousness of Reality through these opposites; which is also the case for the other "dyads": subjective-objective; self-not-self.

It is out of practical needs (but a *method* is not a theoretical *truth*) that thought *separates* and divides up what it ought only to *distinguish* and creates these entities that are then said to be separated in reality: God *and* the world; the soul *and* the body, etc.

The thrust of modern thought is to move from separation toward simple distinction. But then should one say *God* or *the Divine*?

For the philosopher, this is not terribly important. For him, to personify God is only to assert the *reality*, the *objectivity* of the Ideal, of the Divine, of the Absolute. But popular thought is like a muddy torrent in which water is inseparable from clay:

> This great God is corrupted in you, foolish race,
> He enters into your soul an idea and leaves an idol.

For the masses, the mere use of the word *God* which, in its customary usage implies personality, prejudges the question. There is thus a *verbal* vicious circle which is tantamount to the same more subtle (?) result reached by the theologians and philosophers, and given above.

Moreover, as Renan has aptly noted, "The word God having

taken possession of the respect of humanity, this word having a long prescription in its favour . . . , it would perplex humanity to suppress it. . . . Suppose even that we philosophers should prefer another word, *reason* for example, besides the fact that these words are too abstract and do not sufficiently express real existence, it would be very inconvenient to separate ourselves by our language from the simple who worship so well after their fashion. Tell the simple to live by aspiring to truth and beauty; these words would have no meaning for them. Tell them to love God, not to offend God; they will understand you perfectly. . . . One must not fear to ascribe (to God) all the goodness and beauty that can be imagined. But it is contrary to all criticism to erect such a method into a scientific method and to make an ideal construction into a discussion on the qualities of a being."[9]

But we would not say: "God fashions himself [se fait]. . . . The world is the reality of God" ambiguous expressions, which imply an essential contradiction; we would rather accept the definition: God is "the category of the Ideal,"[10] on the express condition of not considering this category as a *purely subjective* form of thought, but as our intellectual mode of adaptation to an *objective* aspect of Reality, just as objective, as for example, the aspect of *unity* in our psychic activity; objective, but eluding us as it is in itself, all of which justifies the use of the word, *Unknowable*.

Above all, we would consider it an error against reason not to teach humanity, little by little, to accustom itself to a religious formula more faithful and less dangerous in its practical consequences than that of the past. We said it at the start: primitive humanity conceived and the great majority of civilized humanity

9. Ernest Renan, *Avenir de la science* (Paris: Calmann-Lévy, n.d.), pp. 475, 480 [Eng. trans. *The Future of Science* (Boston: Roberts Brothers, 1891), 445, 448–49].

10. Ibid., p. 476 [446, 445]. *Dialogues philosophiques* (Paris: Calmann-Lévy, 1876), pp. 25, 145.

still conceives "divine government" according to the barbarous despots of Chaldee and their arbitrary, tyrannical type of government. The implacable Yahweh no doubt became the "heavenly Father" in passing through the consciousness of the Prophets and of Christ; but the oriental despot so often reappears beneath the Father! Then reflective humanity energetically protests, at the risk of rejecting simultaneously the image and the idea. To say: *the Divine* instead of *God* is to sacrifice the image to save the idea. A question of terminology, some will object. We shall reply as does a modern thinker: "It is indeed rare for a mystery to disappear; it usually only shifts its ground. But it is often very important, very desirable to make it shift ground. From a certain standpoint, all progress in human thought boils down to two or three changes of this kind; to have dislodged two or three mysteries from a place where they were doing ill in order to move them to another where they become inoffensive, where they can do good. Sometimes even, when the mystery does not shift ground, it suffices to give it another name. What was called 'the gods' is today called 'life.' And if life is as inexplicable as the gods, we have at least arrived at a point where no one has the right to speak or to harm in its name."[11] This is the practical side of the issue; we merely point it out.

The despotism of "Yahweh" has perennially been used to justify abuses of power:

These two halves of God: the Pope and the Emperor.

Nothing surprising in the fact that these interpreters of an absolute Will should themselves be absolute in their commandments and their doctrine. The partisans of an imperfect Reality's evolution toward the perfect Ideal will at least be more humble.

11. Maeterlinck, *Le Temple enseveli*, p. 27 of the fine treatise on *Justice*.

They will understand that everything here-below, every institution like every being, the product of an imperfect Activity aspiring to the Perfect, can have only a relative value; solely the orientation (of the being, or the doctrine, or the work) can claim an absolute value. Thus no authority has the right to assume an *absolute* power in its commandments; all it is allowed to do is to appeal to us, through all possible means, to participate in the direction, the orientation it represents; no more intrusion of man into the domain of conscience, no more despotism, no more superstition, either of the verbal formula or of the ceremonial form. The essential practice of religion, the "one thing necessary," is to consider every being, especially every man *sub specie Perfecti;* what is or is not religious is the act by which the Ideal is embodied in the achievement of small parts of the best, particularly when this progress occurs in the order of science, of art, or of justice.

IV

For those who accept and for those who reject the teachings of revealed faith, it is interesting to ask what happens to Christian theology, Catholic theology in particular, once *God* has been replaced by *the Divine.*

Let us first recollect that, in order to avoid falling into "fideism"[12] or into a vicious circle, the theologian must grant reason the right to inquire into the existence and nature of God; anything theology later adds can and ought to be accepted only as a function of what reason will have found. So because reason in no way demonstrates the personality of God as an existence separate from that of creatures, this affirmation cannot be accepted from the theologian's mouth in any other way than as a metaphor, an

12. "Rationis usus fidem praecedit" ["The use of reason precedes faith"]. Proposition subscribed to by Bautain (1840) and Bonnetty (1855).

analogy, an anthropomorphic way of affirming that the Divine is "that which we are able to conceive of the greatest" since we represent it to ourselves under the form of the most elevated being that we can grasp through experience.

Texts abound in which theologians affirm, as does Saint Thomas, "that we know more what God is not than what he is";[13] however, rather than linger on this, we find it more interesting to investigate what becomes, in this conception, of the dogmatic formulas relating to Divinity, those, for example, of the Vatican Council on *Deo verum omnium creatore.*[14]

Let us take the definition which seems to contradict directly our way of viewing the Divine: "If anyone says that God and all things possess one and the same substance and essence: let him be anathema."[15]

We agree: it is, in fact, wrong, and an immense danger, after having formed ideas and concepts, in generalizing about the data of the senses or of psychological consciousness, to apply them to reality *in itself* and not as it *appears* in our imperfect and fragmentary experiences. The Divine is beyond everything we know as *substance* and as *essence;* these terms are of the order of the imperfect, it is thus necessary to refrain from transporting them into the order of the perfect; consequently, to say, as do the pantheists, that God and the creature are one and the same being, have the same essence, the same substance, would be to say that the imperfect and the perfect are of the same order.

This understood, the other prohibitions of the Council make sense, since they all suppose the same initial confusion.

13. Magis nobis manifestatur de ipso (Deo) quid non est quam quid est ["What He is not is clearer to us than what He is"] *Summa Theologica* 1 p. 2 1, a. IX ad. 3, p. 7.

14. Denzinger, *Enchiridion*, p. 392.

15. [Dogmatic Constitution on the Catholic Faith, chap. 1: "God the Creator of All Things," in John F. Clarkson et al., *The Church Teaches* (St. Louis: B. Herder, 1964), 153.]

But, we must remember that metaphysics and religion respond to distinct needs of the human soul. The Divine represented to the mind cannot be expressed by the same words as the Divine "felt by the heart." Theologians need no more worry about metaphysicians who, moreover, acknowledge the practical, popular point of view of religion, than chemists or physicists need worry about the systems of metaphysicians concerning atoms or force. But metaphysicians must not forget that what is possible, easy for them, is not so for others. If they want the common folk to make a distinction, they will often have to speak using terms that do not just *distinguish,* but also *separate,* for example, representing the soul on one side, the body on the other, the soul unifying itself with the body, the soul separating itself from the body. This is what the Church must do with regard to the Divine. It takes the perspective of the masses, it adopts their *practical* habits of representation. And just as, in practice, we objectify the finite in multiple substances, in practice, the Church objectifies the infinite into a single substance, isolated from finite substances.

Care must be taken, however, to avoid inflating what is only a *practical method* into a thesis, into *objective truth.* No doubt, in our consciences formed by long Christian tradition, religious life and piety develop more easily if we conceive the Divine in a personal way: how, we say, could we enter into personal relations with an abstraction? Pantheists and monists would affirm, to the contrary, that it is our personal God that is an abstraction: this is a question of imaginative, intellectual temperament that proves that the divine personality is a construction of the imagination—a very legitimate one at that—and not the result of a constant, universal experience, as one can and, we believe, one must say about the sense of the beyond, of the absolute.

To conclude that the Divine is personal because our religious consciousness forces imagination to represent it in this way, and that, in fact, this is the manner in which it is was conceived in the consciousness of Christ, of the Prophets, is to fall into a triple error:

1. It is to create a new mystical and subtle form of *fideism,* since it is to go from faith to reason, since it is to determine according to faith, to piety, what the rational idea ought to be; or even it is to claim that one cannot resolve the problem of the divine personality by reason, but only by faith; all these are assertions and methods diametrically opposed to the theological principle: "Rationis usus fidem praecedit."

2. It is to forget that we do not know, fundamentally, what this human personality, in whose image we create the object of our piety, really is. An objective reality? Or a simple form of thought? . . . In any case, we perceive it as something essentially variable, in constant creation, development. Thus it follows that we cannot affirm the personality of the Divine, any more than we can apply to it the categories of space and time.

Admittedly, man's personality is still what we know the best, and most, and we understand that the imagination cannot find a more noble element to construct a symbol of the Divine; but we do not in any way contest the right of consciousness to *the image;* we merely affirm that the image is only an image.

3. It is easy to see that one falls back into the *petitio principii* pointed out earlier, for to pose the problem: Are consciousness, will, personality appropriate *to God*? is to suppose it resolved, since it already makes *God* a distinct being, separate from the world.

It remains no less true that the practical formulas of councils and theologians have value, as do those of metaphysicians; they can be reconciled, as we have just seen; the two kinds of affirmation form not two truths, but two aspects of the inexhaustible Truth responding to two aspirations: the human mind's mystical and intellectual aspirations. Humanity will never renounce either one.

The danger in these formulas, especially the theological ones, is that the image, objectified, becomes an idol. The danger is real since there is outrage and anathema as soon as a thinker happens to call an image an image and a symbol a symbol. No doubt, the hour has come when many already worship the Father in spirit and in truth, but for how many does the anthropomorphic metaphor remain a reality as real as the very ideal it symbolizes! It is in the name of this existing metaphor that the right to monopolize the Absolute is claimed presumptuously, to be not only its witness, but its representative armed with full powers. From this point on, in the name of God, one is dogmatizing, legislating, impeding the mind's flight toward progress.

Even so, this is not a matter of breaking with traditional, objective religious forms: the Gospel, the Church, are fountains of living water in which the birds of the sky will always quench their thirst, the only places where many can do so. But one must not transform these forms into fetishes; before anybody who reflects and wants to be clear about his faith one must honestly call an image an image, a legend a legend, leaving each person free to symbolize his religious sense, according to his temperament, and must attribute importance to a given rite, a given formula, only to the degree to which these *means* effectively assist us in becoming better.

4

Anonymous or Polyonymous

Second Study on the "Divine Personality"

The Divinity is called by many names and yet none are suitable. Pseudo-Dionysius the Areopagite noted this apparent contradiction in his time and resolved it by justifying divine appellations by an *analogy* between the Creator and the creature indicated centuries earlier by the author of the Book of Wisdom.[1]

Today the problem remains. Is the Divinity literally *unknowable,* and consequently *anonymous*? But we know what we want to say in formulating the problem of the Divine; so we have at least a minimum knowledge that allows us to distinguish the notion (the feeling if you like) of the infinite, of the perfect, from that of the finite, of the indeterminate, of the imperfect. . . .

["Anonymous or Polyonymous: Second Study on the 'Divine Personality'" was published as "Anonyme ou polyonyme. Seconde étude sur la 'personalité divine,'" *Revue de Métaphysique et de Morale* 11 (March 1903): 231–47.] See "La dernière idole," *Revue de métaphysique et de morale* 10 (July 1902): 397–408.

1. Here is the text of Pseudo-Dionysius, probably at the beginning of the sixth century. "We know him. . . . On the other hand . . . no name can lay hold of him. . . . This is the sort of language we must use about God, for he is praised from all things according to their proportion to him as their Cause." *Des noms divins,* chap. VII §III [*On the Divine Names,* translation from *Pseudo-Dionysius: The Complete Works,* trans. Colm Luibheid (New York: Paulist Press, 1987)]. The words ἀγωνυος and πολυωυμος are equally found in chap. I, §VI and VII. "By the greatness and the beauty of the creature, the creator of them may be known ἀναλόγως." Wisdom 13.5.

Polyonymous then? But how to justify these attributes, these epithets?

To better understand, let us examine the value of the *analogies* discussed by theologians and of the triple method of *causality*, of *negation*, and of *eminence* which they use to establish them.

I

The triple *way* leading to God is very clearly mapped out in the works of the Pseudo-Dionysius.[2]

The gentle and subtle Neoplatonist refrains from doing philosophy: "Let us not rely," he says, "on the persuasive words of human wisdom in what we say about God, but on this solid knowledge that Heaven instilled in our teachers and by which we are united in an ineffable and unknown manner to things that are beyond speech or knowledge, a union certainly superior to anything that our reason and our understanding are capable of and attain." . . . "In our words or conceptions that express the supreme and mysterious nature of God we are allowed to use only what sacred Scripture has revealed."

But Scripture itself invites man to raise himself up to God in contemplating creation; Dionysius does not forget this: "Through the magnificent ordering of the universe that God established, in which shine the images and traces of divine ideas, we are raised to the level of the sovereign being insofar as our capacities allow, denying all that is said of him and placing him above all, being the cause of all."[3] Here the believer has once again become philosopher and we find clear indication of the three *ways*, the three "classic" methods: *via negationis; via eminentiae; via causalitatis:*

2. *Des noms divins* [*On the Divine Names*], chap. I, §I and II.

3. Ibid., chap. VII, §III [our translation; cf. *Pseudo-Dionysius: The Complete Works*, 49, 50 and 108].

God possesses all creatures' qualities since he is their cause; he possesses them without any admixture of imperfection; he possesses them to a supereminent, infinite degree. But Dionysius remains, nonetheless, first and foremost a theologian: he begins as if from an uncontested and incontestable *given,* the existence of a creator God, of a God like the one the Christian tradition has understood until now, that is, having his own substance, "substantia *singularis,*"[4] distinct from created substances; Dionysius does not for an instant dream of questioning this point.

Yet, for a modern theologian this attitude is no longer legitimate. Since the condemnations of Bautain in 1840, Bonnetty in 1855, a theologian must teach that the act of reason precedes the act of faith: *Rationis usus fidem praecedit.* Theologians have rejected those doctrines locating the great criterion of truth in revealed faith alone,[5] or in collective reason. With regard to the fundaments of faith, to the motives of credibility, to the existence and the personality of God, for example, they require this *private examination,* rational and individual, which so terrifies them when it concerns details and various articles of belief. It is the sole means—theologians have sensed and honestly recognized this—of avoiding the vicious circle: I accept the truths of faith because God has revealed them; I believe in God because his existence is a part of said revealed truths.

But things are much less simple than they first appear. What precisely is meant by reason (*rationis usus*)? Is it rough practical common sense or a serious critique? Does the "rationis usus" consist solely in stating the objective value of our belief in phenomena and what is beyond phenomena, in certifying the reality of the external world and of the superior world, or does it consist

4. Council of the Vatican : *De fide catholica,* chap. I.
5. This is what is called *fideism.*

of our attempt to make the intellectual representation of both of these worlds more and more exact and rigorous and not just more practical and useful, more effective or comforting? And should we not recognize from the outset that there are different orders of imaginative and intellectual representations, some more popular and others more scholarly? For example, does the *personality* of God belong to the customary image or to the metaphysical image? If theology acknowledged itself as being *of the popular and practical order* it would no longer have to fear any contradiction between its representations and philosophy's: an image and an idea, both expressing the same sentiment and the same objective and mysterious reality, could not contradict one another. But theologians claim to have an actual metaphysics, with a value related to *theoretical* and not simply *practical* knowledge. This value is consonant with the three methods to which they have recourse: *via causalitatis; via negationis; via eminentiae.*

II

Is the argument from causality any good?

Let us clarify the problem. It is a not matter of knowing whether or not the world considered in its totality, or in its parts, or even in the order that prevails in it, has *a raison d'être.* Thought requires it, true. But does it require this *raison d'être* to be *substantially distinct* from the world? THAT IS THE QUESTION.

Now, of what *causality* do theologians speak? Could it be the causality the notion of which is provided by sensible experience?

But—without examining the critical question: this causality is it not a pure *form* of our representations?—everyone admits that the senses, by themselves, provide mere knowledge of phenomena and here positivism would easily triumph: it would say that what scholars call *cause* is a phenomenon that *conditions* another; it is a contradiction to seek the absolute, the perfect, in a series of phenomena; the absolute cannot be found there, no more in the first than in any other.

Presented in this way, the question would indeed be a simple question of words. Consequently, we do not persist but pass on to another notion of causality, this time real, namely, the causality revealed by inner experience.

All those who allow that at least certain of our actions escape determinism see in free activity something other than a simple phenomenal "conditioning," thus a causality properly speaking.—Certainly, but can one legitimately apply this notion of psychological causality to the Divine? Free acts are not *substantially* distinct from the soul that produces them; the soul and its acts make up only one substance; one cannot thus attribute this kind of cause to the Divine without making it *immanent* cause of the world, bringing forth various beings *from the heart of its own substance* as we bring forth our acts, our thoughts. Now, this *monist* theory is energetically rejected by theologians. If our concept of God, they say, were purely anthropomorphic, we would form the idea of a God immanent in relation to the world, according to the image of a soul which is immanent in relation to its acts and forms only a single substance with them; but this is no more the *psychological* idea of causality applied to God than it is the *scientific* idea; it is the idea of *first* causality, that is to say absolute causality, the idea of *sufficient* reason, that is to say once more: absolute, perfect.

This is done, in fact, in two ways:

First, *Popular argument:* impossibility of an indefinite number of causes, thus the necessity of a first cause.

What is true in this argument is that the mind cannot be satisfied by a simple series of phenomena and that it experiences the need to affirm a beyond; but there is a big step from this obscurely sensed beyond to a personal Creator, "substantia singularis." As for the argument itself, we shall point out: (a) that number is a mental construction of the practical order, which is applied to the world of phenomena with useful results, allowing us to separate clearly, to compare, classify them, etc.; but nothing proves that numbers have the least value relative to what things are *in themselves*;[6] (b) that the impossibility of an infinite or indefinite number of causes in no way leads us to a *unique* cause: many have explained the world through the harmony or the conflict of multiple causes; (c) that it would lead us only, in any case, to a *first* cause in the arithmetical sense, a cause that would come before all others, but not necessarily to a perfect cause.[7] In order to claim this perfect cause, it is therefore necessary to complete the popular argument by the deeper considerations which follow.

Second, *Scholarly form of the argument:*[8] The word *movement* is given the meaning of *change* and the word *first* the metaphysical meaning of perfect, absolute, of which we spoke earlier. And

6. According to Saint Thomas (*Summa Theologica,* I q. 46, art. 1 and 2), faith teaches that the world began, but that reason does not demonstrate it: "By faith alone do we hold, and by no demonstration can it be proved, that the world did not always exist. . . . it cannot be demonstrated that man, or heaven, or a stone were not always" [(New York: Benziger Brothers, 1947), 243]. It is always supposed, in the proof of the first mover, that the initial state of matter is at rest, but this is absolutely gratuitous. Cf. Félix Le Dantec, *Revue blanche* 29 (15 November 1902): 460.

7. We do not explore here the most popular form: the world is a clock which supposes a clockmaker, a palace which supposes an architect.—Why would it not rather be a life, singular and multiple? In any case, the imagined *hypothesis* of a clock, of a palace, obliges us to conclude only a *hypothetical* clockmaker or architect.

8. We have received the articles of M. A. Bouyssonie ("La nouvelle idole," *Annales de philosophie chrétienne* n.s. 1 (Oct. 1902–Mar. 1903): 294–307) and of Mgr Mercier ("La dernière idole," *Revue néo-scholastique* 10 (1903): 73–91) too late to cite them in this study. We would not, at any rate, have had any response to make other than the above reflections in which we have sought to summarize our thought. We have never claimed that Saint Thomas was ignorant of pantheism. What he did not know was the totality of considerations that incline us, today, to consider *mechanical* energy and *psychic* energy as the two humanly knowable manifestations of *perpetually active* energy which is the essence of things. The possibility of the lack of awareness of this energy and of the reciprocal equivalence of its manifestations, deprives us, relative to principles to be formulated, of the fine confidence of the past.

thus it is argued: first cause = absolute cause = cause whose essence is being = cause that has the plenitude of being = perfect cause.—And yet many refuse to admit even this starting point. For twenty years, we have made serious inquiry into this subject and we have been able to establish that a number of good minds, even among sincere believers, acknowledge their lack of this sense of the Perfect, the Absolute. These notions may be due to experience: we acknowledge as perfect any being that seems fully to achieve its essence, which is fully all it can and ought to be. A given melody, a given statue is perfect; perfect the table of Pythagoras, the proof of a given theorem. In this sense, Taine writes: "God can only be the infinite and perfect Whole. Those who deny him as God by saying that he is multiple and imperfect do not know him. Multiplicity, imperfection, contingency are only an illusion of the mind that abstracts.[9] One part of the world calls for the other, as one organ of the human body requires all the others; and the world is one, as is the human body. Each part of the world is imperfect because it has its complement and the rest of its being in the others and thus the Whole is perfect."[10]—There is some truth in this standpoint; the "Whole" corresponds to what we call the absolute, the substance, and thus satisfaction is given to the thought that wants to "remain" in the indefinite progression of phenomena and to find in them a *raison d'être*.

But, satisfaction does not seem equally accorded to our sense of the perfect. In the examples cited above, it is always a question of a being that is fully *that* which it is,[11] namely, some limited as-

9. With regard to this word *contingency*, let us cite an objection brought to our attention: "It is unreasonable to say that the contingent is uncreated, that is, necessary." Accordingly let us not say it; we replace *creation* by *evolution* and attribute necessity only to reality regarded only as substance, as absolute: it cannot not be what it is.

10. Hippolyte Taine, *Sa Vie et correspondance* (Paris: Hachette, 1902), p. 51. This letter to Prévost-Paradol is dated 1851.

11. Generalizing, we would obtain the general idea of a being which fully achieves *its*

pect of that being; it is not a question of the being whose essence is to be in all the fullness of the word, the true meaning of the perfect. Now, with Descartes we accept this notion as being irreducible, as eluding all analysis, all possibility of being explained by a pure imaginative figure. We also admit that man believes in the objective value of the two parts of this pairing: imperfect-perfect, just as immediately[12] and legitimately as in the objective value of these others: self-not-self, subjective-objective. But here is precisely the point at which a sophism arises, namely, when it is said: the Perfect is *real,* therefore it *is realized* in a substance, in a person. For, *real* means merely: that which possesses an objective value. The whiteness of this sheet of paper is *real,* but is not, all the same, a substance. Thus, the notion of the Perfect is a *real* aspect of our intuition of Reality; whether or not it results from an *a priori* form or from a manner of seeing specific to our mental nature, it nonetheless possesses an objective *raison d'être,* just as whiteness, as wholly subjective an impression as it may give, nonetheless possesses an objective *raison d'être* in the physical world. To believe in this objective *raison d'être* is to believe in the reality of the Perfect; why require more and affirm its *substantiality,* its *personality*?

It is by virtue of the following principle: a substance cannot be perfect under one relation, imperfect under another. To claim that Reality can have one perfect aspect, the other imperfect, cannot, they say, truly be thought, it constitutes a real "logomachy."[13]—No more, we shall reply, than claiming that, in

essence, the abstract *concept* of perfection, which must not be confused with the *notion* of a being possessing the fullness of being. If we sometimes say: the concept of the Perfect, it is improperly, speaking without the precision necessary in these delicate matters.

12. This is the ontological argument, without value if one claims to be making a logical argument, excellent and even the only good one if one sees in it an invincible belief of the spirit.

13. "Chronique philosophique," *Revue du clergé français* 32 (15 October 1902): 407. As for

one relation, the soul, psychic activity, falls outside number (is *one*, if you will) and that in another aspect it is *multiple*. We do not *understand* it, but we *remark* it. There would be "contradiction" in identifying abstract concepts: perfection, imperfection—unity, multiplicity; they are opposed when we consider them in a state of abstraction, they are *logical* concepts or formal conditions of intuition, but the opposition, the contradiction, come from the abstraction—the example drawn from psychic activity proves it clearly;—the reconciliation occurs *in fact* in Reality.

The famous principle is therefore a gratuitous hypothesis in which the *logical* order is confused with the *real* order. A *petitio principii* is often grafted onto this first inaccuracy. It is said: The being whose essence is to be, the perfect being, cannot in any way admit imperfection; now . . . therefore. . . . But such introductions claim as a separate being *the being* whose essence is to be; and yet the question itself is to know whether the Divine exists in this way, in a state of *separate being*. Or the *petitio principii* is hidden in a minor premise; a major premise of indeterminate subject is proposed, but next one is obliged to say: and yet *God* . . . or: and yet *the* perfect *being, the* absolute substance. . . . One is thus always obliged to claim without due cause what is in question: the *separate* substantiality ("substantia *singularis*") of the Perfect.

The "*via causalitatis*" consequently provides a mode of *distinguishing* the finite from the infinite, the imperfect from the perfect by way of images; it in no way warrants our *separating* them into beings substantially and personally distinct.[14]

miracles as objection, we reply that, if their existence is proven historically, they can also be interpreted, in our opinion, as *extraordinary* (*mira*) episodes of evolution toward what is better.

14. Of course, nothing is more present to secondary causes than the first, according to Christian theology. If we say that it *separates* them, it is insofar as it is the Perfect substantiam *singularem*.

It thus seems preferable to reduce the anthropomorphism inherent in all human thought to a minimum and to interpret *theoretically* the notion of the Perfect as it appears *practically* in the Conscience as Ideal and Law of improvement. *Evolution* is probably only an *hypothesis,* just like *Creation;*[15] but it allows us to understand the existence of evil, the trial and error of natural selection, and the torments that follow for animals as for man, since it does not in any way hold an intelligent, powerful, and infinitely loving Creator responsible (directly or indirectly) for it.[16] No doubt the very idea of becoming implies a passage from the less good to the best which *seems* an impossibility, but: first, how can we be sure that the idea of creation, in other words, a passage from nothingness to being, does not hide a contradiction in terms that our feeble intellect cannot evaluate and that the idea of an infinite power that we add to it only conceals? Second, the insoluble character of the question results from the impossibility of our comprehending sufficiently the very terms of the problem. Everyday experience shows us that, in the quantitative phenomenal order the passage from less to more cannot take place, but what can we claim of the heart of things and of the qualitative order (where it is a matter of the *best* and not of the *most*), given that we glimpse so obscurely what is hidden under the words: spontaneity, virtuality, power, becoming?

An *hypothesis* is therefore all that we have a right to risk. We make use of this right in formulating our own hypothesis, interpreting the unknown by the better known, namely, the world by

15. We note again that we are adopting here the point of view of reason alone.

16. The *Revue du clergé français* (407) responds to our first objections that "suffering can really be explained by good reasons that have nothing childish about them." But it does not give these "good reasons"; we would like it to respond once and for all to the arguments summarized with such force by Guyau, "Le Théisme, idée de creation," 377ff. of *L'Irreligion de l'avenir* (Paris: Félix Alcan, 1902). We shall return to this subject in part III.

our consciousness. External experience, it is true, would not allow us to speak of the Perfect; it is in our consciousness that we find this claim, as persistent it is irreducible. But, without this claim, we say in all honesty, we would prefer the hypothesis of a world in which the same quantity of energy would prevail under multiple transformations, in which there would be no progress, but changes, in the sense that progress on one point would be compensated, counterbalanced by a retreat, a regression on another. If, then, we dare speak of *progress,* of *evolution,* it is in the name of an Ideal that we carry at the center of our thought; *to believe* in its true objective value is precisely *to believe* that it is not only a psychological law, but the cosmic Law of Evolution. Our mind isolates this Law and artificially makes it into an abstraction, but in reality, it belongs to the very essence of the Life whose direction, whose meaning it expresses.[17]

III

Shall we be happier with the "via negationis" and the "via eminentiae"?

The *via negationis* consists in denying divine qualities all imperfections and all limits.[18] Fundamentally, this amounts to claiming infinite Perfection and the two *ways* (negationis and eminen-

17. If examples of *living laws* are desired, one may want to reread verses 14 and 15 of chapter 2 of the Letter to the Romans and to recall that Saint Thomas frequently availed himself of the expression "*Lex aeterna*" to designate Providence.

18. The Pseudo-Dionysius was fond of this *method;* hence there are many passages similar to the following: "Sublime unity, mother of all other unity, supreme nature, mind beyond comprehension, unsayable word, without reason, without understanding, without name; it exists as does no other being; cause of all things, nevertheless it is not, because it transcends everything that is." (our translation. Cf. *On the Divine Names*, chap. I §I, p. 50.) "He is all that is and is nothing" (§VI). "Better said, he is not, but everything which is has his being in it" (chap. V §IV). And in *Mystical Theology*, chap. V: "God is not soul or mind; nor does he possess imagination, conviction, reason, or understanding. . . . He does not live nor is he life. . . . There is no grasping of him; he is not knowledge, truth, kingship, or wisdom; he is neither one, nor oneness, divinity, or goodness. . . ."

tiae) are psychologically one. And yet, we repeat, to claim infinite Perfection, to distinguish it from imperfect beings, is not at all to establish one or the other into separated *substances*. Always the same confusion between *distinguishing* and *separating*! Always, on the other hand, the same difficulty: either God has his creatures' qualities, or one should no more claim substance and personality for him than intelligence and goodness.

The School claims to resolve this difficulty through the doctrine of *analogical* concepts.[19]

According to Saint Thomas, what is claimed both of God and of creatures is claimed in that way because the mind perceives a relation of effect to cause between creatures and God and because in this cause all the qualities of the effects must preexist to an infinite degree. The creature and the Creator thus participate, to varied degrees, in the same perfections: it is because God is infinite goodness that creatures, made in his image, are also good, but to finite and varied degrees: it is this sharing of a same quality in different proportions that is the basis of *analogy*. Saint Thomas thus clearly distinguishes the *analogical* terms from the *univocal* (the word *man*, for example, applied to all men, all of whom have in them—or are supposed to have—a similar humanity) and the *equivocal* terms founded on what today we would call a simple association of ideas foreign to any similarity, for example, the term dog used both for a barking dog and for the constellation.[20]

19. The Scholastic doctrine of the nature and application of the theodicy of analogical concepts is well summarized in an article in the *Dictionnaire de théologie catholique*, fascicle IV (Paris: Letouzey).

20. "[S]ome things are said of God and creatures analogically, and not in a purely equivocal nor in a purely univocal sense. . . . [W]hatever is said of God and creatures, is said according to the relation of a creature to God as its principle and cause, wherein all perfections of things preexist excellently. Now this mode of community of idea is a mean between pure equivocation and simple univocation. For in *analogies* the idea is not, as it is in *univocals* the same, yet it is not totally diverse as in *equivocals;* but a term which is thus used in a multiple

We choose this example because Spinoza himself used it.[21] For him, the terms used by theologians are purely metaphors, "equivocal" notions. We shall not go so far, as we shall shortly explain.

In any case, this doctrine of *analogy* supposes that one admits in advance the *relation of causality* ("ordo creaturae ad Deum, ut ad principium et causam") *between God and the world,* between a God as perfect substance creating a world composed of imperfect substances and these imperfect substances participate to varied degrees in infinite perfection.

But this relation of *causality* is itself an analogy; God is "*analogical* cause" of the world, say theologians.[22] Thus analogies all rest upon a prime analogy and here theologians only avoid the *petitio principii* by supposing the fact of creation as already certain by other means. That it is certain *by faith* has no bearing upon the question, since at this moment we are concerned only with *rational* certitude. Now, what does reason say about this fundamental problem? We have already seen it: it is not satisfied with a series of phenomena, it requires *an absolute raison d'être, but it does not in any way require that this absolute be realized in a "particular substance" transcendent in relation to the essence of things.*

My critics will reply that at least reason does not contradict the theist-creationist hypothesis, a hypothesis that Faith, situated from a practical and pedagogical standpoint, imposes as a thesis.

This is correct, but we have never denied that it was possible to hold the said *hypothesis a priori,* having for a long time held and defended this view ourselves and only having abandoned it[23]

sense signifies various proportions to some one thing. . . ." *Summa Theologiae* I q. 13, art. 2 and art. 5, p. 64 [emphasis is Hébert's, who cites Aquinas in Latin].

21. *Ethics,* Part I. Proposition XVII.

22. "Therefore the universal cause . . . is not an univocal agent. . . . rather it is to be called an analogical agent." *Summa Theologica* I q. 13, art. 5, ad 1, p. 64.

23. Cf. section II of our previous study.

when compelled, overcome by the insoluble objection of the existence of evil. We are speaking of evil such as it is experienced in the course of living, not such as it appears in the Treatises of Metaphysics where it ends up volatilized into something purely *privative* and *negative.* Long ago the Pseudo-Dionysius discussed at length this facile solution to the problem: Evil is only a deficiency of good (chap. 4, §27); God knows it only under the form of the good (§30); it is "a privation, a mistake, an illusion, it is . . . ugly, lifeless, mindless, unreasonable, imperfect, unfounded, uncaused, indeterminate" (§32).—Yes, but nevertheless it is. . . . No doubt Saint Augustine ingeniously observes that the scorpion's venom is not an absolute venom, since it does not kill the scorpion itself and that we must not judge things solely according to our own benefit or detriment,[24] but he is forced to affirm that God, certainly just, is still such "even when he does what man could not do without injustice."[25] Yes, one can speak of the justice of a "species" as superior to that of an individual,[26] but then one begins by recognizing that there is no infinitely perfect personal God, creator of our consciousness.

The best reply to the terrible objection is to evoke the privileges of freedom. The Creator preferred a free world to an automatic world. God *is the fashioner of workmen.* To M. Fouillée's fine statement, Guyau rightly replies: "The Creator not having been able to create bare and completely potential substances, had to create beings endowed with several existing qualities; but then

24. *Contra Faustum,* XXI, ch. XIII [*Answer to Faustus, a Manichean,* trans. Roland Testle (Hyde Park, N.Y.: New City Press, 2007), 293–94].

25. *Contra Julianum, Oper. Imperf.* 1, III, ch. XXIV. We must say that Saint Augustine does not discuss the question from the rational point of view, but rather the theological; his major arguments are drawn from texts such as Leviticus 14.18 and 26.39, marked with the ancient primitive conception of the Divinity.

26. Maurice Maeterlinck, *Le Temple enseveli,* pp. 84 ff.

these are always works, not workers, at least in this relation."[27] Will the notion of "a *moral test*" be mentioned? First of all, it would not be acceptable for animals, children, or men variously deprived of their reason. How can their sufferings be justified, if not by the blind heredity we are obliged to accept as a fact, but whose appalling consequences we resist admitting as the conduct of an infinite Goodness? Second, as Guyau has also put it well: "One does not fall when there are no stones on the road, when one has sound legs and when one walks under the eye of God."[28] One sins through lack of light or of strength and God who knows the amount of light and of strength necessary to prevent the fault that he, God, is deemed to foresee, thus makes himself responsible for the consequences of withholding them from man.—No, it will be said, for he would thereby annihilate freedom.—We reply that, according to the theologians, God knew how to render Christ perfect without removing his freedom or diminishing his merits.[29] If he has not made this process widespread, if it has pleased him to choose the risks of temptation, he is the first to be accountable for the results. The expedient of eternal hell would thus be barbarism added to a whim, since theologians dare to affirm that God in refusing to co-operate with the freedom of man after testing him,[30] makes it impossible for him to return to the good and thus Himself fixes him in this way and condemns him forever to evil.

The intermediate hypothesis (of Voltaire, of Stuart Mill, of Renan) of a very powerful but not all-powerful God, of a central consciousness, superior but imperfect, of the world (organized or in the course of organizing itself), seems to lay itself open

27. Guyau, *L'Irreligion de l'avenir,* p. 383.
28. Ibid., p. 385.
29. Hurter, *Theol. Dogmatica,* t. II, no. 400.
30. Ibid., t. III, note, on p. 495.

to the same objections as that of the theologians, for the objection of evil preserves a great deal of its value against a consciousness that, while being imperfect, would nonetheless be better than our consciousness which finds this evil repellant.[31] If it is objected that we ourselves thus fall into anthropomorphism in judging God by human feelings, we will reply that we are adopting our contradictors' point of view, that we are engaging their hypothesis, and that they can reject the argument only upon one condition: that they themselves cease to consider human consciousness, in its most profound and most universal sentiments, as "made in the likeness of God."

IV

But does this not demand a radical change in the way the Divinity is represented?

It would be surprising if so many modern theologians, who have no other means of defending their positions against criticism than the theory of the *evolution of dogma,* gratuitously limited this evolution and refused to allow it when it treats the very idea of the Divine and religion. In these matters one cannot indiscriminately draw conclusions from the past toward the future: either evolution is only a trompe-l'oeil, a vain subterfuge, or it applies primarily to the conception man seeks to fashion of the Divinity and of the relations uniting the Perfect to the imperfect. If one went so far as to interpret as purely "*equivocal*" the *divine names* accepted until then as *analogical,* it would not be an *evolution* any more radical than the transformation undergone, for

31. Voltaire, *Dictionnaire philosophique,* article "Puissance"; third letter to Memmius; Deuxième dialogue d'Evhémère, etc.; John Stuart Mill, *Essays on Religion,* Part II: Attributes [(New York: Henry Holt, 1874)]; Ernest Renan, *Dialogues philosophiques,* pp. 52, 54, 144, 146; but cf. Letter to Berthelot (in the same volume pp. 184, 185), in which Renan clearly distinguishes the two meanings that he gives to the word God (total existence and ideal).

example, by the belief of Jesus, the apostles, and the primitive Church in the imminent return of the Messiah on the clouds.[32]

Nothing is farther from our thought than arrogantly rejecting outright a doctrine as fruitful for life as the Christian tradition, or breaking the continuity of the historic evolution of Humanity's religious sense.

On the very point under discussion here, we have not made the foolish presumption of accusing Christian thinkers of complete error. They were correct in seeking something other than *univocal* terms or *equivocal* terms; the former would oblige us to *confuse* the perfect and the imperfect in the same genre; the latter to *isolate* them, to represent them as foreign to one another "as the celestial constellation and the barking animal." On the other hand, the theory of *analogical* terms supposes, as we saw earlier, the fundamental analogy of *causality* admitted in so far as implied in the doctrine of Creation. Thus if the idea of creation is not accepted as a rational hypothesis, this theory retains value only as the dogma's *means of exposition.*

What, then, becomes of the theory from the *rational,* philosophical point of view?

In order not to lapse into Spinoza's exaggeration, it suffices to note that there are possible analogies between the Perfect and the Imperfect other than the ones theologians allow in the name of *efficient* causality. Besides, the traditional analogy rests entirely on the relation of "efficient causality" and on that of "*exemplary* causality": God is given to us both as cause and as model; as cause since he draws creatures forth from nothing; as model, since the effect always resembles the cause, according to the adage[33] which

32. Cf. Matt. 16.28; 24.34; 26.64; 1 Thess. 4.1; 1 Cor. 15; 7.31; Phil. 4.5; James 5.3, 8; 2 Pet. 3.11, 12; Rev. 1.3; 12.12; 22.10, etc.

33. "[E]very agent produces its like." *Summa Theologica* I q. 115, art. 1; q. 10, art. 5, p. 560.

is, incidentally, wrongly considered as self-evident. But if the two concepts are linked in theology, they are not so in themselves; where the relation of "*efficient* causality" fails, the relation of "*exemplary* causality" remains.

Indeed, when *God* is mentioned, attention is drawn either to the idea of universal Life, of unique, absolute Substance, or to that of the Perfect, law of evolution.

In the former case, it would be better to say: *Nature;* we would, with reservations, apply the concept of *efficient* and *immanent* causality. To the Perfect, to the ideal Law, we would reserve the august name of God, and he would appear as *exemplary* cause. The sole defect of this expression is that it seems to imply a Model known and willed by a thought more or less analogous to our own; it thus appears to imply the resolution of the question: Is universal Life a conscious or an unconscious activity? However, without taking sides in a discussion in which hypotheses can only clash against hypotheses, we have the right to state a *fact* and say: an Ideal to be fulfilled, a fulfilled Ideal.[34] These terms thus express a practical relation which is enough to allow us to use the idea of *exemplary* causality and, since the moral realization implies an *internal* resemblance and not merely a completely external and artificial relation of resemblance,[35] to safeguard the *analogical* expressions. Used in this spirit, traditional analogical language would allow thought the complete freedom to construct various intellectual hypotheses. It would provide explanations less frequently than it would suggest practical applications.

34. To require that the imperfect "*conceive*" the Ideal in order that the Ideal can act on it, is obviously to go too far; a much more obscure consciousness, a *tendency* and not an *idea* is enough; our contradictor in the *Revue du clergé français* concedes the elements of a "subconscious."

35. Like the relation between the barking animal and the constellation of the Dog of which Spinoza spoke.

Thus, the Divine would remain *polyonymous*. But let us note that in confining ourselves to saying: an Ideal to be fulfilled, a fulfilled Ideal, we have renounced metaphysical hypotheses and have come back down to the practical level. The traditional divine terms would be Symbols of the Ideal and no longer metaphysical information. And their judicious use would satisfy the needs of the imagination and the heart.

A number of thinkers accept and interpret them in this way. A German scholar has written us that in the religious life of the soul it is not a matter of *knowing* and *comprehending* the Divine, which is impossible, but of *feeling* and *living* it, which is necessary. But if the Perfect does not come into our life as a person, it remains an abstraction; an effective relationship, true religion (*religare*) only occurs if man can maintain personal relations with the beyond. In this case, personality = reality. Is that not the deepest meaning of Christianity: the Divine incarnates itself, anthropomorphizes itself in order to reveal itself to men: not to make itself understood, but to make itself loved. The idea of a personal God thus corresponds, not to the nature of the Divine, but to the nature of man; it is only an *expedient;* let us also say that it is necessary *to believe* in a personal God. It is a belief of a practical order.

There is, we acknowledge, a realism, a *thingism* which can be useful, indispensable, on the practical level, as much for the world of mystical phenomena as for that of physio-chemical phenomena; but it is rather a question of *method* (religious or scientific), which must leave philosophical *speculation* its complete freedom. The day when theology presents itself as a body of popular and practical considerations, all possibility of opposition, of contradiction will cease between it and philosophy, as we have already said. But theology has many other claims and absolutely refuses to accept this thoroughly practical interpretation of *belief* in the divine personality.

Besides, may admitting this belief as an expedient deprive it of its force of moralizing and consoling suggestion? Certainly not for those of us who benefit from fixed hereditary habits, developed and deeply anchored in our sensibility and our imagination through long years of education in which we were taught to take the affirmation of divine personality *literally* and not as an *expedient,* but for young generations. Raised in the full light, with complete honesty and candor, informed that this "personality" is merely an admirable myth, "*the utmost effort of our imagination toward perfection,*"[36] they will become used to seeking their consolation and their strength directly in the Ideal that conscience reveals to man as his own law and authorizes him to consider as the law of the Universe. It will be possible to remind them that "the experience which is the knowledge of the finite is not exhaustive of intellect, that intellect is not exhaustive of man, nor man exhaustive of being,"[37] and that there must always be room in life for this religious spirit "ensemble of aspirations always pushing us toward the beyond, toward that which science does not attain, toward that which experience cannot verify, toward that which practice cannot realize."[38] Then we will be able to convince ourselves that, on this point as on so many others, an evolution was necessary; we will admit the drawbacks of the old method that Taine summarized so well in these few lines: "morality founded on the relations between persons and not on the

36. Montaigne, *Essais,* Book II, chap. XII.

37. Ferdinand Buisson, *La Religion, la Morale et la Science* (Paris: Fischbacher 1900), 3rd Lecture, p. 114.

38. Ibid., 126. We do not have to treat here the question of the *social* character of the religious spirit and of the free associations that will respond to this need for union. Cf. on this subject Guyau, *L'Irreligion de l'avenir,* 3rd part, ch. II.

relations between a person and the absolute Good: it is necessary to love God, not the Good. Consequently, development of faith and love (feminine and passive side); weakness of reason and freedom (virile and active side)."[39]

Abuse, in such matters, is always so close to use that we are not afraid to conclude that, in order to express the sentiment of the Divine, it is better to content oneself with what we have called minimal anthropomorphism, to avoid all that invites idolatry in evoking the human personality, and to limit oneself to terms founded on the practical mode of the Divine's manifestation in consciousness: instead of God, to say the Ideal of the Good, of the True, of Justice. This is certainly not breaking with the past, but a normal evolution of the Christian tradition, according to its own spirit of sincerity and of practical truth.

39. *Vie et correspondence*, p. 357. Cf. p. 150.

5

The Bankruptcy of Despotic Catholicism

Catholic theology has always had the honesty to require that faith *be grounded;* it does not allow one to take advantage of the mysterious character of belief, in order to use it to justify its own existence; it has even condemned this claim under the name of *fideism.*

The grounds on which faith must rest are borrowed, on the one hand, from philosophy: the existence and personality of God; the existence of the soul; the possibility of miracle and of revelation; on the other hand, from history: the authenticity of the Old and New Testaments; the historicity of Christ's Resurrection and the Church's foundation by Christ.

And yet, we must recognize (we have tried to demonstrate this elsewhere)[1] that belief in a personal God, the essential foundation of all theology (Protestant as well as Catholic), is becoming increasingly rare in the minds of those who reflect freely. Traditional proofs succeed in helping us to *distinguish* the abso-

["The Bankruptcy of Despotic Catholicism" was published as "La Faillite du catholicisme despotique," *Revue blanche* 30 (March 1903): 439–57.]

1. "La Dernière Idole" (1902) and "Anonyme ou Polynme" (1903), both in *Revue de métaphysique de de morale.*

lute from the relative, the perfect from the imperfect, but by no means to *separate* them into numerically different substances; the hypothesis of creationism shatters against the insoluble objection of the existence of evil. But, it is always simple to avoid philosophy's conclusions by using as an excuse its obscurities and the subjective character of its assertions. We demand objective facts and conclusions that partake of this objective value.

And yet, from historical criticism's standpoint, what have become of the objective grounds of faith, for example, the Pentateuch's authenticity, that of the fourth gospel, or above all of the fact of a Jesus *really* (interpreted properly in the historical, material sense) conceived and born of a virgin, *really* resurrected, having *really* founded a Church to which he *really* wanted to transmit and did transmit the supernatural powers received from God his Father?

Taken *literally* as in the past, all this has now vanished. Now, these are merely true "*idealizations*" of facts that are real but very different from religious history, true in the sense that these idealizations were necessary for the conservation and evolution of Christian consciousness.[2]

Thus it cannot be hidden: day by day theology is more narrowly caught between the jaws of the vice: philosophy and criticism. The *letter,* unquestionably, will be shattered, but the *spirit* will escape, that is, the indestructible beliefs and the hopes of human conscience, that, long ago, purified the Jewish myths in or-

2. "A work of progressive idealization and of symbolic interpretation of the traditional facts has taken place." Alfred Loisy, "Forward" to *Études Évangéliques* (Paris: Alphonse Picard, 1902), p. 7. And that, from the very outset of Christianity: "Custodians and preachers of a living religion, the first initiates of the Gospel did not for an instant dream that in their teaching they had to be tied down either to the letter of the formulas that Christ had used, or by the material reality of the deeds he accomplished. . . . Jesus was a good deal less the representative of a doctrine than the initiator of a religious movement," p. 13.

der to create Christian myths and transformed and idealized the historical Jesus into Christ.

These assertions will cease to appear daring if we consult two recent works by a Catholic critic-theologian, M. Loisy and a Protestant critic-theologian, M. Harnack.[3] M. Loisy seeks to refute M. Harnack. We shall summarize their principal theses.

I

A profound and conscientious study of facts, of documents, courageous candor, sincere and infectious faith, all this is clearly found in Abbé Loisy's work. Never before has he written anything as lively, as vibrant, and as important in its consequences.

M. Harnack's book, he says, presents itself as *historical;* it may thus be discussed exclusively in terms of historical data. And yet, there is something immediately surprising in the eminent professor's work: namely, that a movement as considerable, as complex as Christianity be related to *a single* idea, *a single* sentiment: faith in God the Father, in the merciful Father. Can such a surprising simplification really come from an *historian*? Is it not

3. Alfred Loisy, *L'Évangile et l'Église* (Paris: Alphonse Picard, 1902). This work has already suffered several Episcopal censures, that of Cardinal Richard among others; but these censures are not final judgments; only a Council or the Pope speaking *ex cathedra* has the right to decide on the question *definitively;* other judgments can be interpreted in the sense that the work is of a nature that it should not be in the hands of just anyone. Also, in his response to the cardinal, M. Loisy had to disavow only the errors that *could be deduced* from his book. Adolf von Harnack, *Das Wesen des Christentums* (1900) [appeared as *L'Essence du Christianisme* (Paris: Fischbacher, 1902).] The recent letter of William II is further proof that Protestants currently run up against the same difficulties as Catholics, with this difference that their claim to save at least a minimum of orthodoxy ("You must let the Word stand," writes the emperor to Delitzsch) is not logical since they do not admit an infallible teaching authority. Moreover, their method is always the same: to reserve the truth for yourselves and for those initiated, not to speak it to the people! Thus the Church appears as a great conservative machine designed to keep the people in a state of submissiveness out of ignorance or illusion. And this would be the divine work of Christ! . . . As if he had ever attached the least importance to the "pagodas of terminology"! And as if the slightest hygienic or economic progress was not more worthwhile for the people than all these "pagodas"!

rather from a *theologian* who takes from history what suits his theology? Rather than deduce it from history has he not instead *interpreted* history according to a preconceived theory? Indeed:

> In seeking to determine historically the essence of the gospel, the rules of a healthy criticism forbid the resolution to regard as non-essential all that to-day must be judged uncertain or unacceptable.[4]
>
> He who wishes to decide historically the thoughts of the Savior has not first to discover what can suit the mind of man to-day, or what can be held to be unchanged, but must take the texts and interpret them according to their natural meaning and the guarantees of authenticity they present.[5]

To attempt to distinguish what has changed from what has not changed is not the historian's mission, since what has not changed has never presented itself in a pure, abstract state, but in one that is complex, *living*, and therefore always clothed in changeable forms, varying according to time and place.

What! The consubstantiality of the Son, transubstantiation, papal infallibility, the cult of the saints, etc., are not part of the Gospel? These are thus worthless additions, even sacrileges?

No; the error, in similar cases, is to perceive the Gospel as an algebraic equation, an abstract formula fallen from heaven and which has then been passed on from person to person without adding anything, without subtracting anything. The real Gospel is the Gospel living through the Christian faith, in souls; to seek the Gospel elsewhere than in *expressions* of Christian faith (among which it is necessary to include the *four* written Gospels) is as ridiculous and sterile as seeking life outside of living beings.

4. Alfred Loisy, *L'Évangile et l'Église,* p. 14 [Eng. trans. *The Gospel and the Church,* trans. Christopher Home [1903] (Philadelphia: Fortress Press, 1976), 8. In what follows, reference will be made to the English translation, with page reference to the French edition given in parentheses.]

5. Ibid., p. 111 (62).

The Gospel is a faith, a life. All that lives evolves, transforms, and adapts to various environments under pain of death. Thus:

The historian cannot but refuse to regard as the essence of living Christianity a germ that multiplies without growing. Rather he should return to the parable of the mustard seed, comparing[6] the new-born Christianity to a little grain. . . . The grain, nevertheless, enclosed the germ of the tree that we now see; charity was its sap; its life impulse was in the hope of its triumph; its expanding force was in its apostleship, its pledge of success in sacrifice: for its general form this budding religion had its faith in the unity and absolute Sovereignty of God, and for its particular and distinctive feature that faith in the Divine mission of Jesus, which earned it its name of Christianity. All this was in the little seed, and all this was the real essence of the Christian religion, needing only space to grow to reach its present point, still living after all its growth. To understand the essence of Christianity we must look at those vital manifestations which contain its reality, its permanent quintessence, recognizable in them, as the principal features of primitive Christianity are recognizable throughout their development.[7]

And:

There is no institution on the earth or in history whose status and value may not be questioned if the principle is established that nothing may exist except in its original form. Such a principle is contrary to the law of life, which is movement and a continual effort of adaptation to conditions always new and perpetually changing. Christianity has not escaped this law, and cannot be reproached for submission to it. It could not do otherwise than it has done.

The preservation of its primitive state was impossible, its restoration

6. "Imitatur animarum religio rationem corporum," wrote Vincent of Lérins already in the fifth century, "quae licet annorum processu numeros suos evolvant et explicent. Eadem tamen quae erunt permanent" [The growth of religion in the soul must be analogous to the growth of the body, which, though in process of years is developed and attains its full size, yet remains the same]. But the comparison has other significance with M. Loisy [Vincent of Lérins, *Commonotories* §55, in *A Select Library of the Nicene and Post-Nicene Fathers*, 2nd ser., vol. 11 (New York: Christian Literature Company, 1894), 148].

7. Loisy, *The Gospel and the Church*, pp. 17–18 (27, 28).

now is equally out of the question, because the conditions under which the gospel was produced have disappeared for ever. History shows the evolution of the elements that composed it. These elements have undergone, as they could not fail to undergo, many transformations; but they are always recognizable, and it is easy to see in the Catholic Church what stands to-day for the idea of the Heavenly kingdom, for the idea of the Messiah, the maker of the kingdom, and for the idea of the apostolate, or the preaching of the kingdom, that is to say, the three essential elements of the living gospel, which have become what they were forced to be in order to endure at all.[8]

The five chapters: I. The Kingdom of God.—II. The Son of God.—III. The Church.—IV. Christian Dogma.—V. Catholic Worship, are the development of these views, while also constituting a criticism of M. Harnack's overly narrow conception. To give a pale summary of these fact-filled pages, this penetrating criticism, this substantial documentation, would be a betrayal of the author and his cause. And besides readers will have adequately understood the primary idea and anticipated the conclusion: the Gospel has evolved in and through the Catholic Church; to criticize the Church for changes in dogma, worship, or discipline is thus to criticize it for having overflowed and still overflowing with an inexhaustible vitality.

To those preoccupied, however, by such changes (in dogmatic formulae, for example), M. Loisy responds:

It is a fact that the development of dogma is not in the gospel, and could not be there. But it does not follow that the dogma does not proceed from the gospel, and that the gospel has not lived and lives still in the dogma as well as in the Church. Even the teaching and the appearance of Jesus have had perforce to be interpreted; the whole question is to know if the commentary is homogeneous with the text or heterogeneous.[9]

8. Ibid., pp. 166–67 (111–12).
9. Ibid., pp. 180–81 (128).

This is indeed "*the whole question*" and we will insist on it later. Let us end this exposition by indicating M. Loisy's conclusions.

The past and the present guarantee the future.

It is the life and persistence of the gospel, which have made it a permanent principle of religious and moral education, and a spiritual society where the principle is put in force. The principle has no hold without the society, nor the society without the principle. Protestantism and Herr Harnack wish to keep only the principle. It is a conception that lacks consistence and reality. Catholicism stands for both principle and society. Historical circumstances have made the social organization seem to compromise the principle more or less, even in some sort to appear to threaten it still. But it is still the condition of all that lives in the world to be subject to imperfection. Whatever reservations the historian may make in details as to the way in which the action of the Church is or has been exercised, he cannot deny that Catholicism has been, and is still, the service of the gospel, continued since the days of the apostles.

The power of adaptation recognized in the Roman Church is its best title to the admiration of the impartial observer. It does not follow that the Church alters either the Gospel or tradition, but that she knows how to understand the needs of the time. It cannot be too often repeated that the gospel was not an absolute, abstract doctrine, directly applicable at all times and to all men by its essential virtue. It was a living faith, linked everywhere to the time and the circumstances that witnessed its birth. In order to preserve this faith in the world, a work of adaptation has been, and will be, perpetually necessary. Though the Catholic Church has adapted, and still adapts, the faith, though she adapt herself continually to the needs of new ages, that is no proof that she forgets the gospel or despises her own tradition, but that she wishes to display the value of both, and has confidence that they are flexible and capable of further perfection.[10]

It is true that as a result of the evolution, political, intellectual, economic, of the modern world, as a result of all that may be called the modern spirit, a great religious crisis, affecting Churches, orthodoxies,

10. Ibid., pp. 176–78 (123–124).

and forms of worship has arisen to a greater or less extent everywhere. The best means of meeting it does not appear to be the suppression of all ecclesiastical organization, all orthodoxy, and all traditional worship—a process that would thrust Christianity out of life and humanity,—but to take advantage of what is, in view of what should be, to repudiate nothing of the heritage left to our age by former Christian centuries, to recognize how necessary and useful is the immense development accomplished in the Church, to gather the fruits of it and continue it, since the adaptation of the gospel to the changing conditions of humanity is as pressing a need to-day as it ever was and ever will be.[11]

There, indeed, are conservative and orthodox conclusions, if not yesterday's orthodoxy, at least tomorrow's; invoking the old adage, "*Amicus Plato, magis amica Veritas,*"[12] we will explain the grounds that do not allow us to accept them outright.

II

First, some remarks on the subject of M. Harnack's ideas or their refutation.

Historically speaking, "That which has been essential in the gospel of Jesus, is all that holds the first and most considerable place in His authentic teaching, the ideas for which He strove and for which He died, not only such part of them as is held to be vital today."[13] But, in that case, historically speaking, the proximity of the Messiah's return on the clouds is essential, as is the very hope of the Kingdom, for Jesus never stopped proclaiming it as very near: "*this generation of men*" should not pass away before everything would be accomplished. Such was the conviction of Jesus and the first believers.[14] It was, nevertheless, sincerely

11. Ibid., p. 276 (final pages).
12. [The friend of Plato, still more the friend of truth.]
13. Loisy, *The Gospel and the Church*, p. 8 (xiv).
14. Cf. 1 Thess. 4; 1 Cor. 15; 7.31; 16.22; Matt. 16.28; 24.34; 26.64; James 5.3, 8; Rev. 1.3; 22.10, etc.

and frankly speaking, an ERROR. Try as one might to assure us that "[w]hen Jesus said, in all solemnity, 'Verily I say unto you, There be some of them that stand here, which shall in no wise taste of death, till they see the Son of man coming in His kingdom,' the idea of the kingdom and of its proximity were two very simple symbols of very complex matters,"[15] it is nonetheless true that as "necessary for the success of the gospel"[16] as was this illusion, "even those who were the first to believe must have attached their minds more to the spirit than to the letter of this statement, to find it always true."[17] That Jesus could or could not conceive it otherwise, that he may even have *had* to conceive it thus, does not affect there being *already a mixing together* in what Christ taught, a mixture of divine and human, of true and false, and if the first disciples needed to sort it out, it is understandable that M. Harnack also identified this discrimination, labeling what the Gospel contained of the really and eternally true as *essence* of Christianity.

Moreover, it is not necessary to take the amalgamation, the simplification effected by M. Harnack so literally. Otherwise, M. Harnack could direct the same criticism to M. Loisy when the latter asserts that "[t]*he* thought that the Saviour left to them was that they must continue to wish, to prepare, to await and to realize the kingdom of God."[18]

And M. Harnack could add that the unity of which he speaks is not in any way a mathematical unity; it is the unity of a central truth, around which a rich and complex multiplicity is grouped; this is how it appears to us in these lines, for example:

15. Loisy, *The Gospel and the Church*, p. 218 (166–167).

16. Ibid., p. 76 (26).

17. Ibid., p. 218 (167).

18. Ibid., pp. 167–68 (113). This is even more evident in the citation given by Caird on p. 82 [of the French text; the quotation is lacking in the English translation] where it concerns only a "germ" of a "vague and rudimentary" sentiment.

If we were right in saying that the Gospel is the knowledge and recognition of God as the Father, the certainty of redemption, humility and joy in God, energy and brotherly love; if it is essential to this religion that the founder must not be forgotten over his message, history shows us that the Gospel has, in point of fact, remained in force, struggling again and again to the surface.[19]

M. Loisy seems to have too narrowly represented M. Harnack's thought on another point as well.

"It is," he says, "the life and persistence of the gospel, which have made of it a permanent principle of religious and moral education, and a spiritual society where the principle is put in force. The principle has no hold without the society, nor the society without the principle. Protestantism and Herr Harnack wish to keep only the principle. . . . Catholicism stands for both principle and society."[20]

It appears from this that M. Harnack is preaching a purely individualist and subjective Christianity.[21]

No, he does not want to retain *only* the principle; the proof is in his strongly categorical denial that the "society of believers" is an entirely interior and "invisible"[22] society. And a bit farther on:

[Our union] is no fetter, but the condition of our freedom. And when we are reproached with our divisions and told that Protestantism has as many doctrines as heads, we reply, "So it has, but we do not wish it otherwise; on the contrary, we want still more freedom, still greater individuality in utterance and in doctrine; the historical circumstances necessitating the formation of national and free churches have imposed

19. Adolf von Harnack [*Das Wesen des Christentums*. Eng. trans. *What Is Christianity?* trans. Thomas Bailey Saunders (London: Williams & Norgate, 1901), 299. Loisy is citing p. 315 of the French translation].

20. [Loisy, *The Gospel and the Church*, pp. 176–77 (123).]

21. It is the same with M. Sabatier, although the contrary is repeatedly affirmed. On the *objective and social* aspect of Christianity, see *Esquisse d'une philosophie de la Religion* (Paris: Fischbacher, 1897), pp. 55, 56, 405, 406.

22. Harnack, *What Is Christianity?* pp. 273.

only too many rules and limitations upon us, even though they not be proclaimed as divine ordinances; we want still more confidence in the inner strength and unifying power of the Gospel, which is more certain to prevail in free conflict than under guardianship; and we want to be a spiritual realm and we have no desire to return to the fleshpots of Egypt; we are well aware that in the interests of order and instruction outward and visible communities must arise; we are ready to foster their growth, so far as they fulfill these aims and deserve to be fostered; but we do not hang our hearts upon them, for they may exist to-day and to-morrow give place, under other political or social conditions, to new organizations; let anyone who has such a church have it as though he had it not; our Church is not the particular Church in which we are placed, but the 'societas fidei' which has its members everywhere, even among the Greeks and Romans."[23] That is the evangelical answer to the reproach that we are "divided," and that is the language which the liberty that has been given to us employs.[24]

It would seem that this would also be M. Loisy's conclusion, when one reads this quite penetrating and correct observation that he makes regarding the Gospel of Jesus: "neither wholly individualistic in the Protestant sense, nor wholly ecclesiastic in the Catholic sense."[25] All the same, this is not the case. We part company with him regarding the *unique* character of the legitimate form of Christianity, and this is why.

III

Only M. Harnack's conclusion allows us to avoid the famous antinomy: either religion as an individual sentiment, a private affair, or religion as evolution and collective historical institution. It sacrifices neither one nor the other of these two terms; a rec-

23. The author intends to say: the Greek Church and the Roman Church.
24. Harnack, *What Is Christianity?* pp. 276–77.
25. Loisy, *The Gospel and the Church*, p. 176 (123).

onciliation is obtained: the existence of the collective historical tradition is recognized, and the individual consciousness respected since it is believed according to the forms that this consciousness suggests or authorizes. On the contrary, M. Loisy's solution will always come up against the following difficulty: we are no longer in primitive times, or in the Middle Ages; many souls are intellectually "mature" and the admirable diffusion of instruction characterizing our time will increase their number daily. Yet all religious authority, however broad and paternal it imagines itself, will always force "mature" souls to *put on an act as did Galileo:* in the name of the collectivity, they will be required to adhere by faith to certain affirmations, which is possible only in interpreting them, in one's innermost heart, symbolically, ideally, *in one's own way,* in an entirely different sense than that adopted by the masses and *imposed by authority in its official explanations.*[26]

Or, if one believes that God, that the order of things, requires that certain *fictions,* certain "*essential* lies," be offered to and imposed upon an ignorant and weak-minded Humanity, then one should officially admit as corollary the legitimacy of an esoteric teaching.

But let us examine this ingenious *theory* of religious evolution. Is it historical, scientific? This is to play with words. History establishes *facts* and makes judgments regarding *existence,*

26. "If anyone says that as science progresses it is sometimes possible for dogmas that have been proposed by the Church to receive a different meaning from the one which the Church understood and understands, let him be anathema." *Dei Filius*, chap. 4, Vatican I *Meaning*: there is *only one; understood* and *understands:* there is no longer a place for *evolution,* inasmuch as the council explains: "any meaning of the sacred dogmas that has *once* been declared by holy Mother Church, must *always* be retained" [*The Church Teaches,* trans. John Clarkson et al. (St. Louis: B. Herder, 1964), 35 and 34, emphasis is Hébert's]. Like *symbolism, dogmatic evolutionism* is, *from the orthodox point of view,* only a subterfuge. The true orthodox would like to allow only the possibility of a *logical* evolution, the simple passage from principles to conclusion, from implicit to explicit. But the facts are against them; it is not *logic* that allows us to affirm two wills rather than one in Jesus Christ, transubstantiation rather than impanation, etc.

not *value.* Christian faith has evolved, but what is the *value,* from the perspective of conscience, of these new adaptations? Historians establish the first point, the question of *fact;* the question of *right,* of *value* is the domain of thinkers, of moralists, of conscience and not of science.

M. Loisy leaves us with the hope of one day knowing all the reasons on which he bases not his findings but his interpretation of the facts, and why he considers the Catholic adaptation *unparalleled.* While awaiting his evidence and giving our own, let us draw up some objections.

"*The whole question*" is indeed this one: Has the Gospel's evolution been "*homogeneous* or *heterogeneous*" with the initial data?[27] What allows us to answer?

Is it that, in Christianity "if the figure change, its type does not vary, nor the law that governs its evolution."[28]

But this *type,* this *law* is found in all Christian communities, whatever they are; all have faith in the celestial Father, not only in the present, but in the future, all hope for a Reign of God which is in a very real sense "objective" and "collective,"[29] all, in the end, hold from Christ the faith that sustains them, all have "a service of the gospel which ensures the transmission and application of the Master's word."[30] Thus, if we must choose among them, it is by a criterion other than a "type" or a "law" which is identical in all of them.

The old Catholic system was perfectly clear: Jesus received his authority from God; he transmitted it to his apostles; his apostles to the bishops and to the pope, all without resolving continuity. Objective miracles confirmed this objective transmission. But

27. [Loisy, *The Gospel and the Church,* p. 181 (128).]

28. Ibid., p. 18 (xxviii; cf. xv, xxvi, etc.).

29. Ibid., p. 59 (7, 8).

30. Ibid., p. 170 (116).

this is where we encounter a *faith,* a *hope,* a Christian *life* subjective in its essence although tending toward an objective mystical reality. It is true that function creates the organ. Little by little Christian life will form its organs of development and defense. Admittedly, but nothing, absolutely nothing forces us to believe that there will be only *one* type of legitimate Christian life, *one* kind of acceptable organ; feline or canine life, for example, is expressed in a hundred different ways. Likewise, in a different order of things, Christian life, while preserving the same type and the same law, has been able to and has had to evolve in highly diverse and entirely legitimate ways given the irreducible differences in temperaments, in sentiments, in highly pressing or nonexistent needs for direction, for encouragement, etc.

We have said that the *faith,* the *hope* of which we are told, are subjective in essence. For according to modern critics miracles no longer ground faith, rather faith transforms events into miracles through what is correctly called a "true idealization."[31] Historical proofs of the Resurrection are not the basis of our faith in the resurrected Christ, instead our faith in the living Christ gives to all these marvelous accounts their value.[32] But let us say frankly, as do Schleiermacher and his disciples, that faith is justified by itself, that "Christian life stimulated in us by Christ carries with it its own proper and immediate certitude."[33] Let us affirm that dogmas are "*idealizations,*" myths that religious consciousness has created because it needed them in various conditions or circumstances. It is the only way to avoid playing with words in calling *plainly*

31. *Revue d'histoire et de littérature religieuse* 7 (September 1902): p. 453.—But the Buddha, Krishna, etc., were also subject to idealizations *true* in relation to the consciousnesses that idealized them. All passions, religious or otherwise, *idealize* their object. It is a *fact,* but what *value* does it have?

32. Loisy, *The Gospel and the Church,* chap. II §IV.

33. August Twesten, disciple of Schleiermacher.

true what is historically false[34] but "necessary for the success of the Gospel."[35] This theory of justification of the fact by its *success* would be legitimate to the degree that the success is obviously a spontaneous *progress* of an ideal order; but from the moment that this progress requires the intervention of an authority that fulminates and anathematizes, it is prudent to give the matter a second thought. Moreover, the success, the very progress, does not, in any case, allow one to recognize its truth in the habitual sense of the word, but to recognize its truth in the symbolic order. What meaning, if there is one, could a symbolic authority have? Let us then admit that the old objective method alone allowed one to recognize the real and despotic authority of the present-day Church. Another example: Is Jesus God? One replies: Jesus believed himself and presented himself as Messiah. But this Jewish title was not understood by the Greeks. Christian faith, Christian consciousness thus applied the idea of the *Logos* to Christ, then, gradually, required the famous *consubstantiality* with the Father. Consequently, Jesus is God in the sense that the Christian consciousness needs to represent him as such, to define him as such.

—Who will ever believe that the idea of *Logos* is "homogeneous" with that of *Messiah*! If there was a point of contact (for, obviously, with a bit of ingenuity one can prove that everything is homogeneous with everything), it would be that, in both cases, Jesus is conceived as an intermediary, a mediator; but then Arius's conception would be better than that of Athanasius. It

34. Such as, for example, an event clearly predicted, but that did not occur, as the *proximate* coming of Christ.

35. Loisy, *The Gospel and the Church*, p. 76 (26).—In any case, one would still have to pose and to resolve Hartmann's question: "At the end of the day, are we not at one of those historical moments where a great idea has undergone all the phases of its evolution and sees itself irrevocably condemned to quit the stage to be replaced on it by other dominant ideas?" *La religion de l'avenir*, chap. I: "Evolution or Innovation?"

appears that the defenders of consubstantiality reasoned along these lines: Christ could not deify man if he were not God; and they added that this reasoning was grounded on the assertion of the fourth Gospel. This is inaccurate. The fourth Gospel attributes a more submissive attitude to Christ: "*I will ask* the Father, and *he* shall give you another Paraclete";[36] it makes the Logos a "*god*" and not *the* God.[37] If the Christian consciousness of Athanasius had recourse to "consubstantiality," it was because he imagined things in a very material way, according to the practical formula of *nemo dat quod non habet,*[38] just like the Scholastic Christian consciousness later understood and formulated belief in the Eucharist by the material formula of "transubstantiation" which, supposing the "*permanence of the sensible species*": color, taste, smell . . . objectively isolated from substance, is no longer acceptable for a modern thinker.

The Christian faith of Saint Athanasius, the Christian faith of the Scholastics, that is what M. Loisy should say, but under no circumstances Christian faith *alone.* Christian faith could have been as alive in the consciousness of Arius as in that of Athanasius, in the consciousness of Luther as in that of many of the Council Fathers of Trent. The criterion of *faith,* of *life,*[39] is therefore insufficient for resolving such questions if it is, nonetheless, claimed that they must be resolved by a *unique* solution. By that very token, one would moreover be unfaithful to the criterion of life, life being essentially diverse, inexhaustible, in its variations on a same theme.

36. Fourth Gospel 14.16; cf. 5.26 and 15.26.

37. Jn 1.1. Greek text.

38. [No one gives what he does not have.] It is the same kind of argument: the heretic cannot give the Holy Spirit which he does not have, thus the baptism he confers is not valid, which makes Donatists heretics.

39. "[T]he best apology for all that lives lies in the life itself." Loisy, *The Gospel and the Church,* p. 220 (170).

Besides, these famous historical *facts* are truly misleading: what interests us is knowing the innumerable elements of which they are the result. Learned historians know several hundred of them; the others elude them and they makes up the difference with personal interpretations. We establish the influence of Athanasius's piety (most respectable but most ignorant) on the Council of Nicea, but we also need to determine Constantine's influence and it is difficult, without *a priori* belief, to make the Holy Spirit responsible. And yet, without this *a priori* belief, one concludes quite simply: might is always right.

Who, then, would dare to conclude *historically:* might is always right? This could only be asserted by virtue of a belief *according to which* one *would interpret* the facts, thus by virtue of theology. When it is stated that "the Gospel in its full reality is a living faith which, having its origin in Christ's word and action, makes its way through the centuries explaining itself, and assimilating to this operation everything that could assist in becoming aware of its force and developing it,"[40] it is necessary to distinguish between the *facts* to which this affirmation alludes and the *theological perspective* according to which they are considered. The *facts* show the Roman Church, the Greek Church, the Protestant Churches as having their "origin in the word and action of Christ"; to make *one* of these forms the legitimate, the *unique* normal organ of spiritual life, the *unique* truly providential religious magisterium, is to go beyond the facts to appreciate them according to a preconceived theory of what the Church *must* be, what it is to be *united* with the Church or the *solution*

40. Loisy, *Études Évangéliques* (1902), p. xiii. We should, moreover, make a distinction between what really goes back to the "*action*" of the *historical* Jesus and what goes back to the religious consciousness of Humanity which prepared Christianity and, in "idealizing" doctrines and facts, also in great measure, founded it.

of continuity. Whether we speak of the first initiates of the Gospel's "superior instinct of faith" or of the Holy Spirit enlivening a single Church, causing it to assimilate what is good, to reject what is bad, or of Christ living in the Church and channeling his action, so to speak, through a unique hierarchy, all these suppositions introduced under the guise of living faith, living experiences of faith, are only *practical equivalents* of so-called theological theories. Alternatively, it is faith justifying itself by itself, it is the famous *fideism*[41] against which the Catholic Church has always protested. For if the intellectual and other *grounds* of faith are acknowledged, one is by that token forced to rely on *private examination,* on essentially personal appreciation of what faith and religious feeling are, of their real value, of what does or does not suit Humanity, of what Humanity is and can do for itself, of what it can expect from Providence and from various providential religious forms which all, from certain standpoints, have their "transcendence," and above all, of what must be understood by Providence, the Spirit of God. We settle upon the freedom of the individual (we do not say individualist) conscience with regard to these adaptations, having seen the impossibility in such investigations of making use of the *oracular* authority of the Church in determining difficulties in the name of God without falling into a vicious circle, especially in determining on his part what is "homogeneous" or "heterogeneous" in the historical *adaptations* of dogma, of worship, and of discipline. One cannot arbitrarily grant him a role, admitting it when the existence and the nature of God

41. Rational motives must precede faith: "rationis usus fidem praecedit," is the doctrine to which Rome earlier and Bonnetty and Bautain had subscribed, and which was confirmed by the declaration of the Vatican Council. The currently prevailing thesis is: faith justified by "*action,*" that is, more or less unconscious psychic dynamism whose motives are only a very partial expression, is a reissuance of fideism. This doctrine appears true *psychologically* but would not be so *theologically.*

are concerned, no longer admitting it when faith in Christ and in the various forms of its evolution are concerned.

IV

Is this a return to the Protestant idea?

To the old individualist Protestant idea? No. To M. Harnack's idea: adhering to religious tradition in a group freely constituted or chosen according to conscience? Yes; still we are mistaken in saying: M. Harnack's *idea* as if he were a pure philosopher; like M. Loisy, M. Harnack states the facts; like him, he then appraises them; his *idea* thus has *reality* as its basis; if we prefer his idea to that of M. Loisy, it is because it seems impossible that any adaptation of religious life can be considered intrinsically better: perhaps better for a few, for a certain category of minds, but it is impossible to prove it at all times and in all places. Thus we settle on a prudent and conscientious freedom.

Some may say that if the Church has already adapted itself to circumstances, has become more and more authoritarian, it will adapt itself to new needs and consequently become a simple hierarchy "of devotion"?[42] The prophecy, the induction, if you will, is consoling; but this is why, in spite of our desire, we cannot accept it: the hierarchy of authority is conceived as distributing to the spiritually hungry the bread of truth received through the mediation of Christ, the precious "*deposit*"; these truths that the human mind could not have discovered, these supernatural dogmas which must be transmitted and explained, require an organization supplied by God, with supernatural assistance toward this special goal. But devotion is not a supernatural dogma, it is one of the aspects of what Circero already called "*caritas generi*

42. Loisy, *The Gospel and the Church,* p. 148 (92).

humani";[43] organizations of teaching and action spring forth everywhere convinced souls are stirring:[44] Buddhist missionaries preceded gospel missionaries by several centuries.[45] But these organizations must be freely controlled, freely accepted; to incorporate the idea of devotion in an intangible hierarchy, to make of this idea, this feeling, a question of an administration set apart might have been necessary when faced with pagan or barbarous humanity, but cannot be imposed on men imbued with feelings of solidarity. Certainly these ideas of justice, of goodness, are still far from living their full and fruitful life in the heart of all, but Humanity knows them well; largely thanks to the Church, they have, for the most part, *passed into the public domain;* what Humanity needs is no longer an extraordinary, supernatural teaching, but the daily, ordinary, and natural teaching, of parents in families, of teachers in schools, in order to regularly remind Humanity that these inclinations, these virtues (these virtualities, if one prefers) *are* planted in its conscience and that it must develop them.

Shall I speak of the *symbolist* Catholic Church that certain souls demand, some under the influence of unforgettable and respectable memories, others in the name of a nationalism more political than religious? It is an incontestable truth that every expression of religious knowledge must, to some extent, be symbolic, but the Church will never accept that its authority, at least, be treated as a symbol. What happens in the Anglican Church will be raised by my critics as an objection:

43. *De finibus* V, 23.

44. These organizations will respond to the need pointed out more than once by Renan: "Man needs a moral pedagogy, for which the concerns of the family and those of the State are not enough." (*L'Antéchrist,* p. 535; Cf. *Marc-Aurèle,* p. 644.)

45. Cf. Marquis de la Mazellière, *Moines et ascètes indiens* (Paris: Librairie Plon). Their councils, their convents, their hospitals and dispensaries preceded ours by many centuries.

A certain number of priests think quite freely, see in the divinity of Christ merely the highest human manifestation of the divine, and nevertheless maintain their signature at the bottom of the thirty-nine articles, act as officiating priests and preachers. They argue that they are useful at their posts, drawing their salaries, vested in the surplices that secure their prestige. They keep the accustomed forms going, while in the meantime a new and symbolic meaning sinks in little by little, comes to replace the old and literal meaning. Why then sacrifice them, these forms whose efficacy has been proven by time, whose venerable old age only increases their prestige? They hold such powerful sway over our human machine! We are adapted to them ahead of time, by heredity. They impart our habits of feeling; they maintain them; they impose on our soul its ordinary attitude, to all souls analogous attitudes. . . . They are products of life, spontaneous, natural products, elaborated over the course of history, thereby living, effective, of an essence to which no particular invention, no reasoned combination could create analogies, and consequently, they are of inestimable value.[46]

But the glory of the Catholic Church is that it has never accepted, and is unable to accept this utilitarian role as social machinery. Either it possesses a *supernatural* authority, founded on supernatural *facts,* such as the virginal conception and Christ's Resurrection, or it is only a symbolic expression of human consciousness and then, in the interest of the simple faithful who, if they were honestly informed, would not at all care be taken in, as in the interest of educated souls who no longer acknowledge the real authenticity of these facts, it must be declared clearly, openly, so that we may take stock of the situation, no longer compromise the value of conscience in associating it with illusory legends and cease the ambiguous role that claims to safeguard tradition[47] through interpretations that are a veritable negation

46. André Chevrillon, "Foules anglaises" *Revue de Paris* 6 (15 December 1902): pp. 856–58.

47. We want to safeguard less the tradition than the "established order" and especially the economic *status quo.*

of it; for there are not two ways of being or not being conceived virginally or of being or not being resurrected. If *not,* it must be said, according to the method of the Gospel: "But let your speech be yea, yea, no, no." Why impose on one's brothers the yoke that one no longer bears oneself?

Admittedly, in various specific cases, symbolism can be an honorable *expedient,* thanks to which one may use, *through an intelligent choice,* resources that the established churches present, or through which one hides from orthodox harassment in order to continue with some degree of security a ministry of consolation and devotion. But this must be an exceptional approach, not a method to keep using in the future. Indeed, if at present symbolism still seems to show some chance of succeeding, it is because it is practiced by or for men who began by taking dogmatic affirmations *literally;* in so doing they have endowed them with a power of suggestion that they retain even when they are recognized as purely symbolic. But if the enchantment never existed, suggestion cannot occur and from that moment on what extravagant and sterile pedagogy it is to encumber the formation of young consciences through symbols as heavy as the Trinity, the consubstantiality of the Word, transubstantiation, eternal hell!

If absolutely necessary, in return for a series of omissions and intelligent choices a symbolic *Christianity*[48] can be conceived, a traditionally imaged expression of human consciousness, rich in memories and historical experiences; but a symbolic *Catholicism* cannot be conceived. Without abdication, Catholic authority will never accept being considered symbolic, that is, as being fundamentally only a *provisional* pedagogical method for souls who

48. Above all as a *transition.* Recall the symbolic paganism of a Plutarch. Currently it is not a matter of founding a religion, but of clearing the ground in view of the future. Profound social changes will be necessary in order to determine new enthusiasms.

are still "minors." *Sit ut est, aut non sit!*[49] All the rest is equivocation or wordplay.

We must not, in fact, play upon the word "authority" taken in the sense of teaching, of education of immature souls by mature ones (in this sense there will always be a "*spiritual power*" in Humanity) or in the sense of supernatural and infallible power, requiring the absolute submission of all without exception. This latter sense alone is the Catholic meaning; the rights of this power were legitimated by *facts;* yet these facts have become *legends,* at least in their allegedly miraculous elements.

Thus if Harnack does not exclude Roman Catholicism from his unrestricted groupings, he well knows that all Christian communities are descended from it, that they represent varied adaptations, diverse species of a common genus; and yet, as we have already said, outside of the old apologetic based on miracles and formal declarations of the will of the All-powerful, one could not prove that this *unity* of origin and direction is not sufficient and must be completed by the unity of *corporation.* The *separations* brought about by the Church over the course of centuries with regard to a given individual or given groups are, moreover, only *facts* and in order to transform them into the will of the Most High, it would be necessary to apply the old belief, "outside the Church, there is no salvation";[50] but, with our current ideas of Providence, it becomes impossible to justify the old adage; the Catholic Church, having lost its old *miraculous* credentials, cannot have the monopoly of the *providential:* providential is, above all, the instinctively religious human consciousness; providential

49. [Let it be as it is, or let it not be!]

50. Proposition defined against the Albigensians by Lateran IV. Here is the true, rigorous orthodoxy that we defy all partisans of the new apologetic by action or dogmatic evolutionism to establish. Besides, so much the worse for orthodoxy.

are the various organizations through which its inclinations and its beliefs—which, in their essence, never vary and which all, like Catholicism itself, live and evolve unceasingly—are manifested, and fulfilled more imaginally or more abstractly, more popularly or more philosophically. The Word "enlightens every man"; so without superstition one cannot say that *unity* does not exist, not only between Protestant and Catholic, but also between the honest man and the Christian. Consequently, why restrict the meaning of the word *faith* and refuse *catholicity*, that is, universality to the *Society of faith* spoken of by M. Harnack, to the faith of every man whose theoretical or practical belief rises above phenomenon, number, or sensible pleasure? "[W]ith a little good will"—objects M. Loisy against M. Harnack—"the essence of the Koran could readily be discovered to be identical with the essence of the gospel—faith in a benign and merciful God."[51] It is precisely this "good will" that constitutes one of the most pressing duties and it is not to Islam alone that we must apply it, but to all disinterested beliefs. Far, then, from entering into the sphere of *abstractions*, pure ideas, we draw nearer to the true life of Humanity. In our time, indeed, is not the Ideal, living, and active faith, to be found rather in a House of the people than in a cathedral, in a laboratory, in a cooperative grocery-business rather than in many convents? We do not deny that incontestable and admirable faith and zeal can be found on all sides; it is no less true that the laboratory or cooperative work often represent fewer conventions, equivocations, and a superior intellectual and social level, it is no less true that the future lies in this direction and that, consequently, *abstraction*, the abandonment of the truly living and historic terrain, does not lie on this side.

51. Loisy, *The Gospel and the Church*, p. 9 (xvi).

The old objection: in order to be popular philosophy and morality must transform into a positive and authoritarian religion, was valid with regard to uneducated people. This objection no longer holds with well-organized families and schools and Unions for moral and social action established under the most varied names and forms: popular universities, etc. . . . at once conscious *of recognizing and conserving what was good in the past* and adapting the old traditions of beliefs and aspirations to the new conditions of an emancipated people.

Thus on the condition that these social works, even enterprises of pure humanitarian spirit outside of all dogma itself, can be included in the extension of the notion of *faith,* that this notion of *faith* synthesizes all beliefs and inclinations that science itself, which is occupied only with phenomena, especially those that can be schematized by progress and numerical formulas, cannot explain, the *Society of faith* of which M. Harnack speaks clearly explains the facts of history and finds its justification in our consciences. Nevertheless, we would hesitate to give a paradoxical appearance to our conclusion in saying: "To everyone his own doctrine . . . we wish it no different."—No, for once the subtleties of dogma have disappeared, agreement will be increasingly easier and more frequent. The forms of belief and of worship responding to rather particular mental states tend by that very fact to be self-limiting: the Salvation Army has never quite achieved the conquest of Paris.

The religious movement which is becoming more pronounced at this moment, and which consists in rendering faith and religion *immanent* to different responsibilities, to various social functions, to every sincere effort toward the Best, and to eliminate little by little the antique *transcendent* forms which used authority to impose the Best from outside, is, furthermore, the corollary of the intellectual movement that leads thinkers increasingly to consider the Divine as immanent rather than as transcendent to our souls. Consequently, since human consciousness, always one and identical in the depth of its beliefs and hopes, bears and brings the Divine everywhere with it, what good is it to continue arguing whether we must worship at Jerusalem or at Gerazim?

Part II *Pragmatism*

A Study of Its Various Forms, Anglo-American, French, and Italian, and of Its Religious Value

Foreword

When, in an essay on the Divine, I focused on the various forms (emotive, intellectual, active) of religious experience [sentiment], I made a simple allusion to *pragmatism.*[1] At that time I imagined that pragmatist expressions were only a kind of American idiom, common expressions used to make truths accessible to businessmen and men of action little concerned with logic and criticism. The books of Mr. James and Mr. Schiller and the interest they have received in Latin countries have changed my mind. There are, it seems to me, so many good things and also so many paradoxes in these systems, that it is useful to explain their main themes.

The adjective *pragmatic* is borrowed from the Latin *pragmaticus* (Greek πραγματιχος) relating to business, to facts. Stemming from that: "pragmatic" sanction (ordinance), a solemn act regulating the interests of a monarch's family, or of the state.

Edouard Reuss described as *pragmatic* those narratives that aimed less at informing us regarding historical reality (theoretical goal), than instilling in us (practical goal) one or another truth.[2]

Mr. Charles S. Peirce (whose ideas I summarize in Chapter 1) can be credited with bringing in the use of the word pragmatism in the sense of a method which consists in judging the value of

1. Marcel Hébert, *Le Divin* (Paris: Félix Alcan, 1907), p. 285.

2. Translation of the Bible: *Chronique,* Introduction, p. 41; *Livre des Juges,* p. 93, etc. Furthermore, it is good to maintain the distinction between pragmatic and pragmatist.

an assertion by its practical consequences.[3] He set out the system as early as 1871, but only after long use of the word *pragmatism* in conversation did he use it in print in his article in Baldwin's dictionary.[4] Mr. William James has contributed significantly to making it more widely known.[5]

The most important addition to this new edition, is Mr. William James's very interesting response my work. I have also done my best to take into account my critics' objections and observations—with the exception of *quantitative* criticism—remarks, for example, that look on my efforts at conciseness as superficial analysis. I have always felt that it was enough for the thinker to determine clearly and precisely in what way a particular problem is badly formulated and where exactly the crux of a difficulty, the weak point of a system lies: leave glossing to men of letters.

3. [Hébert consistently renders C. S. Peirce as "Pierce." The correct spelling is used throughout the translation.]

4. Cf. Mr. Peirce's article on "A Neglected Argument for the Reality of God" in *The Hibbert Journal* 7 (October 1908): 90–112 in which he gives information on the origins of his theory. [James Mark Baldwin, *Dictionary of Philosophy and Psychology*, 3 vols. (New York: Macmillan, 1901)].

5. At the beginning of chap. 4 we will have to distinguish among *pure* pragmatism, *mitigated* pragmatism, and *partial* pragmatism.

1

Mr. Peirce's "Pragmatism"

I. An Overview of the Doctrine

It is thirty years now since Mr. Peirce set forth his doctrine in an American journal though not yet using the actual term "pragmatism."[1]

He started from the following psychological fact: uncertainty and doubt cause us malaise and irritation, in short, a disagreeable state. Can we emerge from this painful state? Yes, if we succeed in creating a conviction, a "belief." The belief calms the pangs of doubt, which is why we seek it:

"We may fancy that this is not enough for us, and that we seek, not merely an opinion, but a true opinion. But put this fancy to the test, and it proves groundless; for as soon as a firm belief is reached we are entirely satisfied, whether the belief be true or false."[2]

1. "How to Make Our Ideas Clear," *Popular Science Monthly* 13 (January 1878). As early as 1878 he had taught this "in a Metaphysical Club in Cambridge, Mass., . . . as a sort of logical gospel, representing the unformulated method followed by Berkeley." C. S. Peirce, "A Neglected Argument for the Reality of God," *The Hibbert Journal* 7 (October 1908): 109. [Throughout, Hébert renders Peirce as "Pierce."]

2. "Fixation of Belief," orig. pub. in *Popular Science Monthly* 12 (Nov. 1877): 1–15 [Also published in French as "La logique de la science," Part 1: "Comment se fixe la croyance," *Revue philosophique de la France et l'Étranger* 6 (December 1878): 553–69. All references will be to the English version in Christian J. W. Kloesel, ed., *Writings of Charles S. Peirce: A Chronological Edition*, vol. 3 (Bloomington: Indiana University Press, 1986), with the French version following in parentheses. Here, 248 (559)].

Once man possesses the belief that calms him and makes him happy, he no longer wants to let it go; he buries himself in it, as the ostrich buries its head in the sand, thinking to preserve itself from danger. This is "the method of *tenacity*," easy to carry out, but, if experience did not make its universal practice impossible, deplorable in its results, impeding all progress, consecrating all routine. In a great many cases, indeed, man quickly perceives "that other men think differently from him, and it will be apt to occur to him . . . that their opinions are quite as good as his own, and this will shake his confidence in his belief."[3]

This is how the passage from individual belief to collective occurs. But now we avoid Charybdis only to fall into the maw of Scylla: collective beliefs will try to defend themselves, just as did the previously mentioned individual beliefs; they will organize, they will turn into dogmas: State dogmas, Church dogmas, and dogma will bring with it persecutions and inquisitions, inevitable fruits of the "method of authority."

"For the mass of mankind, then," the author gloomily observes, "there is perhaps no better method than this. If it is their highest impulse to be intellectual slaves, then slaves they ought to remain!"[4]

But such a system does not provide a solution to all problems. Questions not settled by the method of authority and needing to be tackled by other methods, will awaken minds. Many, on the other hand, will realize "that men in other countries and in other ages have held to very different doctrines from those which they themselves have been brought up to believe."[5] They will thus lay claim to their freedom. Let natural preferences be left free to act, in the intellectual as in the aesthetic order!

3. Ibid., p. 250 (561–62). [Italics are Hébert's.]

4. Ibid., p. 251 (563).

5. [Ibid., p. 252 (563).]

It is dangerous to assimilate truth to beauty! If the true is a matter of *taste,* if it is *what it pleases us* to think, it means the proliferation of systems to infinity.

"To satisfy our doubts, therefore, it is necessary that a method should be found by which our beliefs may be caused by nothing human, but by some external permanency—by something upon which our thinking has no effect. . . . It must be something which affects, or might affect, every man. . . . Such is the method of science. Its fundamental hypothesis, restated in more familiar language is this: There are real things, whose characters are entirely independent of our opinions about them; those realities affect our senses according to regular laws, and, though our sensations are as different as our relations to the objects, yet, by taking advantage of the laws of perception, we can ascertain by reasoning how things really are, and any man, if he have sufficient experience and reason enough about it, will be led to the one true conclusion."[6]

Aside from the personal manner in which he presents things there is really nothing particularly new in such affirmations. The doctrine becomes clearer in the following article.[7] First of all we find familiar assertions:

"[T]he production of belief is the sole function of thought. . . . Thought in action has for its only possible motive the attainment of thought at rest; and whatever does not refer to belief is no part of the thought itself."[8]

But the psychological analysis is pushed farther:

"The essence of belief is the establishment of a habit. . . . If beliefs do not . . . appease the same doubt by producing the same

6. Ibid., pp. 253–54 (565–66).

7. ["How to Make Our Ideas Clear" was published in the *Revue philosophique de la France et l'Étranger* 7 (January 1879): 39–57 as "La logique de la science," Part 2: "Comment render nos idées claires," and in *Writings of Charles S. Peirce,* 3.355–74. As above, references will be given to the English version first, followed by the French in parentheses.]

8. Ibid., pp. 261, 263 (43, 45).

rule of action, then no mere differences in the manner of consciousness of them can make them different beliefs, any more than playing a tune in different keys is playing different tunes. . . . To develop [the meaning of a thought], we have, therefore, simply to determine what habits it produces, for what a thing means is simply what habits it involves. Now the identity of a habit depends on how it might lead us to act, not merely under such circumstances as are likely to arise, but under such as might possibly occur, no matter how improbable they may be."[9]

"[E]very purpose of action is to produce some sensible result. Thus we come down to what is tangible and practical, as the root of every real distinction of thought, no matter how subtle it may be; and there is no distinction of meaning so fine as to consist in anything but a possible difference of practice."[10]

Example: discussions between Protestants and Catholics on transubstantiation: are bread and wine, once consecrated, bread and wine, or the real body and the real blood (not symbolic) of Christ?

There is only one way of being bread and wine, replies the author; to speak of an object endowed with the material properties of bread and wine as being in reality flesh and blood is only "senseless jargon." Whence the conclusion:

"Our idea of anything is our idea of its sensible effects. . . . It is foolish for Catholics and Protestants to fancy themselves in disagreement about the elements of the sacrament, if they agree in regard to all their sensible effects, here and hereafter."[11]

9. Ibid., pp. 263–65 (45, 47). In the 1908 article referenced earlier, M. Peirce repeats once again that the only manner of completing our knowledge is "to discover and recognize just what general habits of conduct a belief in the truth of the concept . . . would reasonably develop." "A Neglected Argument for the Reality of God," p. 108.

10. "How to Make Our Ideas Clear," pp. 265 (47).

11. Ibid., p. 266 (47, 48).

Other examples:

Can I assert that a diamond is *hard*? That makes no sense before I have touched it, before I have experienced the relation between my touch and its resistance. From this follows the important rule: "Consider what effects, which might conceivably have practical bearings, we conceive the object of our conception to have. Then, our conception of these effects is the whole of our conception of the object."[12]

Let us apply this rule to a problem of the moral order: Is man free? Is he subject to fate?

The author replies:

"Many questions are involved in the free-will discussion, and I am far from desiring to say that both sides are equally right. On the contrary, I am of opinion that one side denies important facts, and that the other does not."[13]

But the question posed differently, as a choice between freedom and destiny, leads to interminable discussions, to insoluble difficulties, while agreement would quickly be reached if one spoke from the perspective of behavior, of practice, asking oneself: "Must I be ashamed for having acted badly?"

The same is true of the notion of force: "In a recent admired work on 'Analytic Mechanics' it is stated that we understand precisely the effect of force, but what force itself is we do not understand! This is simply a self-contradiction. The idea which the word force excites in our minds has no other function than to affect our actions, and these actions can have no reference to force otherwise than through its effects. Consequently, if we know what the effects of force are, we are acquainted with every fact which is implied in saying that a force exists, and there is nothing more to know."[14]

12. Ibid., p. 266 (48).
13. Ibid., p. 267 (49).
14. Ibid., p. 270 (52).

To ask if force *is* or if it *causes* acceleration of movement is a purely verbal question, as if one attributed an importance to the difference between the English expression, It *is* cold, and the French, Il *fait* froid.

And once again Peirce sets forth his rule:

"[R]eality, like every other quality, consists in the peculiar sensible effects which things partaking of it produce."[15]

"The only effect which real things have is to cause belief, for all the sensations they excite emerge into consciousness in the form of beliefs. The question therefore is, how is true belief (or belief in the real) distinguished from false belief (or belief in fiction)."[16]

And yet *scientific* method alone—and we return to the earlier conclusion—can enable the solid establishment of this difference. Those who are fond of *a prioris* are, basically, skeptics:

"[T]hey seem to think that the opinion which is natural for one man is not so for another, and that belief will, consequently, never be settled. In contenting themselves with fixing their own opinions by a method which would lead another man to a different result, they betray their feeble hold of the conception of what truth is."[17]

The man of science, on the contrary, knows that whatever the differences in starting point or method, agreement on certain points will be reached sooner or later. The real in no way depends on the ideas one or another individual or group of individuals may hold of it. "The opinion that is fated to be ultimately agreed to by all who investigate, is what we mean by the truth, and the object represented in this opinion is the real."[18]

15. Ibid., p. 271 (53).

16. Ibid., pp. 271–72 (53).

17. Ibid., p. 273 (55).

18. Ibid., p. 273 (56). In the aforementioned article M. Peirce admits, on the other hand,

2. Some Remarks

The psychological fact that Mr. Peirce uses as a starting point is incontestable: belief makes the pangs of doubt disappear. But when Mr. Peirce adds: "as soon as a firm belief is reached, we are entirely satisfied, whether the belief be true or false" it becomes impossible to follow him. Altogether too often we notice that many people seek only a calming and reassuring opinion, a "conviction"; but why are men not satisfied with the "method of tenacity"? Why do they try to escape it and to reach the "scientific method" if not because the gentle sleep of subjective certitude no longer suffices and because their need for objective certitude has been awakened?

The examples advanced by Mr. Peirce show, moreover, the degree of simplification to which he has reduced the difficulties in order to allow his pragmatism to respond to them. He begins by declaring that theories on the Eucharist are "senseless jargon," after which he affirms that Protestants and Catholics are in agreement since they admit the same practical effects of the elements of the sacrament.

Who would be content with such *vague approximations*? All the same, from here on he reduces us to these extravagant simplifications on every subject. And Mr. Peirce deludes himself when he claims that, as a result, "agreement will soon follow"; for example, regarding the question of free will, from the moment one posits it in these terms: "Must I be ashamed for having acted badly?"—No; the true fatalist, the true determinist replies: I *regret* it, but I do not *blame* myself for it.

that we can choose between certain hypotheses thanks to a kind of "*divinatory power,*" an infallible instinct analogous to that which directs the bee and the bird for other purposes (104 and 106).

Mr. Peirce allows that two theories that have the same practical effects are fundamentally identical.—They contain some common element;[19] which is not the same thing.

We therefore need to analyze the theories instead of taking them thus, all in one piece. Then we will see that it is not the theories, but certain of their elements, that are identical.

Besides, to apply such a rule, people must not only be perfectly logical, but they must also act independently of the feelings, unconscious tendencies, and hereditary influences which are certainly not all-important in our determinations, but which play a large role in them and whose influence we often justify by attributing it to some perfectly blameless theory or idea.

An example. I recall having heard a straightforwardly materialist speech, which concluded with a vibrant exhortation to a noble, disinterested life—a sort of consecration to the Ideal. Did the peroration logically proceed from the speech itself? I shall never believe it—unless one accepts as definition of *matter* the very definition of *spirit*. A triumph of pragmatism, it will be said, which cares little about definitions and considers only conclusions.—No, it is a triumph of equivocation and wordplay. The pragmatists will never recognize that a clear-sighted intellect will demand explanation, analyze various hypotheses on the subject

19. As M. Ménégoz informed me (article in the *Annales de bibliographie théologique* [16 (November 1908)] reproduced in the second volume of *Publications diverses sur le fidéisme* [Paris: Fischbacher, 1909]), I should have insisted on the analogous and well-known case of an error rendered beneficial by the core of truth it contains—an observation that forms "the correct idea serving as point of departure for the false reasonings" of the pragmatists: "Let us take an example. The ancient Romans maintained a relatively moral life as long as they sincerely worshipped Jupiter, Mars, Neptune, Venus, Minerva; but corruption entered the nation from the moment when they lost faith in their mythological divinities. If one wished to apply the pragmatist theory to this historical fact, one would conclude that the pagan religion was true up until the period of decadence and that, afterward, this same religion was false. The conclusion would be in the logic of the principle. However, the pragmatists refrain from drawing it. This should open their eyes to their error" (p. 497).

of the matter, compare them to the psychological data in order to get a clear idea of whether they fit together, or whether they conceal contradictions beneath the words—all things which are of the order of knowledge itself. Which will not, moreover, impede many people, endowed with a particularly practical temperament, from contenting themselves with the pragmatic response of Socrates to Simmias: the soul resists the body and governs it, thus it is not identical. But the one does not negate the other.

Another instance of Mr. Peirce's *approximations:* The reality of things, he says, is made up of the perceptible effects produced by things.

Their reality *in relation to us,* obviously, but can one infer nothing about their reality *in themselves*? Therein lies the difficulty. We shall return to it. Let us declare, at least, that in order to be satisfied with the pragmatist method one must considerably diminish and amputate both things and thought. I am therefore not surprised that pragmatism has been attacked for hiding or veiling skepticism under simple practical expedients.

"Thought in action," we are told, "has for its only possible motive the attainment of thought at rest." As with all Mr. Peirce's assertions, this is *partially* true. Thought in action seeks a provisory and momentary rest only to increase its activity still more, and resolves a question only to create ten new ones. It is that man does not seek knowledge simply to ease his discomfort, his disquiet, or to gain practical utility. That he seeks all these things is incontestable, but he also seeks because he feels that knowledge has a value *in itself.*

Let us say it loudly and clearly: knowing for the sake of knowing; yes, the true for the sake of the true, as the beautiful for the sake of the beautiful, and the good for the sake of the good. As romantic, as declamatory as this motto may appear, it is no less the expression of an aspect of our psychological life: judgment of value, disinterested regard. It would be absurd to claim that one *values* a being because of the emotions or profits that can be drawn from it. No; one values it and respects it for what one knows or imagines that it *is* objectively. Value cannot be confused with appreciation of usefulness. Judgment of value—judgment of usefulness correspond to: disinterested objective element—interested subjective element of knowledge.[20]

Mr. Peirce's pragmatism, in taking into account only an appreciation of usefulness, thus modifies, diminishes, alters the parameters of the problem as it is manifested in all its complex reality. The truth is that Mr. Peirce adopted a special and limited point of view: to determine the clear content of our ideas in order to confine himself to them and to avoid further pointless and purely verbal debates.[21]

It appears to be above all this methodical point of view in Peirce that has won over the young Italian "pragmatists" of the review *Leonardo.*[22] In the multiple forms under which pragmatism appears, the essential for Mr. Papini is to make beliefs and theories "flexible," to recognize that they have only an "instrumental" value, that they are but means relative to a given end, therefore always subject to being modified and transformed when the need is felt.

20. In our essay on the *Forme idéaliste du sentiment religieux,* refer to §3 of the 2nd part: "Du caractère désintéressé de l'amour divin."

21. "Consider what effects that might conceivably have practical bearings you conceive the object of your conception of to have: then your conception of those effects is the whole of your conception of the object." Let us not forget that Mr. Peirce, after having spoken of personal conviction, speaks of unanimous collective conviction; he does not consider the individual alone, but the evolution of "reasonableness," a reality thus endowed with generality and continuity. (Cf. his article "Pragmatism" in Baldwin's *Dictionary of Philosophy and Psychology.*) But can there not be unanimity in error and this identification of the unanimity of thought with *objectivity,* is it not thoroughly Berkeleyian; is it not (except for the idealists) the confusion of effect with cause?

22. This review is published in Florence. M. Papini's article is in the April 1905 issue. These gentlemen have founded a "pragmatist club."

It is precisely because thought is thus completely subordinated to action and is no longer a means to this end that the result of pragmatist methods depends on the goal pursued by each individual will. Hence this comparison of pragmatism to a "corridor" in a large hotel; one hundred doors open on said corridor: those of an oratory in which a man who wants to regain faith is praying, of an office in which a philosopher who wants to destroy all metaphysics is writing, of a laboratory in which a scientist is carrying out his research. . . . And thanks to the corridor, all these rooms are connected and their inhabitants can exchange their opinions.

The allegory is ingenious; but the point is not to invent a means of exchanging ideas; the difficulty would lie in finding a criterion to judge them. Or would one allow every whim equal validity?[23] That would be the worst skepticism. "There is no accounting for taste" is a practical maxim of civility, nothing more. Man is man only because he can bring judgments of value to bear on his taste and desires. Does he appreciate them only from a strictly utilitarian point of view? If he tries to do so he will quick-

23. "Pragmatism," as M. Ruyssen has written me, "is perhaps at heart the suppression of all distinction between fact and right; everything which acts well is true; insofar as the influence of feeling upon thought does not does not lead to miscalculation, it is by that token legitimate. It is besides the inevitable consequence of Mr. Schiller's thesis that between psychology and logic there is room for no essential distinction.—But does one not then slip into the extreme paradoxes of the Italians, of the *Leonardo* or of the *Art de persuader* of Mr. Papini or of Mr. Prezzolini that Mr. James does disavow, but halfheartedly, and sometimes with an obvious sympathy? Mr. Prezzolini ends, it is known, by praising the lie assimilated to scientific hypothesis: 'The scholar is a liar useful to the collectivity; the liar a scholar useful to the individual'; he draws up a program for a 'Clinic of Beliefs,' or an 'Orthopedic Institute for correcting faith'; and he concludes that 'if something eschews intelligence, it is persuasion,' that the dream would be to suppress the word as intermediary between minds, in order to act on them solely via suggestion; and that 'the arbitrary creation of self and the creation and arbitrary transformation of the world' would be the great tasks of the man of the future, magician more than scholar'; 'the rational animal will give way to the creative animal,' 'man will make himself God.'

Faced with such fantasies, Mr. Schiller and Mr. James must indeed protest." D. Parodi, *Bulletin de la Société française de philosophie* 8 (July 1908): 257.

ly break out of the limits he set himself and will set up a qualitative hierarchy of usefulness, recognizing that this one is *of a superior order* to that one, *must* be preferred to the other, is more *noble*, more *worthy* of man.[24] Thus one does not judge uniquely by usefulness, since usefulness itself is judged.

It will be said that the *a priori* has reappeared.—We shall not use this term if it is too off-putting, but let us acknowledge the fact and be aware that pragmatist utilitarianism neglects this aspect of reality.

It remains to be seen whether the intellect procures a real, though imperfect, knowledge of beings which allows the appreciation of values to pass from the instinctive phase to the reflective phase;[25] this question of the objectivity of intellectual knowledge will be raised and discussed in the following chapters.

24. Cf. *La forme idéaliste du sentiment religieux,* Appendix III on "judgments of value."

25. "See clearly in my thought to see clearly in my conscience." Alfred Loisy, *Quelques lettres sur des questions actuelles* (Ceffonds: l'auteur, 1908), p. 183.

2

Mr. W. James's "Pragmatism"

Pragmatists like W. James and F. C. S. Schiller have not in any way repudiated Peirce's Principle: the concept of a thing is only the concept of its effects. But instead of formulating a simple *practical rule* for "rendering our ideas clear"[1] they seek to justify it by a *theory*.[2]

In his recent work on pragmatism, W. James devotes a special chapter to the notion of truth.[3] In it he develops Mr. Schiller's ideas; thus it is not to set these thinkers in opposition that we devote two distinct sections to their theories, but to gain greater clarity in exposition.

Truth, says Mr. James, is not a "static" property of ideas. Ideas come to be true, *become* true, are *made* true by events. The truth

Mr. W. James's reply appeared in the *Journal of Philosophy, Psychology and Scientific Methods* 5 (3 December 1908). We provide it, with our observations, as an appendix.

1. According to Mr. Schiller (*Studies in Humanism*, p. 5 n.), Mr. Peirce realized the full import of the principle he posed, and it is simply to designate his personal manner of expounding the system that he names it *pragmaticism* rather than *pragmatism*—pragmaticism, a term ugly enough, says Mr. Peirce, to render it secure from kidnappers (*Monist* 15 [1905]: 166). Nevertheless, Mr. Schiller (Essay XIX in *Studies in Humanism*, p. 421) indicates the transition from epistemology to a metaphysics as distinguishing *pragmatism* and *humanism* [Ferdinand C. S. Schiller, *Studies in Humanism* (1907) (Elibron Classics, 2003)].

2. William James, *Pragmatism: A New Name for Some Old Ways of Thinking* (New York: Longmans, Green and Co., 1907), pp. 55 and 65: "Such then would be the scope of pragmatism—first a method; and second, a genetic theory of what is meant by truth."

3. James, *Pragmatism*, Lecture VI.

of an idea is itself an event, a process, that of its "veri-*fication,* of its valid-*ation*."[4] What is true is what has been verified.

Until such verification, there is merely a claim to truth; moving from claim to right is necessary. Every proposition contains an assertion, a conviction. But how many times have we not established the falsity of our most solid, most sincere long-standing convictions! Thus there is an "ambiguity" between a nonjustified conviction and a justified, verified conviction. How do we "validate" our convictions, go from a completely subjective truth to a real truth? The old intellectualist school failed in its efforts to furnish a criterion, for what we have just said of conviction can also be said of evidence, of certitude.

Pragmatism takes an entirely different tack: an assertion is justified by its consequences, by its relation to intention, the goal set in formulating the question. Every science truly useful to life and which harmonizes and improves it, responds to its inclinations, stirs them up and broadens them still further;—if, moreover, science does not contradict other acquired parts of experience but leads us, on the contrary, to richer and more fruitful findings and achievements—this science is *verified,* it is *true.*[5]

What we must ask of our ideas is not to be *copies* of reality, but to agree with it *while "adapting"*[6] *us to it* in practice—whether

4. James, *Pragmatism,* p. 201. Lecture VI.

5. Mr. Schiller has summarized his system in terms so clear that I now borrow several of them: "*Truth* will mean primarily a claim which may or may not turn out to be valid. It will mean, secondarily, such a claim *after* it has been tested and ratified, by processes which it behoves us to examine. . . . If and so far as an assertion satisfies or forwards the purpose of the inquiry to which it owes its being, it is so far 'true'; if and so far as it thwarts or baffles it, it is unworkable, unserviceable, 'false.' . . . Or, in other words, a 'truth' is what is useful in building up a science; a 'falsehood' what is useless or noxious for this same purpose. . . . To determine therefore whether any answer to any question is 'true' or 'false,' we have merely to note its effects upon the inquiry in which we are interested, and in relation to which it has arisen. And if these effects are favourable, the answer will be 'true' and 'good' for our purpose, and 'useful' as a means to the end we pursue." *Studies in Humanism*; Essay V, pp. 144–54.

6. James, *Pragmatism,* p. 194, end of the fifth lecture, and p. 213, sixth lecture. "Ideas, cate-

it be a matter of sensations themselves or abstract ideas elaborated in relation to them. Any intrusion of whim, of fancy, would be betrayed and punished by a lack of success in experience: *it would not work.* Thus it is not a question of *the* truth but *truths. The truth* is a collective name (as health, riches) designating a series of processes employed because they "pay,"[7] because they procure useful results for us, reward us for our trouble, reward us for our goodwill in believing and for the risk that every hypothesis entails.

To accept a truth *ante rem* is to produce an abstraction, is to treat as a transcendent being what is no more than a name applied to a collection of affirmations and beliefs having value only to the degree that we can verify them in practice: "A class-name for all sorts of definite working-values in experience."[8]

Here—in its main outline—is W. James's theory. Far be it for me to see in it only a crassly utilitarian or purely subjective and capricious system! On the contrary, I recognize that the system is true in what it affirms; it is false only in what it omits. Furthermore, this is less an omission than an unconscious dissimulation of the old meaning of the word "truth" under cover of the term *experience:* the facts are not *true,* they simply *are.*[9] The "truth" only begins with our beliefs relative to these facts.—Thus here

gories, theories thus have only an *instrumental* value." Cf. pp. 53, 58, and 194 of the same work.

7. Ibid., p. 218. Lecture VI.

8. Ibid., p. 68. Second Lecture. In the third lecture of his *Pragmatism* W. James explains how the pragmatist envisages metaphysical problems. Materialism and spiritualism, for example, do not consist in subtle abstractions on the essence of matter and spirit: "Materialism means simply the denial that the moral order is eternal, and the cutting off of our ultimate hopes; spiritualism means the affirmation of an eternal moral order and giving free rein to hope." It is the "means *simply*" that I contest. Alongside proofs drawn from the analysis of sensory experience or from psychic experience, arguments founded upon the *practical consequences* of a given theory have always been produced. The pragmatists are correct in attaching great importance to these latter, but this is not a reason for disregarding the value of the others.

9. James, *Pragmatism,* p. 225, Lecture VI.

the two meanings (objective and subjective) are no longer distinguished, as before, but separated. On the one hand, the objective meaning ("id quod est") with which I say—by a clever sleight of hand that must not pass unnoticed since it is an illegitimate suppression—the intellectual subjective meaning ("adaequatio rei et intellectus") is confused; on the other, the subjective pragmatic meaning, encompassing the role of inclinations, emotions, desires, wishes, in a word, all that which is not, properly speaking, intellectual. It is agreed that "adaequatio" can no longer be taken in the same sense as the Scholastics; I agree that pure intellectualism, pure logic are insufficient for explaining and justifying our beliefs; but to confine oneself altogether to the nonintellectual subjective meaning goes too far.

W. James certainly gives experience an objective meaning, of this there is no shadow of a doubt,[10] since the said experience constantly exerts an "objective control,"[11] a constraint, a necessary management of our beliefs. But Mr. James is eager to consider only the aforementioned beliefs; of course it is very true that our beliefs, our ideas can always have a *useful effect*—taking *useful* in the fullest sense of the word: not only sensible, material usefulness, but intellectual usefulness (order, clarity in thought), emotional usefulness (satisfaction of certainty, reinvention, elegance of solution, etc.), moral usefulness, etc.;—so it is possible to construct a theory of belief *in terms of this usefulness*. This is precisely what the pragmatists do. Their system can be verified in a number of cases (especially in the case of minds little concerned with criticism, or devoid of any need for logic, or desir-

10. I had sent Mr. James a letter explaining some objections relative to overly subjective aspects of his system. He replied: "I believe in realities independent of the idea that knows them, and in every grade of *approximation* to them by the idea, even eventually totally confluence with them." (5 July 1907.)

11. James, *Pragmatism*, p. 233. Lecture VI.

ous, through discouragement, weariness, or timidity, of avoiding intellectual difficulties), but the question is this: Has pragmatism the right to treat *other aspects* of the problem as null and nonexistent? From the notion that our ideas have a *use value* (pragmatic) does it not follow that they also have an actual *knowledge value*? Everything human is so complex that the temptation to simplify is all too powerful and because an explanation has been provided in terms of one element, we are tempted to deny the no less real intervention and action of the other element. Matter and thought; finite and infinite; real and ideal; disinterest and interest . . . , all these complexities invite unilateral solutions through abstractions and their authors do wrong only when they become systematic and reject the other aspect of reality. Is this not precisely what happens to the pragmatists?

Does not W. James affirm that: an idea is true because it is useful is exactly the same thing as it is useful because it is true?[12]

Admittedly, if we accept the pragmatist meaning: *true* = *verifiable* by its usefulness, *true* and *useful* are only two phases of the same process, but that is to suppose what is in question, that the word *true* does not have any *other* meaning.

The question is, in effect, knowing whether our ideas, our beliefs do not also have a *representative* value that we can, by abstraction, extricate from the use value, appreciate for itself, love for itself, seek for itself.

Admittedly, in seeking the beautiful, the good, and the true, one can isolate through abstraction the satisfaction of tendencies essentially subjective and involved, but one must not forget that the satisfaction of tendencies or inclinations *implies a judgment and that this judgment also bears on the objective character* of what has satisfied the tendencies: when I admire a handsome horse,

12. "Both these phrases mean exactly the same thing." Ibid., p. 204.

I know very well that beyond my impressions the object of my judgment is not the same reality as a poor nag. Perhaps W. James will consider me a Platonist, or an incorrigible realist; perhaps he will also realize that when I say: the beautiful, the good—and also the true, I use expressions that undoubtedly give rise to regrettable exaggerations (as do nearly all our forms of language) but which do not falsify my thought, the unique goal of which is to keep the disinterested objective aspect distinct[13] from the utilitarian subjective aspect.

Besides, W. James admits this objective aspect. Except that the objective he admits would manifest itself only *practically* by the monitoring of the favorable or unfavorable *result* reached by the effective use of our ideas, beliefs, theories. It would not be expressed in any way by actual *knowledge,* informing us in any way of *what*[14] the object *is in itself.* Thus it is a kind of completely negative objectivity. I do not see, do not feel, do not do what I want; this limitation which hems me in, which constrains me, decides my behavior, independently controls my whims, my will, would be the unique manifestation of the objective, of reality.—Does this conform to the common sense that the pragmatists claim to preserve? Is there not a middle ground between the sensation-

13. And separable only through abstraction, not in the complex real life of the mind.

14. The object *is* not, the pragmatist replies, it becomes, it is unceasingly *made;* further, we "*make*" it to a large degree, as we "*make*" our beliefs. . . .—We "*make reality*" in an appreciable sense only through our moral influence on beings capable of being influenced by it; in all other cases, this influence and that of the evolution of beings would raise an objection solely to an *absolute* "adaequatio" between knowledge and reality. But no one supports this. As for the construction of "scientific" reality by the mind, we shall address this in the following chapter.—The pragmatists really abuse certain psychological evidence in and of itself correct. It is certain that believing I can jump over a ditch is a powerful help in crossing it; the *belief* contributes to the realization, but it does not *create* it. If my belief is not accompanied by a certain *objective* relation between my strength and the distance, it will not pull me through. Likewise, the intervention of my will in the form of *attention* is certainly necessary for me to have an exact knowledge of the object, and of one aspect more than another, but it is not the attention that *creates* the object and its action on us.

image and the sensation-state of a subjective self, a simple practical sign, expedient for action? —Experience alone can tell and in the following chapter we shall explore recent discussions on the value of scientific theories.[15]

For the moment, let us note that the problem is poorly formulated, time and again: the knowing mind is placed on one side, reality *in itself* on the other. Consequently, one can no longer fill the space which separates them and render objective what, as a state of consciousness, is only subjective. To know reality as it is *in itself* is a contradiction in terms, since it is *in itself* only insofar as it is not known. It is through abstraction that man is detached from reality; man is part of this reality. Reality knows itself through man, one should say—as well as: is known by man.[16]

Does Mr. W. James admit that sensation is a simple state of purely subjective consciousness? If, in line with common sense, he recognizes something objective there, however little, sensation becomes a relation having meaning only through its two terms: objective and subjective, one as essential as the other. But that is to admit the possibility of a certain value of objective *knowledge.*

Hence the *fact,* synthesis of sensations, will also have an objective worth and, consequently, will also be able to possess it—independent of all utility—the affirmation declaring that facts

15. To be rounded out, of course, by the penetrating analyses of perception by M. Bergson: cf. for example, *Matière et mémoire* (Paris: Alcan), chap. I and II and Summary and Conclusion [Eng. trans. *Matter and Memory,* trans. Nancy M. Paul and W. Scott Palmer (New York: Zone Books, 1991)]; *L'évolution créatrice* (Paris: Alcan), chap. III [Eng. trans. *Creative Evolution,* trans. Arthur Mitchell (Mineola, N.Y.: Dover Publications, 1998). Page references that follow are to the English translation.] M. Bergson does not want our knowledge to be called *relative,* but *approximative* (206); what he has in mind is an entirely subjective relativism, not that of which we are speaking on p. 164, which is precisely about the *approximative.* Is perception not *relative* to our "rhythm of duration" (cf. *Matter and Memory,* p. 247)? It seems to me that M. Bergson would not deny that.

16. We shall come back to this question in relation to Schiller's theory.

take place, yes or no, in some order or other, in relation to time, causality, etc.

Example: Is it *true* that these flints were used by prehistoric man? Is it *true* that this primitive being used stones (éoliths) for a long period before sharpening or polishing them? Is it *true* that man's ancestor was an animal more or less resembling a monkey?—I suppose that no document, no trace, no fossil will ever allow us to resolve these questions. What meaning might they have? Hypothetical experience cannot provide verification.—Consequently, the pragmatist will reply, these are pointless hypotheses.—Just the same, I will respond, they either do or do not conform to *what has been*. The conformity to what is or has been is the ancient and forever young notion neglected by and compromised by the pragmatists.[17]

They try hard to show the numerous subjective elements involved in the synthesis called a fact. But no one contests this point. Waterloo is a victory for the English, but for the French, on the contrary, a defeat.—No doubt, but for both it is the same defeat of Napoleon.

I have already observed that what we call *truth of fact*, the pragmatist does admit, indeed preserves it, under the guise of "experience," but "experience" also has a subjective meaning. My experience can be tainted with error and nonetheless satisfy my curiosity and calm my doubt, both of which seem all there is for the pragmatist. So, *in addition*, according to the old way of seeing and saying, my belief must be true *in the sense of* conforming to reality.

When I ask: *Is* there a future life for man *or not*? *Does* his hope correspond to a reality *or not*? I am in such a case taking the

17. Even if the evolution of things one day required a renewal of most of our theories,. classifications, and laws, that would change nothing of accomplished fact.

traditional point of view of the "id quod est," inseparable but distinct (and needing to be kept distinct) from the pragmatist point of view: a relation between future life and our desires and aspirations, embryonic faculties awaiting their full evolution.

Admittedly the thing in itself cannot be compared with knowledge as one would the model with the portrait: the expressions portrait-ideas, image-ideas, copy-ideas must thus be avoided. What I do not allow is that there can be no *resemblance* between two of our representations, for example, between that of the cathedral of Paris whose photograph I am now examining and the sensations I will have in a few minutes when I visit it. Likewise, my descriptions of the appearance of the human species on earth, or of primitives using flints, do or do not resemble those I would have written had I been able to witness these phases of our race's evolution. There is thus, in such cases, resemblance, if not "adaequatio."

The following definitions, useful initially, then more and more objective, allow us to become acquainted with this "adaequatio" by trial and error.

"Do you know what a flower is?" Tell me. Please do not reply that a flower is something pretty of which we make bouquets.—No, without even noting that this definition is too egoistic and too utilitarian, I will have you note that there are many flowers that are not beautiful: has it ever occurred to you to make a bouquet of beetroot or rush flowers? Surely not since these small green flowers have neither fragrance nor pretty coloration.

Here is a better response: The flower is the reproductive organ of higher plants.—This is a purely functional definition. With it we do not say what constitutes a flower.

Here is the true response: "A flower is a branch bearing leaves modified for reproduction. —However pretty and colorful and fragrant it may be, a flower is composed of *leaves*, uniquely of leaves, some of which have been transformed into sepals, others into petals, still others into stamens on which pollen is formed, still others finally into carpels containing ovules."[18]

In a piquant "Dialogue Concerning Gods and Priests" Mr. Schiller distinguishes between the gods who exist "in the opinions of men" and those who exist "on the heights of Olympus," between "gods that live in the hearts of men" and "gods that live above."[19] Hence the question: "Does the belief in inner gods correspond to gods *really* existing above the clouds?" cannot be confused with this one: "Do the inner gods respond to *real* needs, to our hearts' *real aspirations*? Here are two orders of *reality* and consequently of *truth:* the truth "*id quod est,*" such as humanity has always conceived it, and *useful* truth, the truth of parables and myths, that of pragmatists.

This is the only one that men can grasp, the latter will reply. Is this correct? The pragmatist not only affirms the existence of other men but recognizes in them the same faculties. Is this solely because this is useful to him? Or does he truly believe that his "*fellow men*" really possess *in themselves* the same faculties as he? To agree is to admit a *knowledge in and of itself* and then we are beyond pure pragmatism. And if this relation of resemblance between our knowledge and reality is admitted, why would we not apply to animals and to the rest of the external world the reasoning by analogy which has been so successful in relation to our fellow men? I intentionally use this pragmatist expression to show that pragmatist utility is perfectly compatible with the other aspect: *true* knowledge—in the true meaning of the word.

Knowledge is *intuitive,* at least in the case of direct, personal—or even *analogical* consciousness. And analogy itself has a double

18. Joséphine (Schouteden)-Wéry, "Excursions scientifiques dans le Brabant," *Revue de l'Université de Bruxelles* 13 (March 1908): 498.

19. *Studies in Humanism,* pp. 338–41.

meaning: actual analogy, that is, sharing in a same quality, to various degrees, by different beings (the consciousness, sensibility, for example, that I note in myself, conceived as shared by other men, animals, and perhaps plants). Secondly, analogy in the broad, metaphorical sense; for instance, to give to someone blind from birth an idea of the difference between blue and red I will tell him that these are visual impressions analogous to hearing a flute compared to hearing a bugle. All human theology is constructed with analogies of these two types.

Imperfect,[20] impoverished knowledge, but knowledge all the same; a glimmering more than a light, but glimmering is already immense progress. *Videmus nunc per speculum in aenigmate,* but *videmus. Ex parte cognoscimus,* but *cognoscimus.*[21] "Man does not see falsely," said Renan, "he sees in a limited way."[22]

I shall return to this in the final chapter: the pragmatic method, in fact, plays a major role in the choice of metaphysical, moral, and religious beliefs. Few intellects escape the confusion caused by so many systems, interminable discussions, insoluble objections. Consequently, many will take up pragmatist "attitudes," will adopt the pragmatist expedient: "What is it better for me to believe?" (*Better,* in the highest sense of the word.) However, it is unnecessary, along with W. James, to exalt this *practical rule* into a theory and to make the *true* into a species of the genus *good:* the good in the order of belief.[23] Once again, we admit this aspect of truth, but it is not a motive for doing away with the other aspect:

20. Hence the necessity of constant effort, never satisfied. Consequently I do not see why pragmatism would assign itself a sort of monopoly (W. James, *Pragmatism,* p. 69) of being plastic, dynamic, "a rich and active commerce" between our minds and reality instead of an "empty notion of a static relation of '*correspondence*'" [emphasis is Hébert's]. It is true that James particularly combats a kind of abstract Scholasticism claiming to subsist *a priori.*

21. 1 Cor. 13.9–12 [Now we see as in a mirror darkly, but we see. We know in part, but we know].

22. Ernest Renan, *Examen de conscience philosophique* (Paris: A. Franck, 1889) §I.

23. *Pragmatism,* p. 76, Lecture II.

knowledge.[24] If the pragmatists only want to maintain the "primacy" of activity, we will agree wholeheartedly (as will be seen in the following chapter) but if they want to suppress a strand of consciousness, an aspect of reality, we must ask leave to protest.

24. ". . . Luce veritatis et fruge utilitatis" ["Light of truth and fruitfulness of profit"]. Saint Augustine, *Confessions*, Book XII: XXX [Eng. trans. W. Watts (Cambridge, Mass.: Harvard University Press, 1970), 2.367]. Cf. our essay: *La Forme idéaliste du sentiment religieux*, Part I, §2 (Consequences relative to pragmatism).

3

Mr. F. C. S. Schiller's "Humanism"

1. Explanation of the Word "Humanism"

"Humanism," states Mr. Schiller, "is simply being aware that the philosophic problem concerns *human* beings striving to comprehend a world of *human* experience by the resources of *human* minds."[1] The emphasis is ours, serving in this way merely to highlight Mr. Schiller's primary goal which is: to rule out the *absolute*, the *a priori*, and take the side of human beings who interpret human experience by purely human means.

To render his exposition more striking, more lively, he fleshes out his doctrine in the person of Protagoras—"Protagoras the humanist."[2] It is well known that only one line remains from the beginning of his Καταβάλλοντες:[3] "Man is the measure of all

1. Mr. Schiller (*Studies in Humanism*, note p. 5) seems to attach very little importance to the distinction between *pragmatism and humanism*. Nevertheless he upholds it and observes that humanism is more encompassing, that its method is applicable to everything: ethics, aesthetics, metaphysics, theology, practical life—in such a way that the pragmatism (of Peirce) would be a humanism limited to the theory of knowledge (epistemology).—In a lecture given recently in Rome (15 April 1909) and published in the June fascicle of *Coenobium* (Lugano) Mr. Schiller insists on this difference. [The citation is taken from Ferdinand C. S. Schiller, *Studies in Humanism* (New York: Macmillan, 1907), 12.]

2. This is the title of Essay XIX in *Studies in Humanism*, p. 302. Mr. Schiller calls his own system "Neo-Protagoreanism," p. 36.

3. This work also bore the titles *On Being* or *The Truth*. [Καταβάλλοντες is a metaphor derived from wrestling, meaning "arguments which overthrow others"; see W. K. C. Guthrie, *A History of Greek Philosophy*, vol. 3 (Cambridge: Cambridge University Press, 1969), p. 183 n. 1.]

things; of those which are, that they are, and of those which are not, that they are not."

Commentators are divided between an individualist interpretation and the generic meaning of the word: "man."[4] Both explanations are correct, asserts Mr. Schiller. Protagoras's humanism was broad enough to encompass both man (individual) and men (human nature in general). . . . But what connection must be established between these two meanings for Protagoras's statement to be true? Protagoras himself—at least according to the *Theaetetus* (166–68)—appealed to the "wise" man and not to the average one and by so doing recognized distinctions of *value* among varied individual perceptions. From the mass of subjective judgments of very variable value, he thus settled upon a selection of the best, the most useful; these will thus endure constituting little by little ever-expanding systems of objective truths that will be accepted by all.[5]

Did Protagoras *really* think all that? The question cannot be settled because the documents are insufficient. At least this kind of myth allows Mr. Schiller to help others better understand what he calls, not without pride, "the new ideas," "the new philosophy."[6]

Let us leave Plato and return to Protagoras! he concludes. Plato "dehumanized"[7] truth; he made it *independent* of the goals man pursues, *absolute,* separated from life, soaring above things, *eternal.* Let us keep, if you will, these hallowed terms, but take them

4. Théodore Gomperz, *Les Penseurs de la Grèce* (Lausanne: Payot, 1904, reprinted), vol. I, p. 478, adopts the generic interpretation. In this he was preceded by Goethe, whose text he cites: "We can observe, measure, calculate, weigh Nature; but it is only according to our measure and our weight, since man is the measure of things."

5. Schiller, *Studies in Humanism,* pp. 33ff. The translation *Études sur l'Humanisme* has just been published by Alcan (1909).

6. Schiller, *Studies in Humanism*, p. 2.

7. Ibid., Essay III, p. 111.

in their *human* sense; independence will result from selection in favor of elements of superior value supplied by experience; the absolute will be the ideal of complete satisfaction for every human tendency; eternity, the perpetual applicability of the true.[8] Like Protagoras, let us start with individual judgments in order to ascend, through the process of "verification,"[9] to assertions of real value. This kind of subjectivism is certainly not skepticism.

It is, in any case, relativism. We would prefer this name which asserts a relation between the two terms and, thereby, the existence of both. The word *humanism* has the unfortunate effect of drawing attention exclusively to the contribution of the human mind in knowing.[10] Let us repeat it: a "sensation," a "thing," a "fact" result from the collaboration and fusion of two activities, the subjective and the objective. Can one analyze this combination and untangle the elements of which it is composed, as Kant attempted for the subjective element, Bergson for the objective?[11] The term "humanism" seems to prejudge the question and to condemn any effort to know anything other than the human element. Yet the humanist affirms (like Protagoras) the *existence* of things.—The existence, he will say, but not the essence, the nature.—So would this be a purely abstract existence? . . . Consequently, not "*humanism*" either, we would say, nor "thingism,"

8. Ibid., Essay II, "From Plato to Protagoras," §18.

9. We have summarized this in the preceding chapter.

10. We do not claim that Mr. Schiller does not preserve *any* objective element. According to him, the mind does not construct, does not "create" reality or truth *ex nihilo;* there is an initial given ("datum"), a "primary reality," a kind of "chaos" that serves all subsequent construction and organization. (Cf. *Humanism,* p. 192; *Studies in Humanism,* Essay VII, §5 and §14; Essay XIX, §7, etc.) But it would seem that the *datum* was, subsequently, as if annihilated by the mind's constructions and that the mind may not truly *know* what it has added. The discussion relative to MM. Le Roy and Poincaré will show us what can be asserted on this subject. Let us also remark that we are speaking here particularly of *science* and of *scientific facts;* in the final chapter we shall study the application of pragmatism to moral and religious beliefs.

11. Cf. Chap. IV and above, note.

but relativism, and, in consequence, the upholding of a certain value "of knowledge in human experience."[12]

This relativism fits very well with the experience of the senses. When activity relies directly on itself it is led to make use of notions very different from those provided by sensations—for example, that of the absolute in the qualitative order, the perfect. I know how the absolute exasperates Mr. Schiller. It is true that among the neo-Hegelians he is refuting it always seems to be a matter of an abstract absolute, of an empty unity, too unreal to explain anything real. But were Mr. Schiller to observe the absolute, the perfect, alive and active in the consciousness of a mystic,[13] would he have the right to say the same thing? Let us try to be "humanist" right to the end; since there are various types of consciousnesses and mentalities,[14] let Mr. Schiller resign himself to the fact that, for many, the absolute is altogether different from "the ideal adequacy for every human purpose" to which he chooses to limit himself.

Instead of dwelling on the fine spear thrusts with which Mr. Schiller and Mr. James pierce the partisans of the absolute, let us say a few words about the "humanist" movement recently introduced in the scientific milieu of our countries in tandem with the Anglo-American movement.

I limit myself to two representative theories: those of MM. Edouard Le Roy and Henri Poincaré.

According to M. Le Roy, it is "*the scientist who makes scientific facts.*" [15] In the complexity of sensations that nature provides,

12. We will see, in relation to M. Le Roy's theory, what this value can be.

13. I am convinced that it was the same for a Plato, a Hegel. It is the systematic verbal expression of sentiment that quickly becomes ridiculous and "objectionable."

14. I have particularly insisted on the various "*species*" of the same sentiment in my recent essay on the *Forme idéaliste du sentiment religieux*.

15. I shall note several of M. Le Roy's articles below. Here I am making use principally of the summary of a discussion which was held on 28 March 1901 between M. Le Roy and mem-

he chooses various details according to his purpose, leaving others aside; those he compares with one another using measures he has also chosen and made (the meter, the gram, the minute, the hour, etc.). He then groups the similarities and neglects the differences, thus establishing classifications and laws under a general form because they do not govern true reality (life always changing, in perpetual evolution, to the degree that the *same* circumstances, the *same* entities, the *same* properties are never repeated), but a pseudoreality where the alleged identities result from considering only averages imagined by the mind and from satisfying oneself with simple approximations sufficient in practice. Science thus regulates our *action* upon reality much more than it enables us to *know* reality. It is an ensemble of *effective* methods, of formulas *useful* rather than *true*.

—It is irrefutable that man does not see the external world in the same way as an animal or a young child; that the external world may thus be, largely, a construct of the mind; that thought may be active in science; that thought brings its own processes, its own measures to science. But why take a paradoxical formula and, instead of saying: there are artificial, arbitrary elements in science (thus indeterminacy, contingency), foster the belief that science is only artificial and arbitrary?

Such is not, I know, M. Le Roy's intention, but exaggerated turns of phrase, intended to impress people, to shake up old prejudices, and to demolish dogmatic metaphysics, scientific sectarianism, and intolerance, run considerable risk of producing the opposite effect.

It would be far too easy to respond to M. Le Roy that neither an eye nor a telescope cause an eclipse. He knows this quite well

bers of the *Société française de philosophie* (*Bulletin* of this society, May 1901); the objections and responses to the objections facilitate understanding of the doctrine. For the definitive essence of pragmatism in M. Le Roy's view, see Appendix IV.

and distinguishes between the *crude* fact that anyone, even animals, can observe, and the fact rendered *scientific* by the manner in which the intellectual activity of the scientist views it or measures it. But then he would be obliged to correct his paradox and to say more simply: "the scientist *makes facts scientific*."[16]

Certainly, "there is an inextricable intermeshing of fact and thought." But this is no reason for seeing only the human and subjective side of sensation and of science—no more than to consider them as wholly objective. I would be uncomfortable specifying what, in the quality of sound, comes from a violinist himself and what comes from his instrument. The two attributes are also true in that case; we strike a balance as well as we can. And, to a certain degree, we can: "According to you," M. Le Roy was asked, "there is in nature an aptitude to accommodate determinism, something like a capacity for laws." He replies, "I admit it: these are the very expressions I used in a presentation at the last Philosophical Congress." "You say that this allows you to know something of reality?" "Again I agree."

We require no more. Our science thus has a certain *knowledge* value and not simply a *use* value. What could be called M. Le Roy's *humanism* is therefore only a mitigated pragmatism.

M. Le Roy has not distinguished clearly enough between the mind's attitude when observing a *fact* (the fall of a body), and its attitude when it constructs a hypothesis (various atomic theories). In the second case, the mind has greater freedom of choice,[17] yet is still obliged, if it wants to reach its end, to draw

16. The same expression, well-analyzed in *Dogme et critique*, p. 334: "a fact only has existence and scientific value in and through a theory, from which it strictly follows that it is the scientist who makes the facts scientific facts or, if you prefer, who makes the facts scientific." Yes. We prefer this, and also this mitigation: "Science leads to what is useful *more than* to what is true, it attains truth only via its useful aspect" (p. 333). The *two* points of view remain clearly distinguished.

17. But, it must be an unlimited freedom, that is why it happens that certain hypotheses

its materials from experience; then, its choices and creations are only provisory and destined to disappear, if necessary, before the objective results of experimentation. Where facts are concerned, the mind "chooses" in the sense that it eliminates things not germane to the object of its search; but what it conserves and what it eliminates do not come from a real "choice"; these are "givens" *imposed* by nature from the very outset. One does not "choose" a fish's gills, a whale's lungs, a rose's smell, lead's heaviness. . . . It is the imprecise term "choose" that sustains the whole paradox.

It might be supposed that whoever wrote "[o]ne geometry cannot be more *true* than another; it can only be more *convenient*,"[18] would share the views of M. Le Roy. Not in any way. M. Poincaré stalwartly rejects them.[19] For him, "*The scientific fact is only the crude fact translated into a convenient language. . . . all the scientist creates in a fact is the language in which he enunciates it*[20] . . . facts are facts, and *if it happens that they satisfy a prediction, this is not an effect of our free activity.* There is no precise frontier between the crude fact and the scientific fact; it can only be said that such-and-such an enunciation of fact is *more crude* or, on the contrary, *more scientific* than such another."[21]

After this beginning, one would expect a clearly objectivist conclusion. Above all, it is clear that M. Poincaré recognizes and defends the *knowledge value* of the intellect, of science. But when

are constructed simultaneously and independently by several scientists. Pierre Duhem, *La Théorie physique* (Paris: Chevalier & Rivière, 1906), Part 2, chap. VII, §2 and 3.

18. Henri Poincaré, *La Science et l'hypothèse* (Paris: Flammarion, 1903), pp. 66–67 [Eng. trans. *Science and Hypothesis* (1952), in *The Value of Science: Essential Writings of Henri Poincaré,* ed. Stephen Jay Gould (New York: Modern Library, 2001), 45; emphasis is Hébert's].

19. Henri Poincaré, *La Valeur de la science* (Paris: Flammarion, 1905), especially the third part: "The Objective Value of Science."

20. Poincaré, *La Valeur de la science*, pp. 231–33 [Eng. trans. *The Value of Science* (1958), in Gould, ed., *The Value of Science: Essential Writings of Henri Poincaré,* 327–28; emphasis in original. References to Poincaré's work will be to the French edition, with reference to the English translation given in parentheses following].

21. Ibid., p. 235 (327) [emphasis in original].

objectivity is concerned, the expressions used by M. Poincaré certainly lend themselves to equivocation. "Nothing is objective except what is identical for all. . . ." "The thing essential is that there are points on which all those acquainted with the experiments made can reach accord."[22] These points are the *relations* of things. "Have these relations an objective value? This means: Are these relations the same for all? Will they still be the same for those who shall come after us?"[23]

—Is the agreement of minds an effect of objectivity? Is it the very essence of this objectivity? In the second case M. Poincaré would be an idealist,[24] even less objectivist than M. Le Roy.

I do not believe his statements should be taken in this sense: "What is science?" he says. "It is above all a classification, a manner of bringing together facts which appearances separate, *even though they might be bound together by some natural and hidden kinship.*" And farther on: "It will be said that science is only a classification and that a classification cannot be true but convenient. But it is true that it is convenient, it is true that it is so not only for me, but for all men; it is true that it will remain convenient for our descendents; *it is true finally that this cannot be by chance.*"[25] In these two passages M. Poincaré envisages real objectivity. Let us provide an example: Fresnel seeks to explain light by the vibrating movements of the ether; Maxwell by oscillations of electrical current. But, whatever the differences between these two hypotheses, calculation shows that in assimilating these movements and these oscillations, one finds that they are governed by the same laws. The mechanical formulas that translate the former are the same for the latter: "between the hypothetical

22. Ibid., pp. 264–65, 268 (346, 348). 23. Ibid., p. 267 (348).

24. In the sense of Berkeley's doctrine.

25. Poincaré, *La Valeur de la science*, pp. 265–66, 271 (347, 350) [emphasis added].

currents which Maxwell supposes there are the same relations as between the hypothetical motions that Fresnel supposes."[26] What should be made of this consistency in spite of the diverse approaches supplied by thought? Is it not the manifestation of an element external to thought and imposed on thought? The order of scientific thought would thus be a very imperfect, indefinitely perfectible translation of a real order among things. The classification of living beings, for example, is not a simple cabinet of drawers, but a genealogical tree always better expressing a more and more perfected knowledge of real relations of descent. In order to escape from this sensible view, one must imagine such a monism among entities that under the pretext of "continuity" they revert to a primitive chaos, losing everything that allows one to distinguish one from another.

So the objective does not intervene in knowledge merely through a simple negative "monitoring"[27] in order to limit the arbitrariness of representations and hypotheses, but inasmuch as it shows the mind—through human methods, of course, and in human language—an order which finds expression, rather than explanation in mechanism and in numerical formulas. This finding no more destroys human relativism than it compromises the existence of the "primary reality" acknowledged by Mr. Schiller; but it preserves a real objective *value of knowledge* for our human science.

A French scientist, M. Duhem, exaggerates when he says "that it would be unreasonable to work toward the progress of physical theory if this theory were not the increasingly clear and increasingly precise reflection of a metaphysics; belief in an order transcendent to the physical is the sole justification for physical

26. Ibid., p. 269 (349).
27. See p. 154.

theory."[28] I prefer the following formulation: "The reflection of an ontological order shines through the theory of a physicist. Thus everything pressures the physicist to affirm: Little by little, as it progresses, physical theory becomes more like a natural classification, which is its ideal and goal."[29]

Where my understanding fails is that, in this very learned study devoted to the long history of the varying fortunes of this Platonist theory, the astronomical hypotheses have no other goal nor currency than to "save the phenomena," to explain the appearances,[30] M. Duhem concludes that "the hypotheses of physics *are only mathematical expediencies meant to save . . . all the phenomena of the inanimate Universe.*"

Here we are again, it would seem, in full-blown idealism issuing from Platonist idealism according to which sensible knowledge is only of "appearances" lacking real value. But who today agrees with such an exaggeration? Our sensible knowledge is reality itself living and acting in us, and of which we are thus conscious in a relative, inadequate way; this is irrefutable, but not uniquely subjective; that is why it shows us, if imperfectly, an objective order and why we can speak of natural classifications, establish the main outlines of the real evolution of the universe, for example: that birds came from reptiles, not reptiles from birds, that the formation of coal preceded that of chalk, etc., etc.

Scientific pragmatism is always fundamentally an idealism (Platonist or Berkeleyan) and varies, in the mind of the authors, with the extent to which they adopt this last. And yet, nothing is more hypothetical and debatable than these various forms of

28. In *Revue générale des Sciences pures et appliquées* 19 (18 Jan. 1908): 17–19 at 18.

29. Duhem, "Physique de croyant" in *Annales de philosophie chrétienne* [n.s. 1 (October 1905–March 1906): 44–67, 133–59 at 143].

30. Pierre Duhem, ΣΩΖΕΙΝ ΤΑ ΦΑΙΝΟΜΕΝΑ. *Essai sur la notion de théorie physique de Platon à Galilée* (Paris: A. Hermann, 1908).

idealism. There is nothing, above all, more false than the identification of terms such as inadequate, approximate, relative knowledge, with nonexistent or completely subjective knowledge.

2. The Teleological Point of View

One of the most interesting originalities of pragmatism is its formulation in terms of finality. Here are seven definitions that Mr. Schiller has brought together as a series in order to bring out their intimate relations:

I. "*Pragmatism is the doctrine which teaches that truths are 'logical values' and the method which systematically tests claims to truth in accordance with this principle.*"[31]

No "pure" intellect. Man never thinks in order to think. He thinks because he pursues a goal, an end. A proposition is good if its consequences are good,[32] that is, conforming to the proposed goal. This conformity is their *value,* their value in the order of the true and the false (= logic).

However, the consequences of an assertion can only be verified in practice by applying it to a concrete experience; hence this definition given by Mr. Alfred Sidgwick:

II. "[*T*]*he 'truth' of an assertion depends on its application.*"[33] Or again: III. "[*T*]*he meaning of a rule lies in its application.*" But said experience serving as test is only possible if it has a precise goal:

31. Schiller, *Studies in Humanism,* Lecture I, 7 [emphasis is Hébert's, who has modified the text slightly].

32. Hence, W. James's assertion that the *true* is a species of the genus *good:* "the true," he adds, "is the name of whatever proves itself to be good in the way of belief, and good, too, for definite, assignable reasons" (*Pragmatism,* p. 76). And later: "What would be better for us to believe? This sounds very like a definition of truth."—Believing what is *better* for us to believe; yes, certainly in morality, in religion, but in scientific matters? . . . And scientific integrity? I do not deny this moral aspect of science, I deny merely that scientific truth can be reduced to this single element.

33. Mr. Schiller refers to Mr. Sidgwick's article, "Applied Axioms" in *Mind,* n. s. 53 [quoted in *Studies in Humanism,* 8–12; emphasis in original].

IV. "[A]*ll meaning depends on purpose*"; in consequence: V. "[A]*ll mental life is purposive*." Thus pragmatism is: VI. "[A] *systematic protest against all ignoring of the purposiveness of actual knowing*"; our intellectual life is completely permeated by interests, inclinations, desires, emotions, goals, goods, choices, etc; the pure reason of the intellectualists is only an abstraction as is the pure determinism or the pure mechanism of the materialists. The will is everywhere: thus if we urge our thought to the point of constructing a metaphysics, the voluntarism that we have established in psychology will be found in said metaphysics; pragmatism is thus: VII. "[A] *conscious application to epistemology (or logic) of a teleological psychology, which implies, ultimately, a voluntaristic metaphysic*."[34]

—All this is true. One can, as we have already argued, organize an explanation of things as a function of usefulness, just as one could construct another as a function of aesthetic feeling. There is no opposition between these attempts since they are merely different aspects, all legitimate, of the same reality. Error only begins with exclusivism.

Pragmatism, it is true, does not take a voluntarist metaphysics as *starting point;* this would be an *a priori* just as assailable as that of the neo-Hegelians. Its metaphysic is a luxury, a surplus expansion. At least it indicates that the mind, beyond simple practical solutions, seeks to know for the sake of knowing, to understand for the sake of understanding. A metaphysics is the revenge of the intellect on an overly exclusive voluntarist and utilitarian psychology. "Surely," says M. Poincaré quite correctly, "in man there are other forces besides his intellect, no one has ever been mad enough to deny that. The first comer makes these

34. Schiller, *Studies in Humanism,* Essay I, §II and "The Definitions of Pragmatism" in *Leonardo* (April 1905).

blind forces act or lets them act; the philosopher must *speak* of them, he must know of them the little that can be known, he should therefore *watch* them *act*. How? With what eyes, if not with his intellect? Heart, instinct may guide it, but not render it useless; they may direct the gaze, but not replace the eye. It may be granted that the heart is the workman, and the intellect only the instrument. Yet is it an indispensable instrument if not for action, at least for philosophizing? Therefore this is why a truly anti-intellectualistic philosopher is impossible. Perhaps we should declare the *primacy* of action; it is always our intellect which will thus conclude; in allowing precedence to action it will thus retain the superiority of the thinking reed. This also is a 'primacy' not to be disdained."[35]

Certainly, I acknowledge the "primacy of action"[36]: the priority, over reflective intellect, of a richer activity that we call unconscious (through a wholly negative approach, a simple admission of ignorance), unconscious at first, then (partially at least) conscious of itself; the anteriority and the superiority (in certain respects) of this reservoir of energy from which our discursive thought, our feelings, and our acts perpetually spring, without ever being exhausted; the primacy of thought-force over thought-representation. Thus I would not object to Mr. Schiller

35. Poincaré, *La Valeur de la science*, pp. 216–17 (319) [emphasis on primacy is Hébert's].

36. "I understand by action," says M. Blondel, "what encompasses the intellect, preceding it, following it, and surpassing it; what, consequently, in thought is internal synthesis more than objective representation." (Text taken from the "Vocabulaire technique et critique de la philosophie," *Bulletin de la Société française de la philosophie* [2 (July 1902)].) [Published originally in fascicles in the bulletin between 1902 and 1926, the "Vocabulaire technique" was later published in book form in 1926, and subsequently reprinted.] From a psychological point of view more or less the same is true of this primordial activity as of protoplasm from a physiological point of view. One can just as well say that it is nothing of what it will later become, thanks to differentiation, or that it is already all that. "Action," "life" is ante-intellectual, not anti-intellectual, for it is the same reality that we call "action" under its nondifferentiated form and "intellect" under one of its differentiated forms.

on this point; what I do contest is that one must derive the pragmatist theory of truth from the primacy of activity and from the essential teleologism of our interior life. Every inclination, indeed, as soon as conscious, is knowledge. Certainly not yet clear and distinct knowledge, but already knowledge: *actio quaerens intellectum.*[37] We act initially with an obscure consciousness; a clearer consciousness allows us to take fuller possession of our inclinations and to judge them—*otherwise the end would always seem to us to justify the means.*[38] If the will, in the form of attention, causes the intellect itself to blossom, the latter, in turn, appreciating the proportion of means to ends, allows the will to assert itself and to come to fruition through acts. This is the story of the blind man and the paralytic—but in a single entity, the same activity.

What in all this would authorize one to conclude that the intellect has no value *from knowledge.* Nothing, certainly, and we have already seen that one should not claim it relative to the sciences themselves. Just as, at a given moment, among certain of our ancestors, aesthetic sensibility developed in the midst of purely utilitarian ornamentation, true religious sensibility in the midst of a kind of magical utilitarianism, so the disinterested appreciation of truth considered as representative of reality disengaged itself from utilitarian appreciation, from truth considered as adapting us to the reality responding to our needs.

The desire of the true for the truth is still an inclination, the pragmatist will reply.—No doubt, but it implies an objective judg-

37. [Action in search of understanding—a play on *fides quaerens intellectum,* faith in search of understanding.]

38. And as consequences: truths "good for the people," the God that, if he did not exist, we would have to invent; the so-called Catholicism of certain nationalists, notorious atheists, etc. I do not insist; these are "*tricks,*" not ideas. However, a justification could be attempted thanks to the social pragmatism of M. Durkheim. (Cf. Appendix VI.)

ment, and insofar as objective, disinterested. Then we appreciate the value of the true, insofar as it corresponds to objective reality and reveals it to us, and not as it corresponds to our inclination and satisfies it. Let us not unify this duality by force!

It is precisely this artificial unity which makes the pragmatist theory exaggerated and partially false. Mr. Schiller wanted "to overcome the anti-thesis between theory and practice" and "to unify human life" in showing its all-pervading purposiveness.[39] And just as our own Condillac has claimed to unify everything by making the whole of mental life a transformation of sensation, Schiller claims to bring everything back to inclination, to desire (whose satisfaction is the very essence of *utility*). Illusion! What meaning could esteem-desire, respect-desire have? . . . And a fortiori, comparison-desire, judgment- desire? M. Ribot has written remarkable pages about this "logic of feelings" whose core is desire, and which, founded on the principle of finality, should not be confused with the other logic founded on the principle of contradiction.[40]

The sophism thus consists of making inclination the center, the very essence of activity, while it is only its first and continuous manifestation. The allegedly "unconscious" center of our being is neither desire, nor thought, nor will,[41] it is that which is expressed in desires, in thoughts, in creative instinct, in free will, and which, no doubt, could be expressed (and is perhaps expressed outside our consciousness) by many other kinds of phenomena. A voluntarist metaphysics is thus unilateral, artificial; we address the same criticism to teleological pragmatism as soon as it attempts to exclude—and it does exclude—different points of view.

39. Schiller, *Studies in Humanism,* Essay IV §10, p. 128.

40. In *La Logique des sentiments* (Paris: Alcan, 1905), chap. II.

41. Schopenhauer finally recognized this. Cf. p. 186, note 21, of the following chapter.

Psychic phenomena seem to be transformed into others, to be the cause of one another—a causality of pure representation: the only true causality is the mysterious synthetic activity from which everything proceeds.

Thus whatever the predominance of inclination, of desire, in our psychic life, nothing justifies us in blaming everything on inclination and explaining everything by inclination and its satisfaction, as the pragmatists claim. There is room for other manifestations having their own nuance *and their own value.* No doubt the continuity of psychic life does not allow *pure* thought, *pure* freedom, in the absolute sense of the word, but no one has ever understood it that way.

Consequently, one understands the appearance of a thought, of a judgment taking an *objective and disinterested* point of view. From this position stems the disinterested evaluation of truth, of science.[42] From this position, first of all, stems the impersonal attitude with which an inquirer must broach and pursue every question that is not a question of feeling, but of fact. To know whether Moses is the author of the Pentateuch, or if Louis XVII was or was not put to death at the Temple, or if birds are or are not descended from reptiles, of what use is the criterion of the satisfaction of our inclinations? What is necessary is a text, a

42. "[I]f I admire the conquests of industry, it is above all because if they free us from material cares, they will one day provide everyone the leisure to contemplate nature. I do not say: science is useful because it teaches us to construct machines; I say: Machines are useful, because in working for us they will some day leave us more time for science. But finally it is worth remarking that between two points of view there is no antagonism, and that man having pursued a disinterested aim, all else has been added unto him." Poincaré, "Discourse on Astronomy" in *La Valeur de la science*, p. 166. [287] "If performance, practice," as Bacon said, "must be held in higher regard than speculation, this is not insofar as they multiply the comforts of life, but insofar as these useful applications of theory are so many pledges or guarantees of truth" [trans.] "[T]he contemplation of things as they are, free from superstition or imposture, error or confusion, much more dignified in itself than all the advantage to be derived from discoveries" [Francis Bacon, *The Advancement of Learning and Novum Organum* (New York: Colonial Press, 1899), §§124 and 129, p. 366].

fossil. Is the painting *Le Soir* by Corot or by Trouillebert? Is it through the pragmatist method that we will dispute the attribution? This method explained the owner's faith—and his error came from not having used the objective method.

If I am reminded that I have recognized the pragmatists' acknowledgment of what we call the objective method of knowledge, etc. under the name of *experience* I will respond: the owner of the false Corot is troubled; he tries to resolve this trouble through an investigation: his calm returns. . . . That may all be true, but then one then persists in confusing two parallel questions: dispositions and subjective emotions with the question of objective truth. It is not *because* the owner is troubled that *it is* not true that the painting *is* Corot's, nor *because* his calm returns and with it the equilibrium of his inclinations that *it is true* that the painting is by another painter.

Mr. Schiller reveals, we believe, the center of his thought when (in the lecture I cited in note 1, p. 161) he concludes thus:

"By his life the skeptic *should* (is even obliged to) affirm a practical truth that runs *parallel* to the theoretical truth that he claims to doubt. He can only doubt this (practical) truth verbally, not in fact; he cannot disregard it without renouncing his own life. If he consented to admit that this practical truth is the sole truth that exists, that all real truth has a relation to life, enters into its structure, the foundations of his skepticism would be completely destroyed." For Mr. Schiller, "theoretical" truth is confused with the results of "formal logic," and, according to him, this logic consists of "determining the truth by means of the simple examination or simple contemplation of the forms of our thought." If logic applied only to *a priori* forms I would understand Mr. Schiller's apprehensions and condemnations, but it is applied *to our ideas, abstracted from experience,* thus still containing reality, constituting exact, though fragmentary, aspects of reality. This confusion is the cause of Mr. Schiller's exaggerations.

We find a similar negation of theoretical truth (at least inasmuch as the *intellect recognizes it as such*) in the writings of Mr. Royce,[43] with an admission of the single practical truth under the name of *voluntarism*. According to him, *instrumentalism* (truth adapting us to life), *individualism* (truth responding to the needs of the individual) are insufficient; there are, in addition, absolute truths, these are the "universal forms of the will," assertions that cannot be denied without contradicting oneself and reaffirming them subsequently in practice, assertions that one thus cannot not will.

—Certainly, but this is simply what we call "primacy of will." In addition, what is this contradiction to be avoided? A simple discomfort about sensitivity? One cannot, in this case, mistake it for "truth." The *intellectual* principle of contradiction then?

I can thus conclude that if pragmatism is a legitimate reaction to an exaggerated intellectualism, it has gone to the other extreme in making itself an exclusive voluntarism: *it has become a paradox*. But, in popularizing the idea (often presented abstractly in France) of the "primacy" of the will, it will nonetheless have provided real service.

43. Report on the Heidelberg Congress, *Revue de Métaphysique et de Morale* 16 (Nov. 1908): 930–37. Mr. W. James acknowledges in his last work a *theoretical truth;* see p. 237.

4

Pragmatism

"A New Name for Some Old Ways of Thinking"

I would like to contribute some points and some reservations relative to the subtitle W. James gave to his work on pragmatism: "A *new name,* etc." It is important to begin by distinguishing among the rather varied types of doctrines that go by the same name. I will distinguish them thus:

pure pragmatism;
mitigated pragmatism;
partial pragmatism.

First, pure pragmatism consists of leaving out (pragmatism as method) or denying (pragmatism as theory) the *representative* value of knowledge; knowledge has only an "instrumental" value as means of action; this value can thus be judged and verified only by practical consequences.

Peirce provides a good example of *method.*

If pragmatism is looked upon as *theory,* will it be said that it is to be found in such-and-such an author in its pure state? Or more likely, is it not a goal to which they aspire? Mr. Schiller comes closest. His intention of "rethinking the traditional formulas in pragmatic terms" is very clear.[1]

Second, mitigated pragmatism: more or less mitigated, depending on the degree to which knowledge of the nature of reality is accepted. W. James admits this knowledge with increasing approximation[2]—without, being any more precise; M. Le Roy also makes some concessions; M. Poincaré loudly proclaims that we know the "relations." So many mitigations.

Third, partial pragmatism (mitigated with regard to extension). One can, in effect, restrict pragmatism to scientific fact insofar as *scientific* (by distinguishing it from crude fact); or apply it to theories, to hypotheses, and not to facts, etc. One can be a pragmatist with regard to metaphysics, or in morality or religion, even if not with regard to science. And here again there are distinctions to make. The "symbolism" of which we shall speak in the following chapter can be only a partial religious pragmatism when it admits religious realities proper and supposes them, if not known, at least glimpsed, suspected "*per speculum, in aenigmate.*"[3]

There are, on the same subject, varying degrees, from a minimum: a tendency to attach more importance to life and to practice[4] than to doctrine,—up to a maximum: to accept only moral truths as the content of religious assertions or practices (= "mor-

1. *Studies in Humanism*, p. 432. The best example we can cite of *pure pragmatism* is that of Nietzsche (p. 189); as *pure religious pragmatism*, the "moralism" of Louis Ménard (p. 195) and the declaration of an Italian modernist (p. 181).

2. Cf. p. 152, note 10.

3. 1 Cor. 13.12.

4. A very clear perception of the superiority of the practical point of view over pure theory, and of our need to adopt this point of view, can be found in the original, profound, and too little-known work by Abbé Gabriel, *Principes généraux d'une théodicée pratique* (Paris: Albanel, 1866): "Man is not put here to reason about abstractions but to act in the midst of the reality of things, developing himself according to the laws of his nature and his final destiny. Practice is the law of life. But one does not draw life from food by looking at it but by assimilating it: theory contemplates, practice alone assimilates" (96).

alism"; I cite, on page 195, a typical statement by Louis Ménard), or truths of the social order; here is a striking example of this last variation:

"Above all, with respect to the fundamental theoretical principles of Catholicism, the doctrine of the immortality of the soul, of the existence of a personal God, of the divinity of Christ, we see in them pragmatist attitudes, stripped of all abstract and objective value, and only expressing particular dispositions of the religious soul. In examining the historical development of Christianity, we see that the initial hope of the kingdom has, with time and a slow process of disillusion, been transformed into the hope for paradise; that the imminent expectation of the Christ Messiah has, through a natural evolution in the minds of the faithful, given way to faith in the Christ God; that the vague sense of dependence on divinity has ended by being delimited and circumscribed in Catholic theodicy, initially on a Platonic foundation, later on an Aristotelian basis.

"We insist on drawing attention to the relativity of dogmatic conceptions, their purely practical value, their obsolescence. They have, in fact, long fed human religiosity. But today, when new content, namely the hope of the progressive improvement of man, has insinuated itself into this religiosity, their practical value declines. Nevertheless we have no right to make a boast of abandoning them, thoughtlessly renouncing our entire religious past. We merely want to establish a persevering work of erosion around these conceptions. When it succeeds, they will fall on their own, and the new religiosity will find new attitudes of thought to anchor its living expansion."[5]

5. These lines are taken from *Lettere di un prete modernista* (Letters of a Modernist Priest), published in Rome in 1908 by Liberia editrice romana. Letter IX, pp. 125, 126 (also in the journal *Nova et vetera* [10 April 1908] which, in its first issue, had made a pragmatist declaration).

What kind of pragmatism does W. James envisage in his subtitle? Is it pragmatism as a *method*? If it were a matter of "judging a tree by its fruits,"[6] the approach, certainly, would not be new. Yet it is not certain: it is a sort of plant whose fruits have a repellant odor, but whose subterranean stems, swollen with reserves, nourish a part of humanity. Judging a doctrine *by its consequences*—this argument is found in very many elementary treatises, proposing freedom, atheism, etc.

Rousseau said, "Flee those who sow dispiriting doctrines in men's hearts under the pretext of explaining nature. Their apparent skepticism is a hundred times more assertive and more dogmatic than the decided tone of their adversaries. Under the haughty pretext that they alone are enlightened, true, and of good faith, they imperiously subject us to their peremptory decisions and claim to give us as the true principles of things the unintelligible systems they have built in their imaginations. Moreover, by overturning, destroying, and trampling on all that men respect, they deprive the afflicted of the last consolation of their misery, and the powerful and the rich of the only brake on their passions. They tear out from the depths of our hearts remorse for crime and hope of virtue, and yet boast that they are the benefactors of mankind. I believe it as much as they do, and in my opinion this is a great proof that what they teach is not the truth."[7]

Same doctrine, Letter III, p. 53, Letter X, p. 148. In his *Filosophia della Fede,* Murri exhibits a sort of pragmatism, in insisting on the point that faith is an assurance of things *hoped for,* not of things *known,* but things *willed;* nevertheless, this is a mitigated pragmatism, for, a bit farther on, he affirms that "the world is not thinkable without the notion of the absolute."

6. Mt. 12.33. The gospel is practical, not pragmatist. When it speaks of "doing the truth" (Jn 3.21) it is a not a matter of putting it together, but of putting it into practice. For its part, *Knowledge* must lead to practice, but it remains real knowledge; if it is not formulated in abstract theories, it is expressed in parables and popular images, the seed of future theories. (Cf. *Evolution de la foi catholique,* chap. I and II.) The importance of "gnosis" only increases: cf. Mt. 11.22; Jn. 17.3.

7. Jean-Jacques Rousseau, *Emile* [Eng. trans. *Emile; or, On Education,* trans. Allan Bloom (New York: Basic Books, 1979), 312].

And Renan: "The most vigorous way of emphasizing an idea's importance is to suppress it and to show what the world becomes without it. One day I hope to apply this mode of philosophical exposition in a book entitled: *Hypotheses*, in which I shall outline seven or eight systems of the world in each of which a major element is missing. This way the role of these elements will be highlighted extraordinarily, visible even to the poorest of vision."[8]

What was for Renan only a "way of emphasizing an idea's importance" is not a *theory* of truth.—Without claiming to treat the question of pragmatism's *origins*, I would like to make several observations relative to what can be considered its precursors.

I. Socrates, in maintaining the role of love alongside that of thought[9]; Plato, in making the idea of the Good the center of the intellectual world; Aristotle, in giving as supreme explanation the attraction of the Perfect to all beings, expressed and established the principle of a *teleological* theory. But do I need to add that they placed full confidence in the intellect in order to straighten out the chaos of the unconscious?

However this may be, a great deal of Platonist idealism can be found in the pragmatists' minds. The idealism of which I am speaking does not come from the tendency to consider every being as belonging fundamentally to the psychic order, but from that which so long ago induced Plato to discredit sensory data, considering them simple appearances, nonbeings behind which true being dwells, hidden and inaccessible.

Mr. James would not go that far. Nevertheless, he insists

8. Preface to *Dialogues philosophiques* (Paris: Calman-Lévy, 1876), p. xii.

9. One of the precursors of the current movement against exaggerated intellectualism was Claude Charles Charaux; he liked to call himself a *Socratic* philosopher. His thesis, "Thought and Love," can be found in *La Pensée* (Durand and Pedone; 2nd ed. 1884). Cf. at the end of this volume, Appendix I: "Pragmatism and Aesthetics."

strongly on this point: that in sensation we do not go beyond the "surface" of reality.[10] Is he not, in the circumstances, partially deceived by this spatial metaphor? If sensation is a communion, a co-consciousness with reality, does the common act of sensing and of sensed stay at this "surface"?

But, it is obvious that if nothing deep or essential is perceived in sensation (in spite of its subjective and relative aspect), one easily comes to consider the world as a construction of the mind,—analogous to the Brahma's dream without its pessimism. That the mind *makes* truth, the theory dear to the pragmatists[11]—would spring directly from it. Thus the mind could, at its personal convenience, alter, modify the construction. Mr. W. James does not allow, on this point, the absolute freedom of mind;—this is to admit that reality also *makes* our thought, that there is a perpetual interaction, and thus the pragmatist thesis (the mind makes truth) would be a paradox.

II. I do not in any way deny that the Scholastics have exaggerated the role of the intellect, especially syllogistic reasoning. At least, we find the very principle of "humanism" at the root of their theory of knowledge: "*The known is in the knowing, according to the mode, the nature, of the knowing.*"[12] This is on a par with Protagoras's equivocal formula. The two terms of the relationship are clearly upheld. Certain of the Scholastics, the nominalists, rigorously applied the idea of a purely human value to our generalizations. The Italian pragmatists are correct to say that modern pragmatism asserts of *theories* what the nominalists held

10. William James, *A Pluralistic Universe* (London: Longmans, 1909), Lecture VI, p. 250.

11. See above, p. 154, note 14.

12. Cf. Joseph Kleutgen, *La philosophie scholastique,* vol. I, p. 41.—Saint Thomas, *De Veritate*, Q. X, art. 4. It is the principle itself that is interesting, for the Scholastics explained it by the baroque theory of "species." Cf. Chareyre, "L'assimilation scolastique" in *Annales de philosophie chrétienne* n.s. 3 (January–March 1907).

of *general terms*.[13] On the other hand, the pragmatists[14] appear to admit a kind of realism, according to which, given the unity and continuity of experience, it is only through abstraction that one can say: *a* phenomenon. Every phenomenon closely observed is like a cog in the great machine that is the whole of experience, and thus must, of necessity, reappear when the same conditions recur. The pragmatists are thus dispensed from explaining the "*relations*" as disengaged from the rest and formulated through a special activity: intellectual activity. But I do not see how one can count on the return of the *same* conditions and of the *same* phenomenon if everything is formed and evolves unceasingly.

III. Was Kant a precursor of pragmatism? For us French, yes, undoubtedly; as for Anglo-American pragmatists, they show such terror of the *a priori* that they seem to me to issue rather from the empiricists.[15] However, Mr. Schiller cites[16] this significant assertion from Kant: "all interest is ultimately practical, and even that of the speculative reason is only conditional, and is complete in practical use alone." This sentence ends the paragraph (of the third chapter, Book II) devoted to the "primacy of pure practical reason."[17] In the same chapter, Kant sets forth his doctrine of the postulates of practical reason,[18] "hypotheses" of which, of itself,

13. *Leonardo* (April 1905): 45.

14. Peirce, "What Pragmatism Is" in *Monist* 15 (April 1905).—M. Lalande refers for W. James to the *Journal of Philosophy, Psychology and Scientific Methods* 1 (September and October 1904, January 1905), which I have not been able to read.

15. *Leonardo* (April 1905): 45.—I shall note, however, that, in *The Reasonableness of Christianity*, Locke seeks to limit the number of truths that must be believed, but in no way reduces speculative truths to purely practical symbols.

16. *Studies in Humanism*, p. 128 n. [italics in original omitted by Hébert].

17. *Critique de la raison pratique*, Book II, chap. 3. [Immanuel Kant, *Critique of Practical Reason*, in The Cambridge Edition of the Works of Immanuel Kant: *Practical Philosophy*, trans. Mary J. Gregor (Cambridge: Cambridge University Press, 1996), 238.]

18. Immortality, freedom, the existence of God.—Kant is also rather close to pragmatism (in the form we shall indicate later on (pp. 193, 195: religious moralism), in the work: *Religion within the Limits of Reason Alone*, that I've summarized on pp. 151 ff. of *L'Évolution de la foi catholique*. It is also quite striking in a letter to Lavater of 28 April 1775.

speculative reason could not even venture to assert the possibility, but that it does not *choose*, however arbitrarily: they appear as "practically necessary conditions" of the moral law's fulfillment; the will desires them at the same time it desires the Good; it is the will thus which gives a practical content, and consequently reality, to these thoughts which, without it, would remain empty forms, that no intuition could fill. There is thus no acquisition of theoretical knowledge in this. Kant repeats this in every possible way; nevertheless, he feels compelled to express a reservation: "If there is no extension of the cognition of given supersensible objects, there is nevertheless an extension of theoretical reason and of its cognition with respect to the supersensible in general, inasmuch as theoretical reason is forced to grant *that there are such objects*, though it cannot determine them more closely."[19] There indeed is the seductive pragmatist distinction: one knows *existence*, one does not know *nature*. But, if one knew nothing, nothing at all of nature, existence would be the most empty of forms, the most indigent of abstractions!

IV. It is surprising to see Schopenhauer included among the precursors of pragmatism.[20] His metaphysic is certainly voluntarist, but the renowned will to live[21] neither pauses nor stops until it is objectivated in intellect; it is the intellect which brings about the redemption of the will, in leading it through disinterested art and the morality of renunciation, to deny and efface itself. And yet, intellect is not only an instrument of redemption; it possesses a real value in itself, when it has shaken the tyranny of said will:

19. *Critique de la raison pratique*, 245–46. [Immanuel Kant, *Critique of Practical Reason*, 248–49 (translation modified).] Also read the chapter "On the Wise Adaptation of the Human Being's Cognitive Faculties to His Practical Vocation."

20. *Leonardo* article cited above.

21. In the Supplements added long after the publication of *The World as Will and Presentation*, Schopenhauer concluded that the will is less the true thing in itself than the most immediate of its phenomena. (Book III, chap. XVII).

When, raised up by the power of the mind, we abandon the ordinary way of considering things . . . , when we devote the whole power of our mind to perception, become entirely absorbed in the latter and let our whole consciousness be filled with restful contemplation of the natural object actually present—be it a landscape, a tree, a rock, a building, or whatever; from the moment we lose ourselves in this object as the Germans so profoundly observe; i.e., from the moment we forget our individuality, our will, and remaining only as pure subject, as clear mirror of the object, so that it is as if the object alone existed without anyone perceiving it, and it is no longer possible to separate the perceiver from the perception, but the two have become one, in a single consciousness entirely filled and occupied by a single perceptual image; when the object has been removed to this extent from all relation to something outside it, and the subject from all relation to the will, then what is thus known is no longer the individual thing as such; rather, it is the Idea, eternal form, immediate objectivization of the will; and just by that fact, anyone caught up in this contemplation is no longer an individual, it is pure, will-less, painless, timeless, subject of cognition.[22]

Here, truth certainly is "depersonalized" and "etherealized"[23] just as with Plato.

V. Positivism itself is far from the complete subordination of theory to practice, science to action:

"*From Science comes prevision,*" says A. Comte; "*from prevision comes action*"; such is the very simple formulation for expressing the general relation between *science* and *art* in an exact way, taking these two expressions in their fullest sense.

But in spite of the major importance of this relation which must never be misconstrued, conceiving the sciences as the bases of the arts, which is very much the tendency of our day, is to fos-

22. *Le Monde comme volunté et comme representation,* 3 vols. (Paris: Félix Alcan, 1888–1890). [Arthur Schopenhauer, *The World as Will and Presentation,* trans. Richard E. Aquila, in collaboration with David Carus (New York: Pearson Longman, 2008), vol. 1, §34, 221–22.]

23. Schiller, *Studies in Humanism,* Essay XII, pp. 111–12.

ter a rather imperfect idea of the sciences.[24] Whatever immense services scientific theories contribute to *industry*, although according to the vigorous expression of Bacon, power is necessarily proportionate to knowledge, we must not forget that the sciences have, above all, a more direct and more elevated purpose, that of satisfying the fundamental need our intellect feels for the laws of phenomena.

". . . It is clear that after having conceived, in a general way, the study of nature as serving as rational basis of action on nature, the human mind must move on to theoretical inquiry, in complete abstraction from any practical consideration; for our means for discovering truth are so weak that, if we did not concentrate them exclusively on this goal, and if, in searching for the truth, we at the same time imposed on ourselves the unfamiliar condition of finding in it an immediate practical utility, it would be nearly always impossible for us to succeed."[25]

VI. Rather, the precursors of pragmatism must be sought from the ranks of empiricist and utilitarian philosophers. This exercise has been very thoroughly carried out by M. René Berthelot.[26] I highlight here what I see as his main idea:

Pleasure (goal of *utility*) is, for Hobbes, a movement favorable to the functions of life—and that remains true when, with Helvetius and Bentham, one adds the consideration of general interest to that of particular interest. Because scientists, Lamarkists or Darwinians, have explained the transformation and the fixation of instincts, of inclinations, by their utility for the individual

24. Note that it is not a matter of fine arts here, but of the practical arts: the engineer's art, etc.

25. Auguste Comte, *Cours de philosophie positive*, second lesson.

26. Articles on the Pragmatism of Nietzsche in the *Revue de Métaphysique et de Morale* ["Sur le pragmatism de Nietzsche," 16 (July 1908: 403–47, May and September 1909: 386–412 and 654–702)]. I cite a passage in Appendix V.

and the species, it is understandably tempting to conclude that intellectual and moral inclinations and beliefs gain their worth from this biological utility: "It is finally time," said Nietzsche, "to replace the Kantian question, 'How are synthetic *a priori* judgments possible?' with another question: 'Why is it *necessary* to believe in such judgments?' It is time for us to comprehend that such judgments must be believed *true* (*false* as they may actually be!) in order to preserve creatures such as we are. Or, to say it more plainly, rudely, and forthrightly: synthetic *a priori* judgments should not 'be possible' at all; we have no right to them; coming from us they are all false judgments. Only it must not be forgotten that faith in their truth is necessary as a provisional faith . . . that has its place in the perspectivity-optics of life." [27]

And further:

> The whole of life would be possible without its seeing itself as it were in a mirror: as in fact even at present the far greater part of our life still goes on without this mirroring. . . . I can proceed further to the conjecture that consciousness generally has only been developed under the pressure of the necessity for communication,—that from the first it has been necessary and useful only between man and man . . . and has only been developed in proportion to its utility. . . . [C]onsciousness does not properly belong to the individual existence of man, but rather to the social and gregarious nature in him. . . . [W]e have not any organ at all for knowing, or for "truth": we "know" (or believe, or fancy) just as much as may be of use in the interest of the human herd, the species; and even what is here called "usefulness" is ultimately only a belief, a fancy, and perhaps precisely the most fatal stupidity by which we shall one day be ruined.[28]

These paradoxes of the poet-thinker constitute a fine example of absolute pragmatism. Nevertheless not so absolute that it

27. [Nietzsche, *Beyond Good and Evil* (Chicago: Henry Regnery, 1955), pp. 12–13.]

28. [Nietzsche, *The Joyful Wisdom* (Frederick Ungar, 1971), Aphorism 354, pp. 296–300.] Cf. Appendix VI. "The Social Pragmatism of M. Durkheim."

does not imply full confidence in this intellect which constructs, explains, seeks to justify the system. It also implies the hypothesis of the "epiphenomenism" of consciousness—once more the hypothesis (Nietzsche asserts it) of the purely utilitarian character of knowledge, not only at its beginnings, but throughout the course of its evolution.

VII. Must one call philosophers such as MM. Blondel and Bergson, who have spoken so much of "action" in such different ways, *pragmatists*?[29]

Yes, if one were restricted to etymology alone,[30] but this would introduce a new ambiguity into philosophical language.

Whoever claims a value *of knowledge* for thought is definitely not a pragmatist (in the Anglo-American sense). And yet this is indeed what M. Blondel does: "Theory and practice neither duplicate, nor are exterior to one another. . . . [I]t is because 'action and the idea of action' are not equivalent that nothing dispenses the practitioner from thinking nor the thinker from practicing. . . . [K]nowledge constitutes real progress; indeed, it produces a form of existence which would not exist without knowledge but which,

29. For the meaning of "action" for M. Blondel see p. 173, note 36.

30. "A curious thing" (writes M. Lalande), "the subtle and profound author of *l'Action*, M. Maurice Blondel, has been led to avail himself of this word without being aware of the use the Americans have made of it. In a session of the Société de philosophie (29 May 1902), I used the term *alogism* to characterize the doctrine; he protested against this word, which he found completely improper, and proposed the term *pragmatism* (cf. *Bulletin de la Société français de philosophie* 1 [1902]: 191–92). Recently, when the word became popular, I asked him if he had borrowed or created it and this is how he replied: 'I suggested the name *pragmatism* to myself in 1888 and I was clearly conscious of coining it, never having encountered this word which has recently been used in England, in America, in Germany. . . . And if I chose the name *pragmatism*, it was to specify the precise character of my study.'" "Pragmatisme et pragmaticisme," (*Revue philosophique* [61 (February 1906)]: pp. 121–46 at 123 n.) I want to point out the article, "Pragmatisme, humanisme et vérité," by the same author in the same journal [65 (January 1908): 1–26]. In the July 1908 issue of the *Bulletin de la Société française de philosophie*, we find on p. 293 a letter in which M. Blondel explains precisely when and how he chose to use the term *pragmatisme* and the great difference that exists between the "philosophy of action" and pragmatism proper, which, he correctly observes, seeks the criterion in success, without being able, from success, to give a criterion and a definition that do not contain a *petitio principii*.

because it is a normal expression, an essential condition, becomes an integral part of the development of being and of the truth of beings in us. Indeed, for man, life is not life without thought, no more than thought is thought without life. We must therefore use what we are and what we have in order to know, and use what we know in order to be and to have in greater depth."[31]

No one has better analyzed the relation between action[32] and thought than M. Bergson, better shown the extent to which the intellect has been subordinated to the requirements of action in its formation, to what extent, therefore, it is exposed to biases when it takes as realities simple practical procedures (time in terms of space, determinism, etc.): "The greatest philosophical difficulties arise, as we have said, from the fact that the forms of human action venture outside of their proper sphere. We are made to act as much as, and more than, in order to think—or rather, when we follow the bent of our nature, it is in order to act that we think. It is therefore no wonder that the habits of action give their tone to those of thought, and that our mind always perceives things in the same order in which we are accustomed to picture them when we propose to act on them."[33]

Yes, but the bondage is not definitive:

"[W]e must accustom ourselves to think Being directly, without making a detour. . . . We must strive to see in order to see, and no longer to see in order to act."[34]

31. Maurice Blondel, "Le Point de départ de la recherché philosophique" in *Annales de philosophie chrétienne* n.s. 2 (Jan. and June 1906), p. 241 [Eng. trans. "The Starting Point of Philosophical Research," trans. Fiachra Long, in *The Idealist Illusion and Other Essays* (Dordrecht: Kluwer Academic Publishers, 2000), 139 (translation modified)]. Cf. *L'Action*, Part 5, chap. III. [Eng. trans. *Action (1893): Essay on a Critique of Life and a Science of Practice,* trans. Oliva Blanchette (South Bend, Ind.: University of Notre Dame Press, 1984)].

32. In the usual meaning of the word.

33. Henri Bergson, *L'Evolution créatrice* [Eng. trans. *Creative Evolution* (1911), trans. Arthur Mitchell (Mineola, N.Y.: Dover Publications, 1998), 297].

34. Ibid., p. 298.

Pure perception,[35] intuition of the absolute,[36] these are all things which establish essential divisions between M. Bergson's doctrine and Anglo-American pragmatism.

It is rather where specifically moral[37] or religious theories are concerned that the subtitle of W. James's book can easily be justified.

35. Henri Bergson, *Matière et mémoire* [Eng. trans. *Matter and Memory*, trans. N. M. Paul and W. S. Palmer (New York: Zone Books, 1991)]. Ch. I and II and Summary and Conclusion.

36. Bergson, *L'Evolution créatrice* [*Creative Evolution*, 199, 298–99, etc.].

37. Cf. at the end of this study Appendix II: "*Pragmatism* and Morality."

5

Religious Pragmatism

1. Various Forms of Religious Pragmatism

In our countries, the pragmatic tendency seems to be manifested in forms more or less linked with one of three modes of expression of religious experience: moralism, fideism, symbolism.[1]

I. Pure *moralism* would consist in granting value to religious dogmas and ceremonies only insofar as they inculcate moral lessons, stimulate us, and help us practice them.[2] They do not in any way augment our knowledge; they make us better.[3]

When the apostle St. James[4] asserts that true devotion, pure and undefiled, consists in knowing how to hold one's tongue, visiting the unfortunate, avoiding the defilements of the world, he is practical, pragmatic if you like, but not pragmatist, for he would be averse[5] to admitting that he who values this worship, our God and Father, is himself scarcely more than a kind of moral myth.

But let us take Charles Secrétan's work, *La Civilisation et la Croyance;*[6] he certainly approximates the "moralism" type.

1. In reality, these forms are intertwined and pass imperceptibly from one to another.

2. It is not a question of a purely *ethical* morality, but of a morality touched by emotion, as wrote Matthew Arnold, penetrated, enlivened by an emotion from beyond. This *emotion,* moreover, is already a germ of *knowledge.*

3. Cf. the end of this study, Appendix III, devoted to J.-J. Rousseau.

4. Epistle, 1.26–27.

5. Recall also the "quod notum est Dei" of St. Paul, Rom. 1.19.

6. Paris: Alcan, 1887.—Cf. also "The Moral Mysticism of Tolstoy" (*Le Divin,* chap. IV).

"All the old proofs (of the existence of God) are good, provided that one understand them without pedantry and that one does not grant them a constringent value; but the true proof, the one that circulates in all the others and gives them strength, is impulse, desire. We strain toward perfection with every breath, our eyes seeking it in the sky, our heart invoking it in silence; we do not assert it as a cold conclusion of thought, we assert it in order to be connected to it, for it to penetrate us and to live in it. Our interior experience thus confirms the history lesson that shows civilizations dying without God; it illuminates, it fulfils Aristotle's lofty abstraction: matter assumes a form, the animal that we are becomes spirit in yielding to the allurement of perfection."[7]

"Perfection is the eternal, immutable will that the good be. . . . The very name of God precisely signifies for us: I desire that the good be."[8]

"Finally, we know nothing whatsoever, we understand nothing whatsoever, we must believe and we do believe, in the face of all appearances to the contrary, that the good is willed by an absolute will; because we must invariably will it ourselves and because we are not able to will it thus, unless we see in it the truth."[9]

What is more "pragmatic" than this first rule of religious method:

From the outset, one goes astray and runs risk of great failure when the problem of truth is separated from the problem of behavior, and when one thinks oneself free to accept a conception as expressing the order of the world, before having examined the

7. *La Civilisation et la Croyance,* second part, chap. III, p. 249.

8. Ibid., chap. III, p. 257.

9. Ibid., chap. III, p. 257.—Cf. also *Lettres* to Renouvier published in the *Revue de Métaphysique et de Morale,* 17 (January, May, July 1909): 1–47, 367–85 and 501–551 [Nov. 1909: 824–35 18 (May, Sept. 1910): 302–17 and 648–70]; for example, letters XXVI and XXVIII.

probable consequences of its adoption for the conduct of life. . . . The choice between two unverifiable hypotheses depends, fundamentally, on what one *wants*."[10]

The entire volume is little more than an application of this rule. Of special note, however, is this superiority over Anglo-American pragmatism: even if Secrétan maintained the intimate union of *truth* and *behavior,* he did distinguish them and would never have made "truth" a synonym for simple moral utility.

But here is the pure expression of moralism: "You see in religion only a group of dogmas to varying degrees unacceptable to a philosopher's reason. I see in them something more important than that: an ideal rule for the conduct of life. Those who have accepted that rule form a social group, an assembly—that is the meaning of the word Church—and feel themselves bound to one another in a common aspiration."[11] "Let us take prayer as a meditation, or, what amounts to the same, as the dialogue of man with the internal law he calls his God."[12]

As early as 1849 Renan said:

"Religion is not the true; it is the instrument of the ideal life of Humanity."[13] "Legend is not factually true, but it is always true as an idea."[14] "Religion is false from the object's point of view . . .

10. *La Civilisation et la Croynace,* 3rd part, chap. I, p. 343; chap. IV, p. 434.

11. Louis Ménard, *Rêveries d'un païen mystique* (Paris: Edition Duret, 1876), p. 136.

12. Ibid., p. 111. Singular juxtapositions of intellectualism and pragmatism sometimes arise. Saint-Simon, for example, declares in his *Nouveau Christianisme* that "God has necessarily brought everything back to a single principle; he has necessarily deduced everything from the same principle; without which his will in relation to men would not have been systematic. It would be blasphemy to claim that the All-Powerful had founded religion on several principles" (p. 11). This principle is that men must conduct themselves as brothers in relation to one another. "Worship and dogma will be viewed only as accessories having as their principal object focusing the attention of the faithful of all classes on morality" (p. 20). "Religion must direct society toward the great goal of improving the lot of the poorest classes as quickly as possible."

13. Ernest Renan, *Patrice* [1849] (Paris: Calmann-Lévy, 1908), p. 42.

14. Ibid., p. 78.

but is eternally true from the subject's point of view, that is to say from our need for it and from the religious feeling to which it corresponds. And yet, this point of view is the most important from the perspective of the philosopher who knows that dogma plays only a very secondary role in religion, a kind of insignificant algebra accepted in view of meaning and the moral life, which form its essential part."[15]

A few years earlier (1843) the two points of view were clearly traced by Alfred de Vigny:

"When men like Descartes and Spinoza buried their head in their hands, they must have been seeking in all sincerity: First, how did creation appear to them? Second, what were the causes and the goal of creation, according to the most probable and most likely reckoning?

"It was belief they sought. When men like Saint Augustine, Bossuet, and Fénelon think about religious matters, I find them much more human and more superficial; they consider the universe as constructed for a certain small clan and God himself is going to descend on a small privileged planet to give them particular laws.

"It was religion they sought. The question, when one digs into these things, is whether one should adopt a general perspective from the immensity in which the universe floats and do one's best to adopt a viewpoint as it were from a planet like Saturn or Jupiter, or whether instead one should adopt a viewpoint from the midst of the human species populating tiny Earth, and from there consider religion according to its usefulness as reference point for morality.

"The first point of view is obviously the grander, the more *di-*

15. Ibid., p. 54.

vine of the two, in that it is inspired solely by a sacred love of the truth which raises the soul toward the Creator and the center of creation.

"The second point of view is incontestably better for the improvement of human society, and, from this perspective, Christianity until now has been the system whose truth is more desirable than that of all the other systems. But one senses how narrow and impoverished the pursuit of this concern is compared to the pursuit of truth." [16]

Our time is characterized by the eagerness that an adult and self-conscious Humanity experiences to separate the two points of view no longer. *Actual* pragmatism commits it to continuing to make do with the second. This is why we are protesting; in religion, as in every other determination of his activity, man no longer wishes to accept expedients through which he is reduced to servitude under the pretext of being served: truths "for the people," truths "by command," truths "from headquarters," as a spiritual prelate once said to me.

II. Originally, *fideism* consisted in not admitting (at least in certain matters) any source of knowledge and certitude other than divine revelation. But it is given a much broader meaning in attributing the term *faith,* not only to adherence to divine revelation, but to *natural faith,* that is, to belief founded on elements other than discursive intelligence: some will call them: *heart, feeling* (not to be confused[17] with *emotions*), others *life,* still others *action.* . . . To assimilate this prereflective belief to an *instinct,* as Jacobi has claimed, would perhaps be preferable, an instinct

16. "We speak of faith. In the end, what is this rarity?—A fervent hope.—I have sounded it and have found only that. Never certitude." A. de Vigny, *Journal d'un poete,* Edit. Ratisbonne (Paris: Fasquelle, 1904), p. 194; and ibid., pp. 187, 188.

17. As the theologians of Pius X have done in the encyclical *Pascendi dominici gregis.*

that would build the varied images, myths, dogmas according to temperaments, as well as organize physical movements if it were a matter of adaptation to the physical world.[18]

However, the fideist can grant a certain *knowledge* value to myths or to dogmas, in which case he is no longer a pure pragmatist.

Or, again, like Pascal,[19] he can mistrust reason solely *in the order of "salvation,"*[20] relative to that which concerns the *supernatural* end of man, the *supernatural* love of God. Only there is Pascal thoroughly pragmatic: "The God of Christians is a God of love and consolation; this is a God who fills the soul and the heart that he possesses; this is a God who makes them feel their misery and his infinite mercy; who unites himself in the depth of their soul, who fills it with humility, joy, confidence, love, who renders them incapable of any end other than himself. . . . Here is what faith is: God sensible to the heart, not to reason. . . . When the truthful word of God is literally false, it is true spiritually. Everything that does not lead to charity is appearance. The unique object of Scripture is Charity."[21]

"God alone can put (divine truths) in the soul and in whatever way he pleases. I know he wanted them to penetrate the mind from the heart and not the heart from the mind, in order to humble the proud power of reasoning that claims to judge things

18. I have studied the various forms of fideism in *Évolution de la foi catholique*: Jacobi's System, p. 155.

19. *L'Évolution de la foi catholique*: Pascal, pp. 132ff.

20. Ernest Havet, ed. *Pensées de Pascal* (Paris: Librairie Ch. Delgrave, 1881), art. X, no. 2.

21. Ibid., art. XXII, no. 1; XXIV, no. 5; XVI, nos. 12, 13; and art. XXIV, no. 26: "One must begin by showing that religion is not in any way contrary to reason: next that it is venerable and to respect it; to represent it as agreeable, to make good people desire that it be true." A pure pragmatist would find that "desire" suffices. Pascal still requires an *objective* proof ("through Scripture," art. XXII, 1). It is true that (in the texts) "each finds what is in the depths of his heart" (art. XVI, 9) and that only those "truly see miracles whom miracles benefit." (Letter 9 to Mlle de Roannez).

that the will chooses, and in order to heal the weak will thoroughly corrupted by its squalid attachments. And it follows that, instead of speaking as one does of human things by saying one must know them before loving them, which has become proverbial (Ignoti nulla cupido), the saints, on the contrary, in speaking of divine things, say that one must love them in order to know them and that the truth is attained only through charity."[22]

—*Fideism* closely resembles pragmatism, not, however, in the sense in which the Catholic Church seems to have adopted the term, but in the sense Protestants often use it, and chief among them, M. E. Ménégoz, who formulates it thus: "Salvation through faith, independently of beliefs."[23]

M. Ménégoz does not say: faith *without* beliefs; in a number of places he has explained himself on this point: "I have always taught that the faith that saves is the heart's gift to God: a decision of the *self* in its unity. And yet the *self* in its unity includes thought, emotion, and will. Thus in the decision that is faith there is a triple factor: an element of thought, of emotion, and of will."[24] "Beliefs" fall under the element of thought. Knowledge, as such does not "*save*" us, but rather the "movement" of the inmost being toward God; therein lies a mystical form of as-

22. *De l'esprit géométrique,* Edit. Havet, p. 549. Remember that for Descartes, judgment is an act of the *will.*

23. In the article that M. Ménégoz devoted to our essay on *pragmatism* (*Publications diverses sur le fidéisme* [Paris: Fischbacher, 1909], vol. 2, p. 498), he explains that in using this word as early as 1879, he was unaware that Catholics had sometimes used it and he thought he was coining it. Among Catholics the word *fideism* designates the doctrine according to which, without depending on previous *intellectual* certitudes, faith possesses its own certitude, sufficient in itself, self-justifying. (Cf. our *Évolution de la foi catholique,* chap. VIII and IX.) This doctrine was condemned in Bautain and Bonnety; in 1855 the latter was made to subscribe to the following proposition: "Rationis usus fidem praecedit" (Denzinger, *Enchiridion,* No. 1507) as a retraction of his theory.

24. E. Ménégoz, *Publications diverses sur le fidéisme,* vol. 1, pp. 244, 255, 261, and vol. 2, pp. 90, 130, 135, 330, 356, 533, etc. A good resumé of M. Ménégoz's ideas by Haldimann has been published by Fischbacher under the title *Le Fidéisme* (1907).

sertion of the "primacy" of activity over intellectuality; however, M. Ménégoz does not for all that contest the value of knowledge. Those who represent "revelation" as a kind of stock of ready-made statements, furnished by God himself and that we must accept as such, would not approve of him. M. Ménégoz adheres to the doctrine of Auguste Sabatier who sees in these truths *symbols* that each conscience interprets as best it can. Hence the name "*symbolo-fideism*" which he accepts for his doctrine and which would have, at least, the advantage of distinguishing it from *fideism* in the Catholic sense.

It is not easy to say precisely what the symbolo-fideists accept of *knowledge* properly so called in dogmas and beliefs.[25] They would approach pure religious pragmatism insofar as they diminish its measure in order to see in dogmas and beliefs merely images orienting our activity without informing us about the fundamental reality of things. They insist a great deal on the incontestable principle that we do not adequately grasp the truth. But an incomplete, inadequate knowledge is not, for all that, *nonexistent*. For example, when M. Ménégoz believes he must affirm the "personality" of God, because "from the intellect we *know* only one thing, namely that he is personal,"[26] he obviously goes beyond pure *symbolism* and pure *pragmatism*.

A kind of proto-pragmatism is presented in Ritschl's doctrine

25. The difficulty stems from different uses by different authors of the terms *objective* and *subjective*. Auguste Sabatier (chap. IV of Book III of *Esquisse d'une philosophie de la religion*) distinguished objective *knowledge* [science] and *subjective* faith. But neither is knowledge completely objective, nor faith completely subjective; that is why there can be an objective aspect of knowledge, properly so called, in religion and why, for example, after having tried to reduce our affirmations regarding God to a practical, "teleological" notion, Sabatier was compelled to add: "It is indeed true that to determine this final cause of the world, is also to determine the first cause" (p. 389). Philosophy! One will say. But for all those endowed with an intellectual temperament, it is a religious need, a religious obligation to reflect on their belief, as much as for others to feel and imagine it.

26. *Publications diverses sur le fidéisme,* vol. 2, pp. 463 and 573.

which has greatly influenced German theologians and which is anterior[27] to Peirce's. Ritschl, too, contested the Hegelian absolute; he, too, insisted on the point that where there is no *interest,* neither is there any effort to know. Alongside any *judgment of existence,* there is then always a *judgment of value* responding to the said interest. "In religion, the subject does not make a judgment that ascertains either the existence of a being or the existence of a relation between two beings (for example: God is; God is spirit; God is the author of the world); but it makes a judgment of value that expresses a knowledge affecting the self, which has for it a value determining variations of its sensibility. Thus, if I say: God is good, God is the judge of sinners, I formulate a judgment of value or a religious judgment, because I do not affirm in a disinterested manner the existence of either a being or of a causal relation between two beings, but a truth that has a direct value for myself, because it is of a nature to affect my sensibility through joy or through sorrow."[28] We can only know the essence of God through the value it has for us; it is manifested to us through its revelation in Jesus Christ. One believes it or one does not; in any

27. Ritschl's great work, *Die christliche Lehre von der Rechtfertigung und Versohnung,* dates from 1874. In *Studies in Humanism* Schiller twice alludes to Ritschl as well as to Newman's *Grammar of Assent.* But Newman always remained convinced of the rights of the intellect, as one may verify by the typical passage cited by William James in Lecture XVIII of the *Varieties of Religious Experience,* where Newman admits a "*Science* of God," theology, as there is science of the stars, astronomy; of the terrestrial crust, geology. As early as 1843, Newman supported the fundamental principles of the "modernist" apologetic: the role of religious experience, the role of subconscious impressions, the symbolic character of our knowledge (sensations, mathematical representations, physical laws, as well as religious dogmas). All these types of knowledge are only "economic" representations, "symbols." By "economy" Newman understands a certain manner of presenting truth, of proportioning it to the weakness of the knower. But it is no less true that, for him, these affirmations "represent the truth to the degree that our minds allow." A quite inadequate, quite imperfect knowledge, but knowledge nonetheless. [Hébert cited Henri Bremond's *Newman. Le développement du dogme chrétien,* which incorporated Abbé Deferrière's 1850 translation of the relevant Oxford University sermon.].

28. Maurice Goguel, *La Théologie d'Albert Ritschl* (Paris: Fischbacher, 1905), p. 11.

case, one cannot believe if it remains indifferent, without relation to our experience and our needs.

—A seductive doctrine, true moreover if it is regarded as a summary observation of what occurs in the majority of cases and not as a rigorous theory. The judgment of existence cannot be the assertion of an abstract existence; it must, in some way or another, represent some mode of existence.[29] And the "value" can only be expressed in terms that invite discussion. For example, when Ritschl says that "the complete name of God which responds to Christian revelation is: the God and Father of our Savior Jesus Christ," who is also known to us as "God of love," he raises the question: Have these terms any "analogical" knowledge value, or are they simply conventional labels through which we designate and distinguish from the rest a mystery of which, fundamentally, we know absolutely nothing?

III. Like the term *fideism,* the term *symbolism* can be taken in various senses.[30]

The symbol can be an image, a parable, a legend, which embodies and from which is drawn a practical truth. Thus Louis Ménard (cf. p. 195) said "that if one wanted to give a living and

29. If only to represent being as active, thus endowed with one or another kind of activity.

30. Perhaps this schema will clarify the question:

	Symbolism	
1st meaning:	A. Through symbolic representation, illusory with regard to what it is supposed to represent, the intellect neither knows nor learns anything; but representation helps it feel, will, act. Cf. p. 203, note 33. B. Through symbolic representation something is known, or learned (or expressed).	
2nd and 3rd	B' through association	a) from resemblance cf. pp. 202, 203 and b) from simple analogy cf. p. 203, note 32
4th	B" through abstract, but inadequate ideas. Cf. pp. 203, 205	

statuesque form to the republican dogma of fraternity, one could not find a finer image than that of the Righteous one dying for the salvation of men.[31]

In this case, the simile—or analogy—is acknowledged.[32] It can, on the contrary, fade into the background,[33] or be misunderstood. This is what happens when one regards the expression of a feeling less as helping to understand than as helping to act.

I think that one must interpret the symbolism of the Italian modernists in the latter sense: "a symbol no longer means a fictitious, and perhaps fraudulent, substitution connected with ignorant or erroneous beliefs. It is a reality of its own peculiar kind whereon faith confers an inestimable value by which it becomes the real vehicle and blessed occasion of an uplifting of the spirit and of a deeper religious insight."[34]

This can be compared to the following assertion: that the activity of knowing is "the result of a laborious effort of the spirit to dominate reality and to turn it to its own service with the aid of whatever mental *schemas* it manages to form of that reality."[35]

Therein lies the difficulty: does one consider these "schemas" as simple means, methods, stimulants, orientations, of action or as enabling us to know, at least to catch a glimpse, of *the nature of* reality?

31. Maurice Barrès, *Voyage de Sparte* (Paris: Juven), p. 25 (Cited in the Preface of Louis Ménard's *Rêveries d'un païen mystique,* Edit. Duret.)

32. Example: the scales as a symbol representing Justice.

33. In this statement, for example, of Barrès: "They [the gods] are all true, because one must see in them the successive affirmations of an eternal need" (*Voyage à Sparte,* p. 26). In this case, there is pure *intellectual* illusion: one feels, one desires, but one knows, one learns nothing.

34. *Le Programme des modernistes. Réplique à l'encyclique Pascendi* (Paris: Nourry, 1908), p. 134. Trans. of *Il Programma dei modernisti* (Rome: Societa internazionale scientifico-religiosa editrice, 1907) [*The Programme of Modernism,* trans. George Tyrrell (New York: G. P. Putnam's Sons, 1908), 114].

35. *Le Programme des modernistes,* p. 115 [*The Programme of Modernism,* 97 (translation modified)].

The first case is one of pure pragmatism. In the second, a certain objective knowledge, however relative or limited it may be, is added to action as its flowering. It is undoubtedly religious experience [sentiment] that fills and enlivens the "schemas": unity, plurality, substance, etc., but in uniting itself with them, it becomes more clearly aware of what it contains, and this is precisely what constitutes an acquisition of *knowledge* (abstract in its form, always living in its content).

This is the way I understand these lines of Loisy's: "The phenomenon of religion cannot be reduced to another form of human activity, nor explained solely by causes pertaining to the social order; but expresses, in its purest manifestations, an endeavour to attain, beyond what is real and tangible, an ideal or a transcendent reality, *conceived as the principle and goal* of a moral life."[36] (The words I emphasize correspond to notions of the intellectual order.)

Not all "modernists" are strict pragmatists. Nevertheless, the decree of the Holy Office *Lamentabili* appears to accuse them of it since it censured the following proposition: "The dogmas of the faith are to be held *only according to their practical sense;* that is to say, as perceptive norms of conduct and not as norms of believing."[37]

An exaggerated interpretation, as M. Loisy has occasion to remark in his work: *Simples réflexions sur le Décret de Saint-Office et sur l'Encyclique.*[38]

M. Loisy has never contested the historical foundation anymore than the psychological or even metaphysical foundation of

36. Alfred Loisy, *La religion d'Israël*, 2nd ed. (Paris: Nourry, 1908), p. 294 [Eng. trans. *The Religion of Israel*, trans. Arthur Galton (London: T. Fisher Unwin, 1910), 275].

37. Prop. XXVI: "Dogmata fidei retinenda sunt tantummodo juxta sunsum practicum, id est tanquam praeceptiva agenda, non vero tanquam credendi." *Lamentabili sane exitu* (3 July 1907).

38. Paris, Librairie Nourry, 1908.

religious beliefs. They are all "constructions of faith,"[39] but faith working from realities. Jesus,[40] his religious consciousness, his influence on his disciples, are facts that believers have idealized, but these facts are objects of *knowledge*.

What M. Loisy has tried to stress is that "truth is in us something necessarily conditioned, relative, always perfectible, and also susceptible to diminution. It seems to be a remainder of repeated, coordinated perceptions, which have the real as their object, which are real in themselves and in the notions that remain of them. But our perceptions do not reach the depths of reality. Still less do notions exhaust it. These are the faded images of subjective impressions that certainly involve the reality of the subject and the object, but which adequately represent to the subject neither the object nor the subject itself."[41]

Loisy continues:

"The ecclesiastical formula is not absolutely true, since it does not define the full reality of the object that it represents; it is no less the *symbol* of an absolute truth; until the Church finds it right to modify and elucidate the formula, it is the best and most secure expression[42] of the truth in question. The faithful adhere by intention to the full and absolute truth represented by the imperfect and relative formula. To adhere to a formula as such, from an assent of divine faith, would be to adhere to its inevitable imperfections, to proclaim them imperfectible and adequate, although they are inadequate and imperfect. Thus the Catholic can believe in the Church's authority and in what the Church

39. Cf. *Évolution de la foi catholique,* p. 194: "La renaissance du fidéisme; forme historique: M. Loisy."

40. Alfred Loisy, *Les Évangiles Synoptiques,* 2 vols. (Ceffonds: Chez l'auteur, 1907–1908), Vol. 1: Introduction; chap. VII and VIII on the teaching and career of Jesus.

41. Alfred Loisy, *Autour d'un petit livre* (Paris: Alphonse Picard, 1903), Letter VI, p. 191.

42. It is a purely oratorical precaution that M. Loisy employs at this point, for this *a priori* assertion was gratuitous.

teaches. Nonetheless, he does not think that the ecclesiastical formulary so perfectly signifies its object that nothing in it will ever be altered by means of interpretation.[43]

There we have still another meaning of "symbolism," the inadequacy of Saint Paul: "*Cognosco ex parte*" [I know in part].

In his remarkable study, *Dogme et critique,* M. Le Roy willingly uses the word *pragmatisme,*[44] but he carefully distinguishes his doctrine from English pragmatism which, it seems "substitutes, in short, a preoccupation with simple *utility* for a concern for the *truth.*"[45]

M. Le Roy does not work by substitution, but complete subordination.

"A dogma has above all a *practical* meaning. It states before all a *prescription of a practical kind.* It is more than all the formula of a *rule of practical conduct.* This is its principal value, this its positive significance.... 'God is a person' means, 'Conduct yourself in your relations to God as in your relations with a human person.' Likewise 'Jesus has risen' means, 'Be in relation to him as you would have been before his death, as you are with a contemporary.' In the same way again the dogma of the real presence means that one must have the same attitude toward the consecrated host as one would have toward Jesus had he become visible."[46]

Does it not then follow that we are in complete subjectivism?

43. *Autour d'un petit livre,* Letter VI, p. 206. Cf. Alfred Loisy, *L'Évangile et l'Église* (Paris: Alphonse Picard, 1902, 2nd ed. 1903), chap. IV, pp. 167 and 174 of the 1st ed. and chap. V, pp. 211 and 218 of the 2nd ed. [*The Gospel and the Church,* 218–19 and 224–25].

44. For example, pp. 51, 105, 114, 133, 150, 252, 302, etc.

45. Édouard Le Roy, *Dogme et critique* (Paris: Librairie Bloud, 1907), p. 332 and note 3, p. 114. [This volume republished Le Roy's 1905 article "Qu'est-ce qu'un dogme?" which originally appeared in *La Quinzaine,* together with critics' replies and Le Roy's responses. Only Le Roy's original article was translated into English; the replies and Le Roy's responses were not.]

46. Ibid., pp. 25–26 [Eng. trans. "What Is a Dogma?" trans. Lydia G. Robinson [1918], republished in Joseph Fitzer, ed., *Romance and the Rock: Nineteenth-Century Catholics on Faith and Reason* (Minneapolis: Fortress Press, 1989), 365–66].

Not at all, for M. Le Roy vigorously maintains this idea that "it is implicitly affirmed by the dogma itself that the reality contains (under one form or another) means to justify the prescribed conduct as reasonable and salutary.[47]. . . By itself and in itself it [dogma] has only a practical meaning. *But there is a mysterious reality corresponding to it and therefore it presents to the intelligence a theoretical problem.* The human intellect at once takes possession of this problem; and obeying simply and solely the laws of its own nature it imagines the explanations, the answers, the systems codified in the precepts of scientific method and the principles of reason. As long as the theory constructed in this way respects the practical significance of the dogma it is given carte blanche. Hence to pass judgment on the theories remains the task of pure human speculation, and any authority exterior to the thought itself has neither the right nor the power to interfere. But once let a theory arise which makes an attack on dogma in its own domain by altering its practical significance, and the dogma would immediately array itself against it and condemn it, thus becoming a negative intellectual statement superimposed upon the rule of conduct which at first it was, purely and simply."[48]

Note the *representative* aspect subordinated to the *practical* aspect, while safeguarded nonetheless. It is because M. Le Roy does not in any way interpret "primacy of action" as annihilation of intellect. He is careful not to relegate pure thought to one side, blind action to the other. As with acting, "to know is a func-

47. *Dogme et critique,* p. 33. Cf. pp. 40, 273, 298.

48. Ibid., p. 33 [in Fitzer, *Romance and the Rock,* 371]. It is more important for the concept, the image, to represent the "corresponding lived reaction" than the intrinsic nature of the object. Thus M. Le Roy does not allow that the cadaver of Jesus was reanimated, but he believes in the Resurrection; this is what that becomes for him: "The present state of Jesus is such that, in order to relate to his ineffable reality, to orient ourselves toward it, to grasp it as much as possible, in order to form a relationship with it in conformity with its true nature, the requisite attitude and conduct on our part are those that would be proper toward a contemporary" (p. 255).

tion of life, a practical act in its way,"[49] but it is not a completely abstract thought, increasingly "thought-action" alone is able to comprehend these assertions whose meaning can only be understood by living and practicing them.[50]

"The Catholic," adds M. Le Roy, "after having accepted the dogmas retains full liberty to make for himself whatever theory, whatever intellectual representation he wishes of the corresponding objects—the divine personality, the real presence, or the Resurrection, for instance.... Only one thing is imposed on him, only one obligation is incumbent upon him; his theory must justify the practical edicts prescribed by the dogma."[51]

The difficulty is not in finding symbolism in Christian beliefs and rituals. They can be invented at will, and of the most elevated kinds. "*But,*" as Louis De Potter said over seventy years ago, with admirable good sense, "*would the Church accept this philosophical recasting? That is the whole question. Of what importance, indeed, the self-styled Catholicism of those philosophers who still fancy themselves Catholics? It is the Church and its visible head that we want to and must hear speaking.*"[52]

49. Ibid., p. 30 [Fitzer, 368].

50. Idem. Cf. pp. 101–5, 114, 125, 301, 332, etc. The charming moral mysticism of Père Laberthonnière claims to show that the ascetical and living method and the speculative and abstract method "are not only interdependent, but complementary," "moral conduct not at all excluding logical methods, but controlling and encompassing them." Dogmas "have a living meaning, accessible to us to varying degrees, according to our degree of spirituality. They express the life of God in itself and in relation to the life of humanity." Lucien Laberthonnière, *Essais de philosophie religieuse* (Paris: P. Lethielleux, 1903), pp. 189, 34, 272. M. Tyrrell maintained the "representative value [of dogmas] as well as practical value. If there is a Pragmatism that denies this, I have nothing to do with it." ("Lex credendi" in the *Annales de philosophie chrétienne* [July 1906], p. 346 [Eng. orig. in George Tyrrell, *Lex Credendi* (London: Longmans, Green, and Co., 1906), 252]. Cf. the same author's "Notre attitude en face du pragmatisme" in *Annales de philosophie chrétienne* (December 1905) [Eng. "Pragmatism" in George Tyrrell, *Through Scylla and Charybdis or the Old Theology and the New* (London: Longmans, 1907), VII].

51. Ibid., p. 32 [Fitzer, 370].

52. Louis De Potter, *Histoire philosophique et critique du Christianisme,* 8 vols. (Librairie historique A. Leclaire, 1836–1837), 1: p. xxiv.

This could not be put better today.

Indeed, the Catholic Church has responded to all these theories only with condemnations. I do not justify this way of acting, but, on this point at least, I am of the opinion that the Church is correct to be against M. Le Roy as it was formerly against the fideists. M. Le Roy neglects reflective thought by divorcing it too far from thought-action. The abstractions are, in short, extracted from reality and, when their contact with reality is maintained, when they are not simply juggled conceptually, they retain the value due in respect to their origin. The Church thus has the right to claim an intellectual content for its dogma—for the Church, moreover, to prove that this intellectual element applies to a reality (this is what historical criticism renders more and more difficult and often impossible for it). There is then, in spite of everything, a substratum of intellectual skepticism in M. Le Roy; nothing proves this better than the following declaration: "My resolve of fidelity to God, to Jesus Christ, to the Church is not connected to any system, even were it my own. . . . My certitude rests—unshakable, by divine grace—on an experience of life stronger than all discourse."[53]

M. Le Roy's case explains many others: one can see the price paid by certain men who remain in the Church: forgetfulness of or disregard for the intellectual part of their nature. Their mysticism is satisfied; pragmatically that suffices. Others, self-assertive and combative, are, fundamentally, skeptics or pessimists: "We believe what we can," wrote Brunetière to one of his disciples, "and it is because I believe I know, as much as anyone, the element of relativity in all my beliefs, that I no longer judge them from the rational, but practical point of view, less in their

53. *Dogme et critique*, p. 39.

principles than in their consequences."[54] Pragmatist utilitarianism, which dispenses them from responding to difficulties arising from historical and philosophical criticism, is, for them, the ultimate refuge.

2. The Religious Pragmatism of Mr. Schiller and Mr. James

M. Schiller's primary concern is to refute neo-Hegelian absolutism[55] and to show that their absolute has nothing religious about it, since it has nothing in common with the openly anthropomorphic God of religion. It is all the easier for him since he views this system from an entirely intellectual point of view, setting aside the emotions that accompany absolutism in the minds of those who affirm it—emotions of which he is nonetheless aware.[56] These discussions do not evoke much interest in France, where nearly everyone is in favor of the primacy of activity, or, at least, are rather mitigated rationalists. I limit myself to the following observations:

First, the God of religions is anthropomorphic, but in the Judeo-Christian religion, God (and this is why one cannot make God into a simple unification of *the gods*) is perceived as *perfect*. In the most typical prayers,[57] he is called *infinitely* good, *infinitely* kind, *sovereign* truth, etc. Among well-educated believers the distinction is thus made between often rough expression and spiritual meaning. Without undertaking here a study of the notion of the perfect,[58] let us recall that man, whatever his theories, his negations, or his doubts, cannot live a truly human life without

54. Letter to M. Arnauld (Maurice Drottin) in "Antée" (1 February), p. 890.

55. Schiller, *Studies in Humanism.* Essay XII: "Absolutism and Religion."

56. Ibid., p. 295, bottom of the page.

57. Acts of faith, hope, and charity.

58. Cf. *Le Divin,* p. 280 and chap. X §4 and 5.

establishing a kind of hierarchy among the qualities of beings, among his own actions, without bringing to bear on them judgments to which he attributes a varying degree of qualitative,[59] *ideal value*—and no longer merely *utilitarian* value. We assert, for example, that altruism is not only more *useful* to people than egoism, but also that it is more *noble, better,* and *must be preferred to it.*[60] And not only can we form an abstract, general idea of the qualitative *value* of an ideal, disinterested order, but we can, without abandoning lived experience, imagine in its continuity what value judgments have given us, in each particular case, as fragmented and divided. This is what should be called the aspiration-sentiment-notion of the *perfect;* it is the living Law[61] of the evolution of the universe, or (if we personify it) of God.

The notion ought not be any more suspect than the aspiration; they are both different, but also legitimate expressions of our interior experience. It is certainly possible to think about the world without employing this form of the perfect; imagine that it represents an aesthetic vogue, that religious thought may be, in this respect, a form of *art;* it is still the case that one has the right to think about *metaphysical theory* in this way, just as one does about *moral practice.* Religious men, in both cases, can say, "*It works,*" as can the pragmatists.

Second, if the notion of faith is exclusively intellectual among the neo-Hegelians, it is hardly the case among Christian theologians. I have studied this question at length in *Évolution de la foi catholique* (notion of faith among the Fathers, among the Scholastics, the Reformers, etc.). "To believe is an act of the intellect

59. Cf. pp. 147–48.

60. Cf. *La forme idéaliste du sentiment religieux,* Part I, pp. 13–29; Part II, §3, and Appendix III.

61. It is indeed in no way a matter of an abstract law, but of an activity developing itself according to a certain orientation that, manifested to our consciousness, we call a *law.*

inasmuch as *the will* moves it to assent," said Saint Thomas Aquinas.[62] "No one believes unless he is willing" Saint Augustine had said.[63]

Third, Mr. Schiller has Protagoras support the thesis that the gods, at least as men imagine them, "are real as the ideal responses to real human needs, which really move us."[64] This explanation of God seems analogous to that of Mr. Leuba[65] who reduces mystical religiosity to the satisfaction of four inclinations:

1. An inclination to organic pleasure;
2. An inclination to calming thought through unification or reduction;
3. An inclination to seek an affective support;
4. An inclination to universalize action (beyond the egotistical personal point of view).

Divine force, it could be said, is employed ("*God is not understood, He is used*"), as are electric power, gravity, etc. without needing to *know* what they are.[66] Mr. Leuba and Mr. Schiller do not seem to suspect that there exists another inclination (the aspiration-sentiment-notion of which I have just spoken), irreducible

62. *Summa Theologica* IIa IIae; q. 4 a. 2. [Vol. 2 (New York; Benziger Brothers, 1947), p. 1191]. Saint Thomas also maintains the *two aspects* of the question: "an act of faith is related both to the object of the *will*, i.e., to the good and the end, and to the object of the *intellect*, i.e., to the true . . . the First Truth is the end of the act of faith, which aspect is that of a thing hoped for." *Summa Theologiae* IIa IIae, q. 4 art. 1 in corp. [Vol. 2, p. 1190. Emphasis Hébert's]. The Scholastics have not developed the finalist point of view, but its beginning nonetheless exists in their theory. We have already had cause to note this: *Évolution de la foi catholique*, pp. 95–99.

63. Tract. 26 *in Joann.* No. 2.

64. *Studies in Humanism*, Essay XV "Gods and Priests," pp. 340–41.

65. On the theories of Mr. James and Mr. Leuba see *Le Divin*, chap. X; *La Forme idéaliste du sentiment religieux*, Part I, §1.

66. "The God of the pragmaticisms," M. Bourdeau rightly says, "does not reside in the Empyrean, behind the veils of the temple. He is an old faithful servant, whose job it is to render us menial services, to help us carry our cross and to drag our trunk in the midst of the sweat and dust of daily trials." (*Journal des Débats*, 18 February 1908.)

to the four noted above, the very same which makes Christian mystics.[67] Here I cannot develop the point sufficiently;[68] I will at least mention that every Christian who has said with sincerity of feeling: "My God, I love you because you are infinitely perfect," has felt what I designate by the notion of the perfect, love of infinite perfection, and has understood my protest against the reduction of this element to the four inclinations noted by Leuba.

It is precisely this mystical declaration that I criticize in Mr. James. After having demolished everything, he excels at reconstructing everything with unexpected and always very interesting "over beliefs." His thought seems to oscillate unceasingly between the traditional affirmations of Christian faith which, after all, if they are useful, are true (according to the theory) and his hypotheses which, likewise, are true, since they are useful to him. Of course, he too refutes the neo-Hegelians,[69] and prefers the hypothesis of a world where unity is not yet achieved, where multiple forces contend and strive without restraint,—and without the salvation of one necessarily implicating that of the other—in order to free it from evil. Nothing prevents our believing that we are aided in our efforts by superior forces. We notice that our ideals coincide with theirs, much as dogs and cats, in our experience, notice it with regard to us.[70]—All this is admissible. My objection, as above, is that in this case God is only "*primus inter pares*" for our consciousness.[71]

67. In a recent article, "Religion as a Factor in the Struggle for Life," *American Journal of Religion, Philosophy and Education* (December 1906, June 1907), Mr. Leuba objects that mystics end by mingling everything in an indivisible unity: Mme Guyon, for example, no longer distinguished between God and her confessor, Père Lacombe.—I reply: at the very first interrogation, Mme Guyon immediately protested that it was Père Lacombe who appeared to merge into divine unity and certainly not the reverse.

68. I have done so in the essay on the *Forme idéaliste du sentiment religieux*.

69. *Pragmatism,* Lecture VIII: "Pragmatism and Religion."

70. Ibid., p. 300.

71. Ibid., p. 298.

As for the formulas expressing our beliefs,[72] they would be true by the same token, since they are useful for a noble goal.

But, one should not slip cheerfully into ambiguity. What is at stake here? Proving that our inclinations and beliefs can play a legitimate role in our life? Showing that there is good, even excellence, in the beliefs of the past? Separating what is true in these myths of "revelation," of "Christ," of "God" (such as he is habitually *imagined*)? Very well, then; the pragmatic point of view assures tolerance and understanding, provides useful compromises for periods of transition. All this already involves working for the free religious associations of the future. But if it is a matter of critiquing or defending religious forms having a history and making use of history, it behooves us to readopt old ideas about objective truth[73] and objective methods; for example, not to ask oneself simply: Is the Resurrection of Jesus a construction of faith, a myth expressing consoling hopes, etc.? but: Is it a fact whose historical reality is proven as is the death of Socrates? Was such an idea of Nirvana really taught by the Buddha? In other words, we must *remedy the deficiencies of the pure pragmatist.*

72. I borrow the following information from an article on pragmatism by M. Dessoulavy (*Revue de philosophie* [6 (1 July 1905)]: 90). "The religious aspect of the system, its capacity as apologetic did not fail to attract the attention of the English religious world. Already, in 1902, the usefulness to be valued in pragmatism was pointed out in the *Monthly Register* (November). A year later, Mr. Vesey Hague, in a series of articles in the *Irish Ecclesiastical Record* considered pragmatism from the religious point of view ["What Is a Reasonable Faith?" 13 (Jan.–June 1903): 510–31; 14 (July–Dec. 1903): 254–72, 325–40. See also J. F. Hogan, "Mr. Hague's Philosophy," also in vol. 14.61–63], and recently an anonymous author did the same in the *Tablet* (February 1905)." M. Dessoulavy appears to value this apologetic. It is, certainly, easy to understand and represents well average requirements. "Godliness is profitable to all things" says the author of 1 Tim. 4.8. But this does not rise above the level of clever pleading.

73. A simple comparison: speaking of *manic patients*, Dr. Regis affirms this: "Often (these sick people) offer a stamp of originality, of innovation, of distinction and of superiority which make them truly remarkable. While in this state the sick have been seen to develop useful inventions, find important solutions, bring about valuable productions, in a word, show themselves more intelligent and more fruitful than they have ever been." *Manuel pratique de médecine mentale*, p. 166. Should one apply the idea of *truth* to the mania because it is accompanied by *useful* excitation?

A long time ago—permit me this digression—I sought proof of the existence of God in the way in which this belief "adapts"[74] us to invisible Reality and I attempted to justify how dogmas "orient"[75] us toward our end. But is this sufficient? We have seen (Chap. 3) that the uniquely practical role of hypotheses and theories is unacceptable with regard to the natural sciences. We assert the same thing in the religious sphere where even should our theories never exceed the level of probability, this probability would not be considered merely *ex consequentiis*, but with arguments implying a certain knowledge value—if only analogical—to human thought.

Finally, speaking from a pragmatic perspective I would say: Since human nature is capable of seeing for the sake of seeing, of knowing for the sake of knowing, let us also affirm it from a *disinterested* angle. There is nothing more "*useful*" for an era when man quite rightly seeks to increase his well-being, to secure it for all. The more human life is enriched with pleasures of every kind, the more "useful" it will be to point out this fissure to the utilitarianism in which we are immersed; a ray of hope and the possibility of another existence shines through this fissure and it is through it that we glimpse the possibility of another existence, less carnal, more imbued with truth, beauty, and goodness, for which the present existence would be but an embryonic and preparatory phase.[76]

I would sum up the preceding arguments in this way:

74. "Platon et Darwin" in *Annales de philosophie chrétienne* 28 (May 1893): 163 ff. [Eng. trans. *Plato and Darwin: A Philosophic Dialogue*, trans. William Gibson (London: Longmans, Green, & Co., 1899)].

75. "Souvenirs d'Assise" (*Revue blanche* of 15 Sept. 1902): 94. This essay was written in 1899. I have already insisted on the importance of making *judgments of quality, of value,* and on the consequences, in *Annales de philosophie chrétienne* 30 (June 1895): 252ff.

76. Ideas developed in *La Forme idéaliste du sentiment religieux,* Part 1, §3; Part 2, p. 81 and Appendix V.

Anglo-American pragmatism has not shown that the *true* can be reduced exclusively to the *useful*, any more than "action" can be to *inclination* alone. This pragmatism thus presents itself as a paradox diametrically opposed to exaggerated intellectualism.

It is important to maintain clearly the distinction between this paradoxical pragmatism and the affirmation of the "primacy of action" or that of the necessary union between speculation and experience (in all its forms, external and internal). If the Anglo-American pragmatists intend to say nothing else, they should at least agree more clearly about it.

It is indispensable when using the word *pragmatism* to explain precisely in what sense, and within what limits. It has become an ambiguous term; there are, alas! hardly any others in philosophy.

Notes

Appendix I. Pragmatism and Aesthetics

Aristippus asked Socrates about beauty. Socrates replied that "everything useful is good and beautiful relative to the use for which it is intended.—Then is a basket used for dung a beautiful thing?—Certainly, if it is suitably made for that use, otherwise no. . . . Socrates also said that the comfort of a house constitutes its true beauty."[1]

This is an early example of *aesthetic pragmatism.* Again we must recognize that the perfect proportion of means to an end truly constitutes for the mind a type of beauty. But who would dare say that beauty is only this?

Appendix II. Pragmatism and Morality

The scope of this little work does not permit me to treat the question from the moral point of view. Without acknowledging all shades of opinion, I refer to Fouillée's *Morale des idées-forces.* M. Fouillée has not made a special study of pragmatism, but nonetheless shows us what is true (verification of moral assertions by their good effects; the *good* considered as the supreme desire and persuasive factor) in moral pragmatism;[2] on the other hand, the rights of the intellect and of theoretical truth (psychological, sociological, etc. fundamentals of morality) are fully safeguarded.[3] "Prag-

1. *Mémorables,* L. III. Chap. VIII.

2. Alfred Fouillée, *Morale des idées forces* (Paris: Alcan, 1909). Cf. p. 382 and Part I, Book 3. The extraintellectual aspect of the moral conscience is set forth well by M. R. Berthelot in the final part of the articles noted on p. 188.

3. Fouillée, Introduction and Part I, Book 1.

matism limits itself to practical results without being concerned about the truth of principles," says M. Fouillée;[4] but if morality is not first truth, who then will sacrifice himself for it?

Appendix III. Notes on J.-J. Rousseau and Chateaubriand

I should recall the considerable influence that J.-J. Rousseau had on Kant.[5] And yet there is no doubt that Rousseau principally values the moral point of view:

"[S]kepticism is in no way painful for me," says the Savoyard Vicar after having noted the "contradictions" of the Gospels, "because it does not extend to the points essential to practice and because I am quite decided on the principles of all my duties. I serve God in the simplicity of my heart. I seek to know only what is important for my conduct. As for the dogmas which have an influence neither on actions nor on morality, and about which so many men torment themselves, I do not trouble myself about them at all. I regard all the particular religions as so many salutary institutions which prescribe in each country a uniform manner of honoring God by public worship. These religions can have their justifications in the climate, the government, the genius of the people, or some other local cause which makes one preferable to another according to the time and place. I believe them all to be right as long as one serves God suitably. The essential worship is that of the heart. God does not reject its homage, if it is sincere, in whatever form it is offered to Him."[6]

And the vicar explains how, in what spirit, he can say the Mass:

"Formerly, I said the Mass with the lightness with which one eventually treats the most serious things when one does them too often. But since adopting my new principles, I celebrate it with more veneration. I am filled with the majesty of the Supreme Being, with

4. Ibid., p. xxxvii.

5. Cf. note 15 at the end of Picavet's translation of the *Critique of Practical Reason.*

6. *Émile,* IV [Jean-Jacques Rousseau, *Emile; or, On Education,* trans. Allen Bloom (New York: Basic Books, 1979), 308].

His presence, and with the insufficiency of the human mind, which has so little conception of what relates to its Author. Bearing in mind that I bring to Him the prayers of the people in a prescribed form, I carefully follow the rites, I recite attentively, I take care never to omit either the least word or the least ceremony. When I approach the moment of consecration, I collect myself so as to perform it in the frame of mind that the Church and the grandeur of the sacrament demand. I try to annihilate my reason before the supreme intelligence. I say to myself: 'Who are you to measure infinite power?' I pronounce the sacramental words with respect, and I put into them all the faith in my power. Whatever may be the case in regard to this inconceivable mystery, I have no fear that I shall be punished on Judgment Day for having profaned it in my heart."[7]

How many "modernist" priests—and the best of them—would recognize their own sentiments here—they could have been and no doubt often were those of the worthy priests of Ammon-Ra or of Zeus!

Nevertheless, Rousseau indeed senses that there are limits to this conservative and ambiguous exegesis, and adds:

"So long as there remains some sound belief among men, one must not disturb peaceful souls or alarm the faith of simple people with difficulties which they cannot resolve and which upset them without enlightening them. But once everything is shaken, one ought to preserve the trunk at the expense of the branches. Consciences which are agitated, uncertain, almost extinguished, . . . need to be reinforced and awakened; and in order to put them back them back on the foundation of eternal truths, it is necessary to complete the job of ripping out the shaky pillars to which they think they are still attached."[8]

—Chateaubriand certainly adopts the pragmatic point of view in the *Génie du Christianisme,* which so strongly influenced our fathers' conscience and, indirectly, our own:

7. [Ibid., 309.]

8. [Ibid., 310.]

"[T]he Christian religion, of all the religions that ever existed, is the most poetic, the most humane, the most favorable to liberty and the arts and sciences. . . . [N]othing is more divine than its morality—nothing more lovely and more sublime than its tenets, its doctrine, and its worship; . . . it encourages genius, corrects the taste, develops the virtuous passions, imparts energy to the ideas, presents noble images to the writer, and perfect models to the artist. . . ."[9]

But he immediately adds: "Surely one great proof of its divine origin is that it will bear the test of the fullest and severest scrutiny of reason."[10]

It is obvious, however, that the first point of view is his own, he who wrote: "I have become Christian. I own that I have not yielded to any great supernatural illumination; my conviction has issued from the heart; I cried and I believed."[11]

Also, in his Appendices the author generally conceals intellectual considerations in order to insist on "The Harmonies of the Christian Religion with the Scenes of Nature and the Passions of the Human Heart."[12] And he concludes in the penultimate chapter:

"The Christian mysteries are the most sublime that can be; they are the archetypes of the system of man and of the world.

"The sacraments are moral laws, and present pictures of a highly poetical character.

"Faith is a force, charity a love, hope complete happiness. . . ."[13]

Here we are far from "intellectualism"!

—I have been asked why I have not spoken of the "pragmatism" of "Modernism's" precursors. It is because I never intended to treat this subject[14] since these thinkers claim to adhere to the "primacy"

9. Viscount de Chateaubriand, *Génie du Christianisme,* Part I, Book I, Chap. I [Eng. trans. *The Genius of Christianity,* trans. Charles I. White (Baltimore: John Murphy Company, 1856), 48–49].

10. [Ibid., 49.]

11. [First Preface of the French edition, quoted by Hébert.]

12. [*The Genius of Christianity,* Title of Book V of Part III.]

13. [Ibid., 664], Part IV, Book VI, Chap. XII.

14. Cf. A. Leclère, "Les initiateurs du modernisme," *Revue bleu* (26 June and 3 July 1909).

of inclinations and will, rather than to pragmatism itself. *Mitigated* pragmatism, yes; I have used this term (pp. 179, 180), while recognizing the ambiguity it creates with more radical forms whose dissemination must be hindered and stopped.

Nearly forty years ago, M. Brugère, a professor of dogma at Saint-Sulpice (Paris) and heir of the doctrine of Pascal, Newman,[15] Dechamps, Gratry, etc., taught the essentials of what has since been developed; but along with the "moral evidence of religious truths,"[16] he acknowledged scientific, physical, or *metaphysical*[17] evidence; along with the "propensity" (to believe), he acknowledged "*reason*."[18] Likewise, as we have seen, neither Blondel, nor Le Roy, or Laberthonnière, for example, contest the possibility and legitimacy of intellectual knowledge. Thus one must not include them in "pragmatism" proper.

Appendix IV. What Pragmatism Amounts to for M. Le Roy

"You ask me what, definitively, pragmatism amounts to? What remains of it in the end? —At least this:

First, experience is everywhere and always the essential verifying procedure, even in areas where one does not generally speak of it, as, for example, in mathematics.

Second, experience is as multiform as the facts that correspond with it and no principle is applicable indiscriminately to every case.

Third, the work of verification requires that one come to actual experience, to experience as practically lived, truly operative, a simple critical essay will never be enough and can never replace the practical testing of hypotheses.

Fourth, experience does not only mutually determine facts and theories; it develops, exercises, refines the mind little by little; it in-

15. Cf. p. 201, note 27.

16. *De verâ religione* (Paris: Jouby, 1873), p. 245, Appendix I: "De evidentiâ morali in veritatibus religiosis" and *De Ecclesiâ Christi* (Paris: Jouby, 1873), p. 319, Epilogue "De fide simplicium."

17. *De verâ religione,* p. 249.

18. Ibid., p. 69.

forms and expands reason in forcing clear-sighted intellect to transcend itself; in short, it constitutes a prolongation of biological evolution in a conscious and reflective form.

In the religious order especially, we cannot confine ourselves to our first instincts for judging; we are obliged to transform ourselves under the very influence of religious reality for the latter to become fully perceptible and verifiable. Undoubtedly the intellect must always be satisfied, but this depends on the intellect being gradually enlarged and modified by lived experience. Religious truth is possessed pragmatically more than speculatively because what is possessed in this name is an inspiring rather than representative principle, a principle of direction and of force that orients and moves one in the ways of increasing spiritual life.

After this you may now say that this is not pragmatism at all. It is a simple question of terminology! If that were the case, I would reply, in conclusion, by imitating one of Jules Lemaître's sayings: "This is not pragmatism? Then it is something else. I care little about the name of what I do."[19]

—Amusing witticism, we will reply, but not terribly serious. The key is to avoid allowing a false notion (insofar as exclusive) of truth to take root, under cover of an affirmation of the *necessity of experience* that all our forms of "philosophy of action" have long formulated. The key is to avoid letting an EQUIVOCATION linger which would render pointless the huge effort toward real truth currently at work in minds today—an equivocation that the Roman Catholic Church, to its credit, also does not want: it has proven this in condemning "Modernism" so rigorously.

Moreover, the criterion proposed by M. Le Roy: religious truth,

19. M. Le Roy's declaration is taken from the *Bulletin de la Société française de philosophie* 10 (July 1908). A very interesting overview of pragmatism, by M. Parodi, then discussion among MM. Parodi, Lalande, Berthelot, Le Roy, Laberthonnière, Blondel (by letter), etc. Also consult the summary of the discussions on pragmatism at the Heidelberg Congress (1908) between Messrs. Schiller, Royce, Armstrong, Jerusalem, Nelson, Itelson, etc.: *Revue de Métaphysique et de Morale* 16 (November 1908).

inspiring and directive principle, is *completely insufficient.* Would it allow, for example, M. Le Roy to choose between the pantheism of a Spinoza and the theism of a Fénelon? Obviously, not; it is, most often, man who sets the value of doctrine. On the other hand, does the high moral value of the teaching of a Guillaume Monod, who, like his disciples, sees it as inseparable from his claim to be Christ reincarnate,[20] justify this bizarre claim? Why then would there be two weights and two measures: one for ancient prophets and another for contemporary prophets? . . . Would the phenomenal success of Joan of Arc at Orléans and at Rouen guarantee the real existence of a Saint Catherine or a Saint Michael? . . . Why give credence to a system that confuses the varied aspects of these questions?

Appendix V. Origins of Pragmatism according to M. R. Berthelot

"After the unleashing of romanticism,[21] which sought to destroy utilitarian and mechanist doctrines and to subordinate idealism to itself, the most vigorous thinkers of Europe, in Germany, in France, in England—those returned or still faithful either to the spirit of rationalism, to that of utilitarianism, or that of mechanism—endeavored to interpret in this spirit results gleaned from the romantic movement. This spirit has not ceased to animate the majority of scientists and philosophers and to direct their efforts. *But a certain number of them, struck by the insufficiencies and the lacunae that rationalist or mechanistic interpretations still represent today, found themselves drawn back, most often without being aware of it, to a state of mind close to that of the romantics and, putting the very ideas they derived from utilitarian empiricism into the service of the romantic ideal, launched*

20. Cf. G. Revault d'Allonnes, *Psychologie d'une religion* (Paris: Alcan, 1908).

21. For the romantics (Novalis, Schlegel, Schelling, for example) life is "an indefinitely creative spontaneity, perpetually and arbitrarily projecting from the interior to the exterior a continually renewed multitude of unforeseeable forms"—there being organic forms, states of consciousness, or physico-chemical phenomena. M. Berthelot explains this point at length in the first part of his study.

these two unexpected allies against rationalism. Nietzsche was one of the first to do so, with an incomparable enthusiasm and tactlessness, and because of this his theory of knowledge reveals with striking clarity the essential tendencies of the pragmatist movement. Wherever it assumes defined forms, pragmatism reveals itself as a utilitarian romanticism; therein resides its clearest originality and no doubt also its secret vice and hidden weakness. . . ."

M. Berthelot excels at discovering and tracing the connections among systems, the impact made by great thinkers on this or that topic. But he is foremost in recognizing that the question is more complex and that many influences[22] other than those of *systems* (utilitarian or romantic) have worked on the authors of the various forms of pragmatism. The fact is that, especially for religious pragmatism, the experience of real life, the immense role in it played by feelings, the great rarity of intellectual demands (as trivial as they may be), more authentically explains the pragmatist tendency than the influence of *systems;* one borrows phrases, expressions from systems, one finds articulation and legitimation through them, but conviction comes from elsewhere. Perhaps he [Berthelot] will allow me to cite a personal fact? In 1893 I studied the development of Richard Wagner's religious thought; I did not take the idea of religious "symbolism" from his work, but finding it clearly and auspiciously formulated there, I used it in order to set out this liberating idea not widely held at the time and I even added a chapter entitled, "The Letter Kills, It Is the Spirit That Gives Life"[23] to a first version that appeared in the *Annales de philosophie chrétienne.*[24]

22. Note p. 403 (of the article cited on p. 188). Is not the ABC of Christian theology that there are "mysteries" that essentially surpass all created reason? Thus a Christian can never be precisely "intellectualist."

23. Published by Fischbacher (1895) as *Le Sentiment religieux dans l'oeuvre de R. Wagner.* Also see "L'Évolution sentimental de la pensée de R. Wagner," *Annales de philosophie de chrétienne* 24 n. s. (June 1896): 246–54.

24. *Annales de philosophie chrétienne* (June–July and August–September 1893).

Appendix VI (Cf. p. 174). The Social Pragmatism of M. Durkheim

It is interesting to compare Nietzsche's biological form of utilitarian pragmatism with the more mystical form that M. Durkheim proposes. For the latter, the something *superior* that we sense in moral obligation, in religious feelings, is the social element, which, in fact, is superior to the individual element. "I see in divinity," he says, "only society transfigured and imagined symbolically."[25] Everything would be explained by a *collective ideation* of men influencing, overexciting one another (an ideation whose laws are still only vaguely defined) and from which derive most of our social, moral, and religious myths. There is a great deal of truth in this *social* view, and I would not dream of contesting it, but I assert that progress, for man, consists of submitting this *social pragmatism* more and more to the control of the individual conscience[26] which purifies it of the innumerable exaggerations, aberrations, follies accumulated in it by "the collective ideation"; thus man passes from "morals" to (individual) "morality," from primitive and barbaric religions to the "worship of spirit and truth."

Whether it pertains, moreover, to private, social, or even cosmic utility, is only *a* point of view that does not authorize making *useful adaptation* the synonym of *truth*. W. James protests, for example, that the moth which deems the flame dangerous and flees from it has more of the truth than one which throws itself into it and is consumed by it.[27] Without a doubt, from the physical point of view, but could one, ought one not to hold that to die for and in beauty, or, as did the martyrs, for a conviction, is another, superior view of life?

25. Cf. *Bulletin de la Société française de philosophie* 6 (April 1906): 29. Also "De la définition des phénomènes religieux" in *L'Année sociologique* 2 (1897–1898). More clearly still in the preface to MM. Hubert and Mauss, *Mélanges d'histoire des religions* (Paris: Alcan, 1909), pp. xxxii and xxxiii.

26. Cf. our essay, *La Forme idéaliste du sentiment religieux*, Appendix VIII.

27. See p. 233.

Professor Hébert on Pragmatism

WILLIAM JAMES

Le pragmatisme et ses diverses formes anglo-américaines. Marcel Hébert. Paris: Librairie critique Émile Nourry. 1908. Pp. 105.

Professor Marcel Hébert is a singularly erudite and liberal thinker (a seceder, I believe, from the Catholic priesthood) and an uncommonly direct and clear writer. His book *Le Divin* is one of the ablest reviews of the general subject of religious philosophy which recent years have produced; and in the small volume the title of which is copied above he has, perhaps, taken more pains not to do injustice to pragmatism than any of its numerous critics. Yet the usual fatal misapprehension of its purposes vitiates his exposition and his critique. His pamphlet seems to me to form a worthy book, as it were, on which to hang one more attempt to tell the reader what the pragmatist account of truth really means.

M. Hébert takes it to mean what most people take it to mean, the doctrine, namely, that whatever proves subjectively expedient in the way of our thinking is "true" in the absolute and unrestricted sense of the word, whether it corresponds to any objective state of things outside of our thought or not. Assuming this to be the pragmatist thesis, M. Hébert opposes it at length. Thought that proves itself to be thus expedient may, indeed, have every *other* kind of value for the thinker, he says, but cognitive value, representative value, *valeur de connaissance proprement dite,* it has not; and when it does have a high degree of general-utility value, this is in every case derived from its previous value in the way of correctly representing independent objects that have an important influence on our lives. Only by thus

A retrieval from the *Journal of Philosophy, Psychology and Scientific Methods* for December 3, 1908 (vol. V, pp. 689–94) of a review of *Le Pragmatisme; étude de ses diverses formes anglo-américaines,* by Marcel Hébert (Paris: Librairie critique Émile Nourry, 1908, pp. 105). [James included this review in his *The Meaning of Truth* (New York: Longmans, Green, and Co., 1914), chap. 12, 230–45, with some small modifications. In the second edition of *Le pragmatisme* Hébert gives James's review in French, noting that James has reviewed his translation.]

representing things truly do we reap the useful fruits. But the fruits follow on the truth, they do not constitute it; and M. Hébert accuses pragmatism of telling us everything about truth except what it essentially is. He admits, indeed, that the world is so framed that when men have true ideas of realities, consequential utilities ensue in abundance; and no one of our critics, I think, has shown as concrete a sense of the variety of these utilities as he has; but he reiterates that, whereas such utilities are secondary, we insist on treating them as primary, and that the *connaissance objective* from which they draw all their being is something which we neglect, exclude, and destroy. The utilitarian value and the strictly cognitive value of our ideas may perfectly well harmonize, he says—and in the main he allows that they do harmonize—but they are not logically identical for that. He admits that subjective interests, desires, impulses have the active "primacy" in our intellectual life. Cognition awakens only at their spur, and follows their cues and aims; yet, when it is awakened, it is objective cognition proper and not merely another name for the impulsive tendencies themselves in the state of satisfaction. The owner of a picture ascribed to Corot gets uneasy when its authenticity is doubted. He looks up its origin and is reassured. But his uneasiness does not make the proposition false, any more than his relief makes the proposition true, that the actual Corot was the painter. Pragmatism, which according to M. Hébert, claims that our sentiments *make* truth and falsehood, would oblige us to conclude that our minds exert no genuinely cognitive function whatever.

This subjectivist interpretation of our position seems to follow from my having happened to write (without supposing it necessary to explain that I was treating of cognition solely on its subjective side) that in the long run the true is the expedient in the way of our thinking, much as the good is the expedient in the way of our behavior! Having previously written that truth means "agreement with reality" and insisted that the chief part of the expediency of any one opinion is its agreement with the rest of acknowledged truth,

I apprehended no exclusively subjectivistic reading of my meaning. My mind was so filled with the notion of objective *reference* that I never dreamed that my hearers would let go of it; and the very last accusation I expected was that in speaking of ideas and their satisfactions, I was denying realities outside. My only wonder now is that critics should have found so silly a personage as I must have seemed in their eyes, worthy of explicit refutation.

The object, for me, is just as much one part of reality as the idea is another part. The truth of the idea is one relation of it to the reality, just as its date and its place are other relations. All three relations *consist* of intervening parts of the universe which can in every particular case be assigned and catalogued, and which differ in every instance of truth, just as they differ with every date and place.

The pragmatist thesis, as Dr. Schiller and I hold it—I prefer to let Professor Dewey speak for himself in these pages—is that the relation called "truth" is thus concretely definable. Ours is the only articulate attempt in the field to say positively what truth actually *consists of*. Our denouncers have literally nothing to oppose to it as an alternative. For them, when an idea is true, it *is* true, and there the matter terminates, the word "true" being indefinable. The relation of the true idea to its object, being, as they think, unique, it can be expressed in terms of nothing else, and needs only to be named for any one to recognize and understand it. Moreover it is invariable and universal, the same in every single instance of truth, however diverse the ideas, the realities, and the other relations between them may be.

Our pragmatist view, on the contrary, is that the truth-relation is a definitely experiencable relation, and therefore describable as well as namable; that it is not unique in kind, and neither invariable nor universal. The relation to its object that makes an idea true in any given instance, is, we say, embodied in intermediate details of reality which lead towards the object, which vary in every instance, and which in every instance can be concretely traced. The chain of workings which an opinion sets up *is* the opinion's truth, falsehood, or irrelevancy, as the case may be. Every idea that a man has works some consequences in him, in the shape either of bodily actions or of other ideas. Through these consequences the man's relations to surrounding realities are modified. He is carried nearer to some of them and farther from others, and gets now the feeling that the idea has worked satisfactorily, now that it has not. The idea has put him into touch with something that fulfils its intent, or it has not.

This something is the *man's object,* primarily. Since the only realities we can talk about are such *objects-believed-in,* the pragmatist, whenever he says "reality," means in the first instance what may count for the man himself as a reality, what he believes at the moment to be such. Sometimes the reality is a concrete sensible presence. The idea, for example, may be that a certain door opens into a room where a glass of beer may be bought. If opening the door leads to the actual sight and taste of the beer, the man calls the idea true. Or his idea may be that of an abstract relation, say of that between the sides and the hypothenuse of a triangle, such a relation being, of course, a reality quite as much as a glass of beer is. If the thought of such a relation leads him to draw auxiliary lines and compare the figures they make, he may at last, perceiving one equality after another, *see* the relation thought of, by a vision quite as particular and direct as was the taste of the beer. If he does so, he calls *that* idea, also, true. His idea has, in each case, brought him into closer touch with a reality felt at the moment to verify just that idea. Each reality verifies and validates its own idea exclusively; and in each case the verification consists in the satisfactorily-ending consequences, mental or physical, which the idea was able to set up. These "workings" differ in every single instance, they never transcend experience, they consist of particulars, mental or sensible, and they admit of concrete description in every individual case. Pragmatists are unable to see what you can possibly *mean* by calling an idea true, unless you mean that between it as a *terminus a quo* in some one's mind and some particular reality as a *terminus ad quem,* such concrete workings do or may intervene. Their direction constitutes the idea's reference to that reality, their satisfactoriness constitutes its adaptation thereto, and the two things together constitute the "truth" of the idea for its possessor. Without such intermediating portions of concretely real experience the pragmatist sees no materials out of which the adaptive relation called truth can be built up.

The anti-pragmatist view is that the workings are but evidences of the truth's previous inherent presence in the idea, and that you can wipe the very possibility of them out of existence and still leave the truth of the idea as solid as ever. But surely this is not a counter-theory of truth to ours. It is the renunciation of all articulate theory. It is but a claim to the right to *call* certain ideas true *anyhow;* and this is what I meant above by saying that the anti-pragmatists offer us no real alternative, and that our account is literally the only positive theory extant. What meaning indeed, can an idea's truth have save its power of adapting us either mentally or physically to a reality?

How comes it, then, that our critics so uniformly accuse us of subjectivism, of denying the reality's existence? It comes, I think, from the necessary predominance of subjective language in our analysis. However independent and ejective realities may be, we can talk about them, in framing our accounts of truth, only as so many objects believed-in. But the process of experience leads men so continually to supercede their older objects by newer ones, which they find it more satisfactory to believe in, that the notion of an absolute reality inevitably arises as a *Grenzbegriff,* equivalent to that of an object that shall never be superceded, and belief in which shall be *endgültig.* Cognitively we thus live under a sort of rule of three: as our private concepts represent the sense-objects to which they lead us, these being public realities independent of the individual, so these sense-realities may, in turn, represent realities of a hypersensible order, electrons, mind-stuff, God, or what not, existing independently of all human thinkers. The notion of such final realities, knowledge of which would be absolute truth, is an outgrowth of our cognitive experience from which neither pragmatists nor anti-pragmatists can escape. It forms an inevitable regulative postulate in everybody's thinking. The belief in it is the most abundantly verified and validated of all beliefs, the last to suffer doubt. The difference is that our critics use this belief as their sole paradigm, and treat anyone who talks of human realities as if he thought the notion of reality "in itself" illegitimate. Meanwhile, reality-in-itself, so far as by them *talked of,* is only a human object; they postulate it just as we postulate it; and if we are subjectivists they are so no less. Realities in themselves can be there *for* anyone, whether pragmatist or anti-pragmatist, only by being believed; they are believed only by their notions appearing true; and their notions appear true only because they work satisfactorily. Satisfactorily, moreover, for the particular thinker's purpose. There is no idea which is *the* true idea, of anything. Whose is *the* true idea of the absolute? Or to take M. Hébert's example, what is *the* true idea of a picture which you possess? It is the idea that most satisfactorily meets your present interest. The interest may be in the picture's place, its age, its "tone," its subject, its dimensions, its authorship, its price, its merit, or what not. If its authorship by Corot have been doubted, what will satisfy your proprietary interest will be to have it confirmed; but, if you have a normal human mind, merely calling it a Corot will not satisfy other demands of your mind at the same time. For them to be satisfied, what you learn of the picture must make smooth connection with what you know of the system of reality in which the actual Corot played his part. M. Hébert accuses us of holding that the proprietary satisfactions are all-sufficient to make the belief true, and that, so far as we are concerned, no actual Corot need ever have existed. Why should we be thus cut off from the more general and intellectual satisfactions, I know not; but whatever the satisfactions may be, intellectual or proprietary, they belong to the subjective side of the truth-relation. They found our beliefs; our beliefs are in realities; if no realities are there, the beliefs are false; but if realities are there, how can they ever be *known* without first being *believed;* or how *believed* except by our first having ideas of them that work satisfactorily, pragmatists find it hard to imagine. They also find it impossible to imagine what makes the anti-pragmatists' dogmatic "ipse dixit" assurance of reality more credible than the pragmatists' conviction based on concrete verifications. M. Hébert will probably agree to this, when put this way, so I do not see our inferiority to him in the matter of *connaissance proprement dite.*

Some readers will say that, although *I* may possibly believe in realities beyond our ideas, Dr. Schiller, at any rate, does not. This is a great misunderstanding, for Schiller's doctrine and mine are identical, only our expositions follow different directions. He starts from the subjective pole of the chain, the individual with his beliefs, as the more concrete and immediately given phenomenon. "An individual claims his belief to be true," Schiller says, "but what does he mean by true? And how does he establish the claim?" With these questions we embark on a psychological inquiry. To be true, it appears, means *for that individual,* to work satisfactorily for him; and the working and the satisfaction, since they vary from case to case, admit of no universal description. What works is true and represents a reality, for the individual for whom it works. If he is infallible, the reality is "really" there; if mistaken it is not there, or not there as he thinks it. We all *believe,* when our ideas work satisfactorily; but we don't yet know who of us is infallible. Schiller, remaining with the fallible individual, and treating only of reality-for-him, seems to many of his readers to ignore reality-in-itself altogether. But that is because he seeks only to tell us how truths are attained, not what the content of those truths, when attained, shall be. It may be that the truest of all beliefs shall be that in trans-subjective realities. It certainly *seems* the truest, for no rival belief is as voluminously satisfactory, and it is probably Dr. Schiller's own belief; but he is not required, for his immediate purpose, to profess it. Still less is he obliged to assume it in advance as the basis of his discussion.

I, however, warned by the ways of critics, adopt different tactics. I start from the object-pole of the idea-reality chain and follow it in the opposite direction from Schiller's. Anticipating the results of the general truth-processes of mankind, I begin with the abstract notion of a reality. I postulate it, and ask on my own account, *I vouching for this reality,* what would make anyone else's idea of it true for me as well as for him. But I find no different answer from that which Schiller gives. If the other man's idea leads him, not only to believe that the reality is there, but to use it as the reality's temporary substitute, by letting it evoke adaptive thoughts and acts similar to those which the reality itself would provoke, then it is true in the only intelligible sense, true through its particular consequences, and true for me as well as for the man. The moth who thinks of a flame as dangerous thinks of it more truly than the moth who only feels its beauty. The workings of such a moth's idea prove more satisfactory in the long run.

My account is more of a logical definition; Schiller's is more of a psychological description. Both treat an absolutely identical matter of experience, only they traverse it in opposite ways.

Possibly these explanations may satisfy M. Hébert, whose little book, apart from the false accusation of subjectivism, gives a fairly instructive account of the pragmatist epistemology.

Author's Reply

It was never my intention to accuse Mr. William James of pure "subjectivism," as the course of my argument (directed primarily against a strict pragmatism rather than against the personal interpretation of the renowned psychologist) led him to believe. I have even said and repeated the contrary,[1] at the same time confessing that I did not see *how* Mr. W. James succeeded in preserving objective reality.

1. See pp. 151, 152, 154, 156, 179. For Mr. Schiller, cf. p. 163 note 10.

Part II: Pragmatism: Its Various Forms

Mr. James has kindly given us a very interesting exposition of this subject. I am not completely won over. Mr. James has created a highly mitigated pragmatism which scarcely asserts more than our various "philosophies of action," namely, that real life, with its practical requirements, in every aspect transcends our strictly *intellectual* resources. However, he seems to me to avoid the principal difficulty by calling into his theory, under the guise of the expressions *reality*, and *experience* (considered as *givens* beyond all discussion), *precisely what we call "intuition" and knowledge properly so called.* I will explain my thought in the following two sections.

1

For me, "reality" is not an object of *belief* in the sense that Mr. James gives the word, namely, an initially hypothetical, problematic belief that becomes certain only at the end of a great deal of trial and error through which one finds that said belief always works.[2]

Certainly I do not in any way separate this belief from experience and do not take it as *a priori*. But I believe it to be accompanied from the outset by an unshakable certitude.

Theoretically, intellectually, it is possible to set two states of mind, problematic belief verifiable by practice, and certain belief derived from intuition, in opposition, like two hypotheses. But, *in fact*, the impossibility of doubting the existence of reality (internal or external), an impossibility already formulated so strongly by Pascal,[3] allows us neither to establish these *two* hypotheses, nor to *choose* between them.

2. This recalls the role attributed to *experiences* by Descartes (sixth part of the *Discourse on Method*): the mind constructs, with its simple ideas, explanations,—then it verifies, by experiences, whether the explanatory construction fits reality.

3. "[S]peaking in good faith and sincerely, we cannot doubt natural principles. . . . I lay it down as a fact that there never has been a real complete sceptic. Nature sustains our feeble reason, and prevents it raving to this extent. . . ." Blaise Pascal, *Pensées* [Eng. trans. W. F. Trotter (New York: Modern Library, 1941), #434, pp. 140–41]. Is this not, it will be said, the "voluntarism" of Mr. Royce (p. 178)? No, for Mr. Royce supposes that one doubts intellectually and that the will virtually causes doubt to cease; Pascal, on the contrary, holds fundamentally that the mind does not doubt.

Analogical induction and hypothesis intervene when it is a question of clarifying *the nature* of the real. Still this is not completely correct. We do not have the *intuition* of an abstract *existence;* we experience a resistance, an energy analogous to our own; it is when we wish to go beyond the limits of our experience, to attempt to get to know more about it, that we turn to hypotheses.

If sensation were only a subjective state of mind, our consciousness would be, in essence, *solipsist.* To acknowledge the nonsolipsism of consciousness is to recognize that sensation, beyond personal impression, shows us something of reality, that it is *intuition,* assuredly inadequate, but accompanied by an immediate certitude, a direct belief without the intervention of a verifiable hypothesis. This belief is not true *because* it works in practice; it works in practice because it corresponds to an intuition.

2

Those who accuse pragmatists of not admitting "reality" will at first have grounds to be shocked: Mr. James offers them two realities instead of one: a phenomenal reality, object of experience, seconded by a reality that could be called *noumenal,* since it is the object of belief alone, since it is simply "postulated."

Upon reflection, this superabundance will appear to them of doubtful quality. Either the phenomenon allows us to *know* nothing of this kind of noumenon so that the relation between the two terms is entirely hypothetical—or the phenomenon is the imperfect, inadequate, but real *knowledge* of the noumenon, and, that being the case, there is room in the intellect for a *value of knowledge properly so called* and not only for practical values (satisfactions, adaptation for action).

These are the *types of knowledge* that constitute the *data of intuition* in our consciousness; data that we can and must analyze and not simply take outright, synthetically, as do the pragmatists without really realizing it, putting everything together and confusing everything in a single word: *reality.* We must analyze these "*immediate data of consciousness*"; in them we will find the experience [sentiment] of what is, at heart, our activity, always unrivaled by, unexhausted by the phenomena through which this activity is expressed (hence the impossibility of reducing the *self* to a simple series of phenomena); in them we will find the living duration, the living *fieri,* the living extension;—from which abstract or idealized representations of unity, identity, substance, time, space will later proceed—and this irreducible experience of the infinite, the perfect, the absolute,[4] unique in its kind, which does not give us the means of defining intellectually *what is,* in this regard, the fundamental activity from which all things come, but allows us to know, at least, *what it is not* (and this is already a real degree of *knowledge*). Besides, inductions based on these relatively limited analogies verified by experience are far from providing us with *only* practical adaptations. Were they no more than probable, they would not be any less of the order of theoretical knowledge. And our certainty that there exist other minds, other human consciousnesses similar to our own, is this not then merely a probability, a simple practical adaptation? Is it not the *knowledge of what is*? This is an excellent example allowing us to see clearly that this belief is not true because it adapts us, but that it usefully adapts us because it represents reality truly, if only inadequately.

Thus there is a *practical* value of truth and a *knowledge* value; the two aspects cannot not be confused. They harmonize admirably in "*experience.*"[5]

I do not in any way dispute that there remains a great deal of imperfection, of relativity, in our way of conceiving individuals and things. But as "relative" as is the manner in which we perceive *expanse,* for example, we know in it—if inadequately but really—a manner of being that does not allow us to attribute to what we call

4. Cf. our Essay, *Le Divin,* chap. X §V and *La "forme idéaliste" du sentiment religieux,* first part, pp. 55ff; second part, pp. 94ff.

5. As M. Le Roy has shown well; cf. Appendix IV.

"material" an act that would involve interior unity: unity that involves the act of "comparison," for example, or of "recognition" in memory. Thus we have a certain *intuition*—inadequate but real, I repeat this intentionally—of this manner of being.

Likewise, I agree that the separation of beings is "relative" and conceals a kind of *monism,* or, if one prefers, a basic *continuum,*[6] but *separation* is one thing and the *distinction* of beings another: the former is relative to the needs of action, it constitutes a utilitarian approach, the latter has objective grounds that any monism must preserve lest it end in a completely abstract unity that the pragmatists are right to detest.

In sum, the pragmatists concede too much or too little to us: *too much,* in the sense that to avoid foundering in subjectivism or solipcism, they deviate from systematic rigor and admit at least *a* "knowledge": that of the *existence* of objective reality (*knowledge* and not simply practical adaptation, or useful illusion); *too little,* because this knowledge is the vaguest, the emptiest, and most unserviceable of categories if it does not include some *knowledge* (through intuition or analogy) of the objective nature of this reality.

These lines were written when I read Mr. James's recent work: *A Pluralistic Universe.* The author concedes a certain degree of *theoretical knowledge,* but "only [of] the outer surface of reality."[7]

This knowledge seems to me to be limited to the scientific phenomenal knowledge which gives us the relations of coexistence and succession; it is, in this sense that it is "enormous in extent"; but "does not penetrate a millimeter into the solid dimension"[8] (the intimate nature of beings).

Yes and no. As we have explained above (pp. 155, 156, 163, 184) it is no less true that therein lies a gap in the paradox of *not-knowing,*

6. Cf. *La "forme idéaliste" et le sentiment religieux,* Part 2, p. 98.

7. [William James, *A Pluralistic Universe* (1909) in *Essays in Radical Empiricism and A Pluralistic Universe* (Gloucester, Mass.: Peter Smith, 1967)] Lecture VI, 250.

8. [Idem.]

a gap that the author widens further in also considering as theoretical, aesthetic impressions revealing a glorious world of *values:*[9] "but value is, in a sense, an objective quality that we perceive," it is not, as he says, that the essence of this quality is its relation with the will, but that it determines *one* or *another* kind of relation with our will.

What we claim in the name of intuition, Mr. James concedes to us under the name of "perception." His bêtes noires are "abstract," utterly intellectual concepts, by whose aid alone certain metaphysicians would claim to fathom every essence, dissipate every mystery, construct every reality.

Thus there is between us little more than a disagreement about words: do we say: perception or intuition?—do we call intelligence, intellectual things,[10] intuition, perception? We could also debate the varying degrees of wealth contained in the data of perception. But what remains then of *pragmatism* in its provoking originality?

9. Ibid., Notes, pp. 340–42.

10. Instead of reserving these terms for abstract concepts and their handling. Three-quarters of all misunderstandings come from such terminological equivocation.

Part III Review of Hébert's *Le Pragmatisme*

1

Pragmatism

EUGÈNE MÉNÉGOZ

The word *pragmatism* has been coined only recently. It entered philosophy to designate a tendency to judge a doctrine's truth or value based on its outcomes in practical life. In the last century, the adjective *pragmatic* was already in use in Germany, but in another sense. It was freely applied to an author's way of writing; one spoke of a *pragmatic style* to designate an energetic, vivid, concrete, gripping style, the opposite of abstract or colorless language.

We are grateful to M. Marcel Hébert for a brief work that provides an illuminating survey of the different meanings certain French and foreign philosophers and theologians attach to the term pragmatism.[1] His short book is a manual that will serve as guide, not only for young people studying philosophy, but for all educated people interested in intellectual matters, and for older scholars who until now have not had opportunity to familiarize

[Appeared originally in *Annales de bibliographie théologique* (1908); reprinted in Eugène Ménégoz, *Publications diverses sur le fidéisme et son application à l'enseignement chrétien traditionnel*, 2 vols. (Paris: Fischbacher, 1909), 2.494–99.]

1. Marcel Hébert, *Le Pragmatisme. Étude de ses diverses formes anglo-américaines, françaises et italiennes, et sa valeur religieuse* (Paris: Émile Nourry, 1908).

themselves with this new term and with the theory or method it represents.

M. Hébert combines criticism with exposition, and this criticism, generally speaking, appears most judicious. One feels the author is at once a thinker well versed in the history of philosophy, and a dialectician who probes systems in depth. He is also a theologian; but I like him better as a philosopher; in his writing, we get to know the philosopher above all.

His book is devoted to the pragmatism of Messrs. Peirce, William James, F. C. S. Schiller, Le Roy, Poincaré, and Bergson. The author investigates the origins of pragmatist philosophy, going back to the Scholastics and to the Greek philosophers. He outlines modern tendencies related to pragmatism, such as moralism, symbolism, fideism. While paying respect to these multiple efforts of modern thought and the elements of truth they have highlighted, he nonetheless judges insufficient the philosophical conception proposed by pragmatism's varied systems.

M. Hébert takes on the very principle of this movement. He does not allow that the useful can be made the criterion of truth. A doctrine is not necessarily true because it is useful. The ideas of usefulness and truth do not overlap, do not derive from one another. They belong to two spheres of a different order; they cannot be interchanged. The true belongs only to reason; it must justify itself for our thought.

In this regard, M. Hébert also examines the capital role that Ritschl and his disciples have made value judgment play in theology, and he mentions the French theologians who have followed in his path. Hébert may not, however, have sufficiently appreciated what separates an Auguste Sabatier from the head of the modern German School, not only in nuances, but in the very conception of religion.

What pleases us in M. Hébert's critique is the energy and talent with which he claims reason's supremacy in philosophy, and the perceptiveness with which he unveils the pragmatist philosophers' error with regard to the principle of knowledge. Pages of his work are remarkable for their incisive and luminous criticism. Philosophers and theologians will do well to take them seriously.

Nevertheless, I am not completely won over by his way of thinking. I see in pragmatism an element of truth that M. Hébert seems to have misunderstood as a result of this movement's excessive exaggerations and generalizations.

At the root of pragmatism lies a correct observation: that truth performs its work in the service of good, and error in the service of harm. A good action, wherever it may be, authorizes us to conclude that it is the fruit of a true idea; and a bad action reveals a bad thought. It is also certain that the *self* always acts in its personal unity. There is no watertight compartment separating the faculties of the soul. They work simultaneously and exercise a permanent and reciprocal action on one another. This is a well-established psychological fact.

The pragmatists recognize this absolutely. But it is a long way from this to the conclusion that when a person performs a good and useful action, all the doctrines that he professes are right and true. And the pragmatists' error lies precisely in drawing this conclusion, if not rigorously, at least in accordance with the general spirit of their principles. This is what M. Hébert has proven so well.

Only he was not able to show how the correct idea that serves as point of departure for these philosophers' false reasoning. Certainly, a doctrine is not true as a whole, because he who professes it performs a good action, but a person performs a good action in allowing himself to be directed by the elements of truth that his beliefs contain, however erroneous they may be.

Let us take an example. The ancient Romans led a relatively moral life as long as they sincerely worshipped Jupiter, Mars, Neptune, Venus, Minerva; but corruption set in when they lost faith in their mythological divinities. If one wished to apply the pragmatist theory to this historical fact, one would have to conclude that the pagan religion was true up until the period of decadence and that, afterward, this same religion was false. The conclusion would follow the principle's logic. However, the pragmatists refrain from drawing it. That should alert them to their error.

Moreover, M. Hébert must concede that in the Romans' ancient convictions there was a power of truth acting on their will in the service of the good, and that, consequently, their belief was not absolutely false when they worshipped Jupiter or idols of stone and wood. This is what Saint Paul clearly saw when he called the idolaters of Athens "religious," and when he wrote to the Romans that God has inscribed his law in the hearts of pagans (Acts 17.23; Rom. 1.19; 2.15). This is an example of the immediate and permanent action that God's spirit works in the conscience of each man, of the internal testimony of the Holy Spirit.

Jesus recognized this fact when he praised the faith of the Canaanite woman and the Roman centurion who entrusted themselves to him although, at that time, they still likely worshipped their national gods. Jesus was not a pragmatist: while admiring the faith of these pagans, he nevertheless did not dream of proclaiming the truth of their religion. On the other hand, he was manifestly fideist, for he made salvation depend on an interior decision, a movement of the heart, of religious faith, and not the correctness of beliefs.

I would introduce here an observation regarding the term "*fideism*." The word *solafideistae* can be found in our forerunners' arguments to designate theologians who teach salvation by faith alone: *sola fide*.[2] More recently, some Catholic theologians, seeing some sincere Christians blindly accepting the doctrine of the Church, *bona fide*, without stopping to examine it, have called them *fideists*. But the latter have in no way accepted this designation, which implies criticism: the reproach of credulity.

This *fideism*, or indeed this *credulism* has not given rise to any theology, any doctrinal system; it is supported neither by the pope, nor by the modernists, nor by any noted theologian. There is no Catholic Fideist School. The word *fideism*—that the pope, in the encyclical *Pascendi dominici gregis*, seems to have borrowed from Protestant theologians—has never enjoyed currency in official Catholic theology.

It was so little used when I availed myself of it for the first time in 1879, in my *Réflexions sur l'Évangile du salut*, that I was in complete ignorance of its existence and believed to have coined it. I have since assured myself that, at that time, French and German Protestant theologians were likewise unaware of its sporadic use by a few scattered Catholic writers. It can be said that the term *fideism* was *res nullius*. Thus we are perfectly authorized in applying this designation to our modern evangelical theology which teaches salvation by faith, independently of beliefs.

M. Hébert mentions the religious symbolism of M. Auguste Sabatier, and he notes the internal relation, the spiritual affinity between *symbolism*, which expresses the formal principle of modern Protestant theology, and *fideism*, which formulates its material principle. He willingly accepts the term *symbolo-fidéisme* to

2. *Evangelische Kirchenzeitung* 24 (1903), col. 571.

designate this tendency. According to him, it approximates pragmatism to the degree that it accentuates *knowledge*.

We must thank M. Hébert for having so clearly drawn attention to the specific value of the intellectual factor, the role of thought, of doctrine, in its religious and moral action, and for having shown the danger of making truth depend upon utility and thought upon action.

Bibliography

A comprehensive bibliography of Marcel Hébert's writings is given in Albert Houtin, *Un prêtre symboliste. Marcel Hébert (1851–1916)* (Paris: F. Rieder, 1925), pages 319–46. Here entries will be confined to a listing of Hébert's books, the articles, and reviews that appeared in the *Annales de philosophie chrétienne* plus others that have a bearing on Modernism, and book reviews of works by those who were involved in the modernist crisis. Hébert also published extensively in newspapers; for those articles the reader may consult Houtin.

Books

1894. *Le sentiment religieux dans l'oeuvre de Richard Wagner.* Paris: Fischbacher. German trans., *Das religiöse Gefühl im Werke Richard Wagners: Jesus von Nazareth. Tetralogie. Tristan und Isolde, Parsifal.* Munich and Leipzig: August Schupp, 1895.

1905. *L'évolution de la Foi catholique.* Paris: Félix Alcan.

1906. *Le Divin. Expériences et hypotheses.* Paris: Félix Alcan.

1908. *Le pragmatisme. Étude de ses diverses formes anglo-américaines, françaises et italiennes et de sa valeur religieuse.* Paris: Nourry, 1908. 2nd ed. 1909.

1914. *Jeanne d'Arc a-t-elle abjuré?* Preceded by *Jeanne d'Arc et ses voix* and *Jeanne d'Arc et les Fées.* Paris: Nourry.

Booklets

1893. *Platon et Darwin. Dialogue philosophique.* Bar-Le-Duc: Imprimierie de l'Oeuvre de Saint-Paul. Eng. trans. *Plato and Darwin, a Philosophic Dialogue.* Translated by William Gibson. London: Longmans, 1899.

1894. *Tétralogie. Tristan et Iseult. Parsifal. Trois moments de la pensée de Richard Wagner.* Paris: Fischbacher.

1899. *Souvenirs d'Assise.* Paris: Imprimierie Bour. Reprinted, Paris: Éditions de la Revue blanche, 1902.

1904. *Comment M. Loisy interprète les dogmes catholiques*. Brusells: Bibliothèque de la propaganda, No. XXV and XXVII).
1905. *Résumé des leçons sur la crise religieuse au début du XXe siècle*. Brusells: Imprimiere Rousche.
1906. *Résumé des leçons sur les equivoques et les malentendus dans la manière de poser le problème religieux*. Brusells: Imprimiere Rouche.

Articles

Annales de philosophie chrétienne

1886 (Jan.). "Thomisme et Kantisme," 364–84.
1886 (Feb.). "Le Darwinisme," review of Mathias Duval, *Leçons professéees à l'École d'Anthropologie*, 487–94.
1886 (July). "Connaissance et certitude," 399–416.
1887 (April). "Du rôle direct de la volunté dans la certitude rationnelle," 54–69.
1887 (Dec.). "Jugements analytiques et synthétiques. Réponse au R. P. O'Mahony," 259–62.
1888 (Feb.) Review of P. Klein, *Le Pape* and Albert Gaudry, *Les ancêtres de nos animaux dans les temps géologiques*, 477–81.
1891 (Feb.). "Métaphysique de l'inconscient dans la doctrine de Schopenhauer," 401–29.
1891 (Nov.–Dec.). "I'dée de Dieu dans les dialogues philosophiques de Voltaire et de M. Renan," 185–205 and 248–64.
1892 (March). "I'dée de Dieu dans le nouveau volume de M. Renan," 595–97.
1892 (May). Reviews of J. Bourdeau, *Le socialisme allemande et le nihilisme russe* and J. Jaurès, *De primis socialisme germanici lineamentis apud Lutherum, Kant, Fichte et Hegel*, 186–90.
1893 (Jan.). "Une conférence de M. Charles Secrétan," 387–96.
1893 (Feb.). Reviews of Henry Joly, *Le socialisme chrétien*; Charles Secrétan, *Études sociales*; Bernard Lavergne, *L'évolution sociale*; and B. Malon, *Précis historique, théoretique et pratique du socialisme*, 484–89.
1893 (May). "Platon et Darwin," 157–74.
1893 (May). Reviews of Paul Leroy-Beaulieu, *Le collectivisme*; Eugène Richter, *Où mene le socialisme*; and Jules Lemaître, *Les Rois*, 189–92.
1893 (June–Oct.) "Trois moments de la pensée de Wagner," 235–48, 335–63; 411–29, 88–91.

1894. "Art et philosophie," 157–62.
1895 (Feb.). Reviews of E. Boirac, *L'idée du phénomène*; and Jean Izoulet, *La cité moderne*, 487–99.
1895 (March). "Science et religion," 570–76.
1895 (March). Review of J. Crépieux-Jamin, *L'écriture et le caractère*, 577.
1895 (June). "L'Union pour l'action morale de M. Paul Desjardins," 242–60.
1896 (June). "L'évolution sentimentale de la pensée de R. Wagner," 246–54.
1900 (May). "Lorsque sera venu le Prafait"

Articles in Other Reviews

"Souvenirs d'Assise." *Revue blanche* 29 (1903): 81–95.
"La Faillite du catholicisme despotique." *Revue blanche* 30 (March 1903): 439–57.
"La Dernière Idole. Étude sur la 'personalité divine.'" *Revue de Métaphysique et de Morale* 10 (July 1902): 397–408.
"Anonyme ou polyonyme. Seconde étude sur la 'personalité divine." *Revue de Métaphysique et de Morale* 11 (March 1903): 231–47.

Reviews of Books by Others Involved in the Modernist Crisis

Review of Albert Houtin, *La Question biblique chez les catholiques de France au XIXe siècle*, 2nd ed. *Revue de Belgique* 104 (1903): 193–209.
Reviews of Alfred Loisy, *Autour d'un petit livre; Le Discours sur la Montagne*; and *Le Quatrième évangile*. *Revue de Belgique* 105 (1903): 292–300.
Reviews of Albert Houtin, *La Question biblique chez les catholiques de France au XIXe siècle* and *L'Americanisme*. *Revue de Belgique* 106 (1904): 178–80.
Review of Joseph Turmel, *Histoire de la théologie positive depuis l'origine jusqu'au concile de Trente*. *Revue de Belgique* 108 (1904): 89–90.
Review of Hippolyte Delehaye, *Les légendes hagiographiques*. *Revue de l'Université de Bruxelles* 11 (1905–1906): 139–49.
Review of Albert Houtin, *La Question biblique au XXe siècle*. *Revue de l'Université de Bruxelles* 11 (1905–1906): 725–77.
Reviews of Albert Leclère, *Pragmatisme, modernisme, protestantisme*; Paul Sabatier, *Les Modernistes*; and George Tyrrell, *Suis-je catholique*

and *Christianity at the Cross-Roads. Revue de l'Université de Bruxelles* 15 (1909–1910): 387–89.

Review of George Tyrrell, *Le Christianisme à la croisée des chemins. Revue de l'Université de Bruxelles* 16 (1910–1911): 497–98.

Reviews of Alfred Loisy, *Jésus et la tradition évangélique* and *A propos d'histoire des religions. Revue de l'Université de Bruxelles* 16 (1910–1911): 671–72.

Review of Alfred Loisy, *Leçon d'ouverture; La religion d'Israël. Revue d'histoire et de littérature religieuses,* n.s., 1 (1910): 69 and 278–79.

Review of Friedrich von Hügel, *Eternal Life. Revue d'histoire et de littérature religieuses,* n.s., 5 (1910): 185–86.

Review of Alfred Loisy, *Guerre et religion. Coenobium* (April–May, 1915): 99ff.

Review of Alfred Loisy, *Guerre et religion,* 2nd. ed. *Coenobium* (Oct.–Dec. 1915): 130–31.

Review of Alfred Loisy, *L'Épître aux Galates. Coenobium* (Jan.–Feb. 1916).

Index

accidents, 36, 40, 42
action, primacy of, 173, 207, 216
Aeterni Patris, 7, 27–28
agent intellect, 8, 32, 33
agnosticism, 17, 18, 23, 67
analogy, 34, 41, 81, 85, 96–97, 100–102, 158–59, 202n, 203, 236–37
Annales de philosophie chrétienne, 3n, 8, 9–10, 224, 247–48
Anselm, St., 74
Aristotle, 29, 183, 194
Arius, 121
Athanasius, St., 121–22
atheism, 182

Barrès, Maurice, 203
Bacon, Francis, 176n, 188
Bautain, Louis, 80, 87, 123, 199
belief, and doubt, 134–43; religious belief, 10, 13, 23, 159; and symbols, 203–15; usefulness of, 152–54, 236. *See also* fideism
Bergson, Henri, 4n, 155n, 163, 190, 192, 242
Berkeley, George, 32, 137n, 146n, 170
Berthelot, René, 188, 217n, 222n, 223–24
Blondel, Maurice, 2, 3, 4, 7, 16, 173n, 190–91, 221, 222n
Bonnetty, Augustin, 80, 87, 123
Bourdeau, J., 23, 212n
Bouyssonie, A., 90n
Brunetière, Ferdinand, 209–10

Catholicism, 3, 4, 5, 10, 11, 13–15, 16, 18, 21–22, 24, 49–50, 55, 106–31, 174n, 181, 208
cause, 38, 41, 44, 63, 73, 85n, 86–91, 146n, 176, 196; and analogy, 95–97, 101; efficient cause, 73, 101–2; final cause, 200n; first cause, 61, 63, 89–91, 200n; secondary cause, 93n
certitude, 8, 11, 31, 43, 45, 48, 97, 120, 143, 150, 197, 199n, 209, 234–35
Chateaubriand, François-René, 219–20
Claire, St., 52, 57, 63
Colin, Pierre, 7
Comte, Auguste, 17n, 187–88
concepts, 3, 63, 73, 81, 89, 93, 96, 102, 140n, 149, 207n, 209, 230, 238
conceptualists, 42
conscience, 48, 65, 66, 70, 80, 94, 104, 107, 118, 123–27, 148n, 200, 217n, 225, 244

Darwin, Charles, 3, 9, 10, 22
Democritus, 29
De Potter, Louis, 208
Descartes, René, 29, 31, 49, 92, 196, 199n, 234n
Dessoulavy, Charles, 214n
Dewey, John, 228
d'Hulst, Maurice, 7
Divine, the, 64, 65–69, 70, 85, 93, 131, 135; personal representation of, 13–14, 105; and the problem of evil, 75–76; as replacement for "God," 77, 79–84, 103
divine types, 37–38
dogma, 50, 65, 101, 111, 130, 138, 198, 218; development of, 14, 112, 120; evolution of, 14, 100, 117n, 128n; moral significance of, 12, 68, 193,

dogma *(cont.)*
195–96, 200; practical meaning of, 204, 206–9, 215;symbolist understanding of, 4–13, 17, 18, 201n
Duhem, Pierre, 169–70
Durkheim, Émile, 174n, 225

École Pratique des Hautes Études, 1n, 50
École Fénelon, 6, 13, 18, 50, 51
essence, 35, 36–39, 41–42, 46, 72, 81, 90n, 91–93, 97, 119, 129, 151n, 163, 168, 201, 238; of Christianity, 110, 114, 119, 129
evolution, 3, 8, 9, 68, 79, 91n, 94, 154n, 157, 165, 170, 222; of faith, 18, 124, 181; laws of, 18, 19, 76, 95, 102, 211; religious evolution, 13, 101, 105, 107, 111, 117, 118, 120n
evolutionism, 9, 18, 23

faith, 17–18, 56, 80, 106–8, 112, 117–24, 129–30, 147, 174n, 181–82, 189, 203–5, 211–14, 219–20, 244–45
fideism, 80, 83, 87, 106, 123, 193, 197–202, 242, 245
Fouillée, Alfred, 98, 217–18
Francis, St., 52–59, 63, 64, 69

Galileo, 117
God, images of, 9, 14, 62, 65–67, 75–84, 89, 104–105, 210
Gregory IX, 54
Guyau, Jean-Marie, 94n, 98, 99, 104n

Harnack, Adolf, 15, 108, 111–17, 124, 128–31
Hébert, Marcel, 2–24, 50–51, 135, 226–27, 231–33, 241–46; "Anonymous or Polyonymous," 4, 14, 21, 85–105; "The Bankruptcy of Despotic Catholicism," 4, 14–15, 21, 106–31; *Le Divin,* 15, 135, 212n, 226; *L'Évolution de la foi catholique,* 15, 182n, 185n, 198n, 199n, 211, 212n; "The Last Idol," 4, 13–14, 20, 70–84; "Memories of Assisi," 3, 4, 11, 12–13, 19, 20–21, 49–99; "Plato and Darwin," 9, 11, 13; *Le Pragmatisme,* 5, 22, 135–238; "Thomism and Kantianism," 3, 7, 11, 27–48
historical consciousness, 3, 21
historical criticism, 12, 16, 107, 209
Hogan, John, 10n
Houtin, Albert, 1, 2n, 5, 8, 9, 11, 24, 50, 247
Hügel, Fredrich von, 20–21
humanism, 23, 149n, 161–78, 184
Hume, David, 30

idealism, 32, 170–71, 183, 223
immanence, 17, 38, 75; divine immanence, 15, 17; method of immanence, 2n; vital immanence, 17, 18
induction, 34, 40–41, 124, 235, 236
Innocent III, 54
instrumentalism, 178
intuition, 32–37, 46, 92, 93, 186, 192, 234–35, 237–38

Jacobi, Friedrich, 197
James, William, 5, 22, 24, 135, 136, 147n, 149–60, 164, 171n, 178n, 179–80, 182–85, 192, 193, 201n, 210, 212n, 213, 225, 226–38, 242
Jesus Christ, 12, 13, 53, 55, 59–60, 64–69, 79, 83, 99, 101, 106–10, 112–14, 116–24, 126, 140, 201–2, 205, 206, 207n, 209, 214, 244
judgments, analytic, 44; synthetic, 44–45, 189; of usefulness, 146, 211; of value, 146–47, 148n, 162, 163, 201, 211, 215n, 242

Kant, Immanuel, 3, 5, 7–9, 13–14, 16, 17, 22, 30–34, 37, 40, 42–47, 163, 185–86, 218
Kantianism, 6–8, 27–48
knowledge, 86, 174, 179, 190, 243, 246; and fideism, 226–38; and Kant, 31–35, 37, 40–48, 186; and Nietzsche,

224; objectivity of, 148, 153–60, 166–71, 177, 200n, 204; subjectivity of, 5, 22, 146, 163–64, 170–71; and Thomas Aquinas, 35–37

Laberthonnière, Lucien, 2–3, 16, 208, 221, 222n
Lamentabili sane exitu, 204
Leclère, Albert, 5, 220n
Le Dantec, Félix, 90n
Leibnitz, Gottfried, 29, 30, 34, 40, 45, 75
Lemaître, Jules, 222
Leo XIII, 27–29, 48
Leonardo, 23, 146, 147n, 185, 186
Le Roy, Édouard, 4, 163n, 164–68, 180, 206–09, 221–23, 236n, 242
Leuba, James, 212–13
Locke, John, 45, 185n
Luther, 121
Lycée Condorcet, 6

Malebranche, Nicolas, 76
Martin du Gard, Roger, 18–19
materialism, 31, 34, 151n, 172
Ménégoz, Eugène, 144n, 199–200, 241–46
Mercier, Désiré-Joseph, 90n
metaphysics, 47, 61, 63, 65, 70, 82, 88, 98, 147, 149n, 165, 169, 180; and Kant, 7, 44; voluntarist metaphysics, 172, 175
miracle, 9n, 66, 92n, 106, 119, 128, 198
Modernism, Roman Catholic, 1, 4, 5, 7, 15–24, 220, 222, 247
modernity, 4, 7, 11
moralism, 180n, 185n, 193–97, 242
morality, 29, 66, 104–105, 130, 171n, 180, 186, 220, 225; and pragmatism, 217–18
mysticism, 59, 63, 208n, 209
myth, 53, 59, 62–65, 104, 107–108, 120, 158, 162, 193, 198, 214, 225

natural theology, 17
Newman, John Henry, 201n, 221
Nietzsche, Friedrich, 180n, 188n, 189–90, 224, 225
nominalists, 44, 184
noumena, 37, 235

ontological argument, 74, 92n

pantheism, 90, 223
Papini, Giovanni, 146, 147n
Pascal, Blaise, 198, 221, 234
Pascendi dominici gregis, 16–18, 21, 197n, 203n, 245
Paul, St., 37, 43, 56, 60, 64–65, 67, 206, 244
Peter, St., 56
Peirce, Charles S., 22, 23n, 135, 137–48, 149, 161n, 179, 185n, 201, 242
phenomena, 17, 38, 41, 61, 73, 87–91, 97, 103, 130, 170, 175, 176, 186n, 188, 203n, 236–37
philosophy. *See* Kantianism, positivism, pragmatism, Scholasticism
Pius X, 197n
Plato, 29, 35, 43, 46, 113, 162, 164n, 183, 187
Poincaré, Henri, 163n, 164, 167–68, 172–73, 176, 180, 242
positivism, 88, 187
positivists, 36, 44
pragmatism, 5, 22–24, 135–225, 226–38, 241–46; aesthetic, 217; and James, 149–60; and Le Roy, 164–68; as method, 139–42, 146–47, 159, 179, 182; mitigated, 179–80, 221–34; and morality, 217–18; partial, 179–80; and Peirce, 137–48; precursors of, 183–92; pure, 179–80, 204; religious, 193–216; and Schiller, 161–78; as term, 135–36; as theory, 149–51, 159, 179, 182
prayer, 63, 66, 195, 210, 219
Prezzolini, Giuseppe, 147
Protagoras, 161–63, 184, 212
Protestantism, 14, 55, 69, 112, 115, 116
Providence, 9n, 95n, 123, 128
Pseudo-Dionysius, 64, 85–87, 95n, 98

Rabier, Elie, 39
realism, 3, 103, 185

Index

reason, 13, 17, 22, 29, 37–38, 48, 53, 63, 68, 74, 75, 78, 80, 94n, 99, 172, 219–22, 224n, 234n, 242–43; practical, 9, 30–31, 46, 180–86; reason and faith, 50–51, 70, 83, 87, 90n, 105, 198; speculative, 17, 185–86; sufficient, 44–47, 61, 72, 89; theoretical, 30–31, 46, 55, 186
relativism, 155n, 163–64, 169
religion, 10, 14, 19, 49–50, 63, 80, 82, 100, 103, 117, 130, 171n, 180, 201, 210, 242; Chateaubriand on, 220; Harnack on, 115, 117; Loisy on, 107, 110, 115–16, 204; reconciliation with science, 68; Renan on, 195–96
Renan, Ernest, 76, 77–78, 99, 100n, 125n, 159, 183, 195
Resurrection, 12, 20, 37, 59–60, 64–65, 106, 119, 126, 207n, 208, 214
Reuss, Édouard, 135
revelation, 66, 71, 106, 197, 200–202, 214
Ribot, Théodule, 175
Richard, François, 21, 108n
Ritschl, Albrecht, 200–201, 202, 242
Rousseau, Jean-Jacques, 182, 218–19
Royce, Josiah, 178, 222n, 234n

Sabatier, Auguste, 115n, 200, 242, 245
Saint-Simon, Claude Henri, 195n
Schiller, Ferdinand C. S., 22, 23n, 135, 147n, 149, 150n, 155n, 158, 161–78, 179, 185, 201n, 210, 212, 222n, 228, 232–33, 242
Schleiermacher, Friedrich, 119–20
Scholasticism, 3, 6, 16, 30, 70–71, 159n
Scholastics, 29, 32, 36, 42, 43, 59, 121, 152, 184, 211, 212n, 242
Schopenhauer, Arthur, 175n, 186–87
Sécretan, Charles, 43n, 193, 195
sensation, 38, 154–55, 157, 163–66, 184, 235; in Kant's philosophy, 8; in Scholastic philosophy, 32–33, in pragmatism, 139, 142, 151
Sidgwick, Alfred, 171
skepticism, 8, 34, 145, 147, 163, 177, 182, 209
skeptics, 31, 142, 209
socialism, 15, 49
Société de Saint-Thomas d'Aquin, 7–8, 27, 48n
Socrates, 35, 145, 183, 214, 217
Spencer, Herbert, 17n
Spinoza, Baruch, 97, 101, 102n, 196, 223
spiritualism, 151n
Stuart Mill, John, 99–100
Suarez, Francisco, 42
subjectivism, 23, 48, 163, 206, 230, 233, 237
substance, 36–37, 40, 42, 63, 81–82, 87, 89–93, 96–98, 102, 107, 121, 204, 236
symbolism, 117n, 127, 180, 193, 202–10; and fideism, 245–46; theological symbolism, 17–18

Taine, Hippolyte, 91, 104
Taylor, Charles, 10
theism, 4, 223
theodicy, 4, 9, 61, 75–76, 96n, 98–100, 181
Thomas Aquinas, St., 28, 29, 33, 35, 37, 43n, 71–74, 81, 90n, 95n, 96, 212
Thomism, 7–8, 27–48
transcendence, 75, 123; divine transcendence, 15
Trent, Council of, 121
truth, 13, 19, 30, 36, 43, 47, 67, 68, 77, 78, 82, 84, 87, 105, 113n, 120, 139, 140n, 142, 149–51, 156, 158–60, 162, 163n, 171, 174–202, 205–6, 212n, 214–19, 221–22, 225–33, 241–46; practical dimensions of, 22, 105, 158, 166n, 236; objectivity of, 47, 82
Turmel, Joseph, 24
Tyrrell, George, 16, 18, 208n

Vatican Council (First), 81, 171n, 123n
via causalitatis, 86–87, 88–95
via eminentiae, 86–88, 95–96
via negationis, 86–88, 95–96
Vincent de Paul, St., 58
Vincent of Lerins, 110n
Voltaire, 99–100
voluntarism, 172, 178, 234n

Wolff, Christian, 30